Critical Studies of the Asia-Pacific

Series Editor
Mark Beeson
University of Western Australia
Crawley, WA, Australia

Critical Studies of the Asia Pacific showcases new research and scholarship on what is arguably the most important region in the world in the twenty-first century. The rise of China and the continuing strategic importance of this dynamic economic area to the United States mean that the Asia-Pacific will remain crucially important to policymakers and scholars alike. The unifying theme of the series is a desire to publish the best theoretically-informed, original research on the region. Titles in the series cover the politics, economics and security of the region, as well as focusing on its institutional processes, individual countries, issues and leaders.

More information about this series at
http://www.palgrave.com/gp/series/14940

Tu Phuong Nguyen

Workplace Justice

Rights and Labour Resistance in Vietnam

palgrave
macmillan

Tu Phuong Nguyen
Centre for Governance and Public Policy
Griffith University
Nathan, QLD, Australia

Critical Studies of the Asia-Pacific
ISBN 978-981-13-3115-2 ISBN 978-981-13-3116-9 (eBook)
https://doi.org/10.1007/978-981-13-3116-9

Library of Congress Control Number: 2018960835

This Palgrave Macmillan imprint is published by the registered company Springer Nature Singapore Pte Ltd.
The registered company address is: 152 Beach Road, #21-01/04 Gateway East, Singapore 189721, Singapore

To Mom and Dad

Copyright Acknowledgements

This book contains materials from the following publications:

1. Nguyen, T. P. (2017). Workers' Strikes in Vietnam from a Regulatory Perspective. *Asian Studies Review* 41 (2), 263–280. <Copyright The Asian Studies Association of Australian>. Available at https://doi.org/10.1080/10357823.2017.1298568
2. Nguyen, T. P. (2017). Legal Consciousness and Workers' Resistance in Đồng Nai Province, Vietnam. *Asian Journal of Comparative Law* 12 (2), 311–333. <Copyright National University of Singapore>. Reprinted with permission. Available at https://doi.org/10.2017/asjcl.2017.18
3. Nguyen, T. P. (2018). Labour Law and (In)justice in Workers' Letters in Vietnam. *Asian Journal of Law and Society* 5 (1), 29–47. <Copyright Cambridge University Press and KoGuan Law School, Shanghai Jiao Tong University 2018>. Reprinted with permission. Available at https://doi.org/10.2017/als.2017.29

Acknowledgements

This book starts as a PhD project that I conducted at the Department of Political and Social Change, Australian National University. I owe a great deal to many people and institutions for their support for the completion of the thesis and subsequent revisions.

I foremost wish to express my sincere gratitude to my thesis panel, Prof Tamara Jacka, Assoc/Prof Sally Sargeson, and Assoc/Prof Philip Taylor, for their tireless intellectual guidance, professional advice, and support. I am especially thankful to Tamara for her patience, dedication, and meticulous editing that have helped tremendously in transforming my ideas and writing. I also thank Dr Kim Huynh for his professional tips and useful questions to push me to go beyond the comfort zones, and Dr Nick Cheesman for his willingness to read short extracts from my thesis and offer important advice on the socio-legal scholarship.

I have also been indebted to various forms of support from people other than my supervisors. Wendy Baker's selfless editorial assistance and our many thought-provoking e-mail exchanges and hour-long conversations have helped me transform my drafts and ideas. Prof Kanishka Jayasuriya, who used to be my honours supervisor, has inspired me to pursue this academic path. In addition, I am also grateful for many advice and suggestions from senior academics at conferences, graduate and young scholars' workshops, and from anonymous reviewers on my journal articles. Academics, colleagues, and administrative staff at the Department of Political and Social Change have also made my research journey fun and memorable.

My revision of the thesis into the book has benefitted greatly from feedback and comments of Assoc/Prof Lynette Chua, Emeritus Prof Benedict Kerkvliet, Dr Kim Huynh, and Prof Tamara Jacka, all of whom I sincerely thank. Prof Haig Patapan, Director at the Centre for Governance and Public Policy, Griffith University, where I work as a postdoc, also provided constant support during the completion of the book manuscript. Many thanks also to the team at Palgrave Macmillan for their editorial assistance.

At the heart of my book are the voices and stories of the factory workers whom I was fortunate to meet, talk, and feel inspired during my field trips in Đồng Nai Province. I thank all of them for sharing their thoughts and extraordinary journeys, as well as people who have helped me make my fieldwork less challenging. Finally, I am indebted to my parents, brother, and husband for always trusting me and meaning so much to my life and imagination.

Contents

List of Tables

CHAPTER 1

Introduction

> Once more, with all respect, I urge the leaders of all state agencies in the province to promptly intervene to save our lives. We are genuine employees who have no rights, lack equality, and experience a lot of coercion by the company.

This desperate plea comes from Mrs Nguyên who has worked for six years in a garment company in Đồng Nai Province. She lodged a complaint and petition against the company management after perceived legal violations and unfair treatment. Mrs Nguyên exhausted her legal arguments accusing the management of illegal wage policies and a lack of transparency in employees' bonus payments. This extract from one of Nguyên's complaint letters is similar to the kind of rightful claims brought against the abusive power of political and economic elites in authoritarian regimes (O'Brien and Li 2006, pp. 2–3). In making these claims, resisters exhibit a consciousness of their legal rights as well as knowledge of appropriate state law and other normative reasoning to mobilise popular support and demand justice. Similar to many other factory workers in Vietnam, Nguyên was abandoned by the trade union that purported to serve in the workers' interests. For the past few decades after the country opening its door to private and foreign investment, Vietnamese workers' struggles to have their voices heard have been both enabled and stifled by the legal and political systems that are supposed to protect their rights. Workers' accounts of resistance, both verbally and in

T. P. Nguyen, *Workplace Justice*, Critical Studies of the Asia-Pacific,
https://doi.org/10.1007/978-981-13-3116-9_1

writing, are underpinned by their consciousness of the socialist state's legal and political structures.

This book seeks to capture and comprehend factory workers' resistance in Vietnam through an examination of their values and ideals of rights and justice. In particular, it investigates the extent to which values, language, and practices derived from the Labour Code, which is the key labour legislation in Vietnam, contribute to shaping workers' views of workplace relations and providing justifications for their resistance. I understand resistance as acts that question or challenge power arrangements, authority, or practices of subjection, and focus on two forms of workers' resistance: factory strikes and complaint writing and petitioning. In Vietnam, strikes, which are largely spontaneous and without union organisation, have been the most popular form of workers' resistance. Strike demands have varied, but they all represent challenges to managers' conduct and policies on the shop floor and, less frequently, state laws and policies (Trần 2013, 2007). Other forms of resistance, such as petitioning and complaint writing, while not as vocal and explicitly confrontational as strikes, also deserve attention as they represent valuable testimonies of workers' experiences on the shop floor in relation to labour law and their desires for justice. As will be shown in subsequent chapters of the book, these actions give expression to workers' grievances and demands that have been either silenced or suppressed, and question or challenge existing practices by company and factory management and, at times, by state authorities.

The 1986 reform in Vietnam, known as *đổi mới* (renovation), gave rise to the development of private domestic and foreign investment and marked a shift in labour relationships from a socialist to a market-based perspective. The Vietnamese Labour Code, passed in 1994 and most recently amended in 2012, laid the groundwork for the state's regulation of labour based on the rights and interests of employing parties within their contractual relationships. In practice, the evasions and violations of labour rights enshrined in the law have led to a rise in factory strikes that bypass the legal procedure for labour dispute resolution. More than 70 per cent of strikes from 1995 to 2010 occurred in foreign enterprises dominated by Taiwanese, Korean, Hong Kong, and Japanese investors (Trần 2013, p. 200). Thus, despite making up less than 4 per cent of all registered businesses in Vietnam,[1] foreign enterprises are central to the prevalence of labour unrest in the country. The government, meanwhile, has continued to promote the importance of attracting foreign investment; a government decree in 2009 includes strike prevention and labour dispute resolution as necessary measures to facilitate foreign-funded production activities.[2] While strikes in state-owned enterprises are undoubtedly under-reported, the cultural alienation between foreign managers/supervisors and Vietnamese workers is an important factor in arousing and escalating shop floor tensions (Trần 2013, p. 197).

The Vietnam General Confederation of Labour (VGCL) remains the only recognised trade union in Vietnam. It claims to represent the entire Vietnamese working class and serves under the agenda of the Communist Party of Vietnam (CPV) in the interest of maintaining regime stability. Under the pressure for reform following the waves of factory strikes, the VGCL has exerted a greater voice in law and policy dialogues for the benefit of employees (Knutsen and Hansson 2010; Do and van den Broek 2013). There are also increasing efforts to enhance the bargaining capacity of company unions affiliated with the VGCL on the shop floors. However, these positions are often filled by management personnel, leaving the workers voiceless. These efforts have neither increased workers' bargaining power nor addressed the persistent distrust between them and the organisation that claims to act in their interests.

The subject matter of this book relates and contributes to the broader literature on labour resistance in post-socialist countries of Vietnam and China. While not presenting a comparative study, it draws from works conducted in China which provide useful perspectives and insights into the case studies in the Vietnamese context. Both China and Vietnam have experienced transition from central planning to a market-based economic system, starting in late 1980s and 1990s, under the leadership of the ruling Communist Party and its socialist legacies. These countries have also reformed their labour law regime following market principles while recognising only one legitimate trade union, the All-China Federation of Trade Unions and the VGCL, respectively.[3] The VGCL to date has had more institutional power than their China counterpart, at least in their capacity to participate in developing key labour policies at the national level (Quan 2015).

The brunt of economic transition in post-socialist Asia falls foremost upon the state workers, who became redundant following the restructuring or dismantling of state-owned enterprises. In the socialist era, employment was based on workers' loyalty and obedience to their managers and the state in exchange for a modest income and guaranteed social welfare, rather than on legality and formal labour contracts (Hurst and O'Brien 2002, p. 357; Walder 1986). As economic reform put to rest the socialist state's promises of welfare and lifelong employment, these workers launched protests and lodged their petitions to call upon the state and management to uphold their moral obligations (Lee 2007; Chen 2000; Hurst and O'Brien 2002; Trần 2013). Viewed from a moral economy perspective,[4] the redundant workers' sense of grief turned into vocal protests in particular when their minimum living needs were no longer secured and when they believed that managerial corruption had added to this situation (Chen 2000, pp. 45–48). Those state workers who demand their pensions also held the state and managers accountable for their now impoverished livelihoods (Hurst and O'Brien 2002). They acutely felt that a breach of reciprocal duties and a denial of the socialist contract had occurred when their pension was not paid in part or in full after all their years of service to the state enterprises.

The next wave of labour unrest was led by a new generation of migrant workers, who left their rural hometown to look for jobs and better incomes in growing urban and industrial areas. In both China and Vietnam, economic reform and integration into the global economy have produced a surge of growth in private domestic and foreign businesses, which are typically labour-intensive and export-oriented, and a high demand for manual, unskilled labour. As businesses have sought to maximise their profits and drive down labour costs, the new, mostly migrant working class, has been subject to exploitation and varying forms of managerial control on and off the shop floor (Chan 2001; Chan 2008; Pun 2005, 2016; Friedman and Lee 2010; Friedman 2014; Trần 2013; Pun and Smith 2007). These workers, at the same time, lack the institutional capacity to organise and collectively bargain with the state and capital. Their experience of a perpetual cycle of exploitation, powerlessness, and desperation has led these workers to take illegal spontaneous action, mostly in the form of strikes and protests, to demand decent wages and working conditions. Since the Labour Code was introduced in Vietnam in 1994, factory strikes have continued to break out in large numbers each year: they climbed to a peak of 993 in 2011, then dropped to 601 in 2012 and 293 in 2014 (VGCL 2015). In China, while official statistics for strikes are unavailable, different sources have suggested that hundreds of thousands of labour disputes took place across the country from 1993 to 2010 (Elfstrom and Kuruvilla 2014, pp. 454–455). The prevalence of workers' collective action against the law is a significant challenge to the legal regime that has endorsed a wide range of employees' rights in accordance with international labour conventions.

From a Marxist political economy perspective, state law is an aspect of the superstructure that controls and immiserates the workforce in the interests of the ruling and powerful classes. Law functions as a political and ideological tool to safeguard the capitalist mode of production and sustain its machine of labour exploitation (Steinberg 2010; Cotterrell 2006). In post-socialist China and Vietnam, the growing political alliance between the state and capital (especially foreign capital) in export-processing zones and industrial regions in the south has significantly constrained workers' institutional power (Pun 2005, 2016; Nghiem 2006; Trần 2013). Consequently, the promulgation of labour laws is rendered unfavourable to the workers' interests and contributes little to protecting or advancing labour rights (Chan and Siu 2012; Chan 2008; Trần 2013). In particular, while employees now in principle have extensive individual rights in accordance with international conventions, the lack of collective rights, such as the right to strike and to form independent unions, serves to entrench workers' disadvantage vis-à-vis the state and capital. The phenomenon of factory workers' disruptive street actions in Vietnam and China during the past few decades is a reaction against the capitalist power structure,[5] of which the law is a part.

Still, disadvantaged workers have shown that state law is neither irrelevant nor detrimental to their aspirations for justice. Workers have become more familiar with the legal language and know how to navigate the legal avenues, thanks to the state's consolidation of its legal regime (Lee 2007), its legal education campaign (Gallagher 2006; Hui and Chan 2012), and a variety of forms of legal support run by non-governmental migrant organisations (Becker 2014). To be clear, the Chinese state is more proactive than Vietnam in disseminating legal knowledge and informing its population of the benefit of using legal avenues, despite both states displaying a similar rhetorical turn towards formal legality in regulating the public sphere. In China, workers' actions such as lodging complaints and disputes via administrative bodies, filing labour lawsuits, and invoking legal labour rights fall within the broader phenomenon of citizens' 'rightful resistance' (O'Brien and Li 2006; Lee and Hsing 2010). Rightful resistance is defined as 'a form of popular contention that operates near the boundary of authorized channels, employs the rhetoric and commitments of the powerful to curb the exercise of power, […] entails the innovative use of laws, policies, and other officially promoted values to defy disloyal political and economic elites' (O'Brien and Li 2006, pp. 2–3). Workers' engagement with law in turn inspires a growing academic interest in 'rights consciousness' (Wong 2011; Lorentzen and Scoggins 2015), which refers to the way a person understands and perceives their *legal* rights. Of course, one's consciousness of law is not static nor does it develop in a linear fashion; it is subject to fluctuation and change as one actually navigates the legal system to demand redress (Gallagher 2006).

From the rightful resistance perspective, law is not just a set of uncontested rules enforced by the state and its legislative bodies. Rather, it can be appropriated by societal actors for purposes that might work against state interests. Analyses informed by this perspective acknowledge the political endorsement of rights within new laws and policies as the key factor that enables rightful claims and individuals' demands for rights protection. These actions indicate individuals' consciousness of their citizen rights, and, at the very least, show that legal institutions have had a certain role to play within contemporary societies that previously were bound by customary moral norms and respect for social hierarchy rather than by codified written laws.[6] The literature therefore lays the ground for further interest in the contribution of state law towards advancing social justice.

While previous studies provide useful insights into the causes and nature of workers' resistance in post-socialist contexts, we need a more holistic approach to understand what state law means and how it matters to Vietnamese workers' notions of justice in their resistance. The main problem with previous studies lies in the way they view and conceptualise state law, and, more importantly, how it relates to other norms and values in shaping the relationship between the state, workers, and management. In particular, while the political economy scholarship takes a top-down approach and examines law predominantly as part of the state-capitalist structure, studies that take a moral economy perspective generally take little interest in state law. Although they offer valid explanations as to how and why the majority of workers in China and Vietnam have bypassed or turned away from legal rules and procedures, they fail to acknowledge, or properly address, practices, values, and meanings derived from the law that underpins workers' expectations, language, and acts of resistance. The rightful resistance literature has brought the law back in, yet it tends to pay attention to instances when citizens deploy the legal system and legal discourse in an explicit manner. This focus also does not produce an adequate assessment of law as it overlooks instances when law contributes to resistance and citizens' consciousness in a subtle and tacit manner.

This book seeks to overcome the analytical shortcomings in previous studies by taking a socio-legal approach that explores the relevance and meaning of law through its interaction with non-legal sets of norms and practices. It takes interest in the different values underpinning workers' framings of workplace problems, demands, and ideals of justice, and the relationship between these values and their experiences and understandings of labour law. In doing so it is able to reflect upon different threads of understandings and perspectives about law, morality, and justice as discussed in previous studies, and evaluate the possibilities and constraints of law in addressing workplace injustice. In this sense, findings of the book also contribute to our understanding of law and society in post-socialist regimes in Asia, which to date tends to treat law and other sets of moral norms and precepts as oppositional, conflicting, or separate from each other (see, e.g., Phạm 2005; Gillespie and Nicholson 2005; Koh 2007; Yang and van der Wal 2014; He and Feng 2016). This book illustrates that law penetrates more deeply into social life than what conventional scholarship has shown. As law interacts with other normative orders in shaping the way workers justify and deal with their grievances, the relationship between law and morality becomes fluid and complex.

A Socio-legal Account of Labour Resistance in Vietnam

Building upon the tradition of socio-legal scholarship[7] that situates law within other cultural and normative understandings, this socio-legal account evaluates to what extent law underpins social interactions and influences individuals' behaviour and consciousness, which ranges from compliance with power and authority to resistance. Different socio-legal scholars have defined law in various ways and examined it through different contexts. Sally Merry (1990, p. 5) defines law as consisting of 'a complex repertoire of meanings and categories understood differently by people depending on their experience with and knowledge of the law,' and explores how the American working class bring their social problems to the courts and/or later confront the court's authority. Michael McCann (1994) studies law through legal conventions, discourses, and practices, examining how rules and communication surrounding state laws inform individuals' understandings of their rights, and how outcomes of litigation reinforce or alter those understandings. Patricia Ewick and Susan Silbey (1992, 1998) treat law as a cultural schema and a resource that shapes individual behaviour and social relations. Their study focuses on how law matters in 'taken-for-granted acts and agreements' (1992, p. 732) outside formal institutional settings and what law means to ordinary people when they encounter or confront problems in everyday situations.

Drawing from these scholars' approaches and focusing on labour relations in Vietnam, this book understands labour law as a combination of three aspects. (1) The labour law regime, that is, legal institutions and processes set out in the Labour Code; state policies and regulations associated with the Code; and measures, such as the establishment of strike action teams and legal aid activities, introduced by the state to enhance implementation of the law and associated policies and regulations. (2) The language used in the Code and other aspects of the labour law regime, and the values and understandings embedded in it. (3) The practices through which law and associated state policies and regulations are implemented (or not implemented) by officials, factory managers, and others. The book examines how these three aspects of labour law influence the way factory workers justify their claims and the type of actions they take to resist and demand justice against abusive management. It argues that labour law is only one factor shaping workers' articulation of what is fair and unfair and one aspect of what generates their resistance to injustice. The way workers turn (or do not turn) to labour law depends on their perceptions of the relationship between the law and the morality of workplace behaviour. These perceptions, in turn, are constructed through their experiences on the shop floor and with legal institutions and processes, and are shaped by both socialist ideology and long-standing cultural norms.

Further analysis of the values and perceptions underpinning workers' resistance, as expressed in interviews and verbal and written accounts, will contribute to addressing the following questions:

- How and to what extent do workers draw on labour law to make sense of their relationship with management, the state, and unions, and of their workplace problems?
- How do workers use the language of labour law to demand justice? In employing that language, do they mean to condemn illegal practices and call for a proper implementation of law, or do they want to convey a different set of norms and expectations about workplace behaviour, or both?

- In their demands for justice and acts of resistance, do workers evoke a sense of legal rights or other notions of rights, and what is the relationship between their different notions of rights?

The answers to these questions will be elaborated along two strands of socio-legal enquiry, concerned with, firstly, how individuals perceive and act in response to grievances in their everyday lives, and, secondly, how they engage with, avoid, or resist law. The first strand of enquiry is informed by Felstiner, Abel, and Sarat's (1980/81) exploration of how disputes emerge from the way affected parties make sense of and interpret their experiences. How people react to an injury incident, from naming to blaming and claiming, is contingent on the subjective views of the injured towards related events and situations. In this social construction of disputes, language and understandings derived from certain state laws and policies provide individuals 'with a powerful set of interpretive tools' (Marshall 2003, p. 661), among other sets of non-legal frames and expressions. Thus, in examining law as part of dispute experiences, scholars have found varying narratives that may be constructed by or clash with particular laws, and these narratives in turn account for individuals' decisions to escalate their grievances or drop their cases.

For instance, Austin Sarat's research (1990) provides insights into the way American welfare recipients navigate the legal service and bureaucracy to claim their benefits. Most frame their problems in terms of their personal needs and based on a sense of urgency, before invoking formal rules as a last resort. Another study of sexual harassment in US workplaces reveals that female employees rely on legal standards as well as other 'interpretative frames' to decide whether their experiences constitute sexual harassment (Marshall 2003, p. 659. See also Quinn 2000; Marshall 2005). These other interpretative frames stem from their views about male dominance in the workplace, professional dignity, and sexual freedom, and often play a major role in their judgements of and reactions to their colleagues' behaviour. Indeed, it is precisely these other non-legal constructions of workplace conduct, which were somehow internalised and tolerated by the harassed, that have limited law's power in protecting female employees against abusive practices.

The second strand of inquiry, on law and resistance, situates law within the nexus of power relations at a micro level and investigates how individuals' actions represent conformity to and/or resistance against the power to which they are subjected. This strand of enquiry investigates resistant acts and behaviour concealed from the public view and, importantly, 'the way in which people make sense of the law and legal institutions' (Ewick and Silbey 1992, p. 734), that is, their legal consciousness. Studies of legal consciousness are not limited to an examination of subjects who have experiences with laws and law enforcement institutions, but also extend to those who refuse to obey or who evade law (Engel 1998; Ewick and Silbey 1998; Gilliom 2001). These varying uses and attitudes towards law can be explained by the social and cultural contexts shaping individuals' lived experiences.

Socio-legal studies also present a critique against those that tend to treat consciousness as a unilinear cognitive development or as epiphenomenal to resistance. Viewing consciousness as embedded within social and cultural practice, Ewick and Silbey (1992, p. 742) highlight that:

> we see legal consciousness as something local, contextual, pluralistic, filled with conflict and contradiction. The ideas, interpretations, actions and ways of operating that collectively represent a person's legal consciousness may vary across time [...] or across interactions [...]. To the extent that consciousness is emergent in social practice and forged in and around situated events and interactions [...], a person may express, through words or actions, a multi-faceted, contradictory, and variable consciousness.

The story of an African-American working-class woman covered in their research exemplifies the various expressions and contingent nature of consciousness. While this woman was incorrectly charged with causing a car accident, she nevertheless accepted and obeyed the court verdicts, but later returned to appeal the verdict with assistance from her employer and a local attorney. In their analysis, Ewick and Silbey attend to not only this woman's concrete actions in response to the charge she faced but also the way she perceived the charge and the court procedures. As her experiences transformed from being subject to the law enforcement authorities to employing available resources to contest their power, her consciousness shifted from conformity with to resistance against law and the power exercised through it.

Research on labour resistance in authoritarian contexts like China has benefitted from disputing and legal consciousness approaches. In her 2006 *Law and Society Review* article, Mary Gallagher notes that the legal consciousness of employees who receive formal legal aid is varied and can be contradictory rather than emerging and developing in a singular linear fashion (2006, pp. 785–787). The author demonstrates that through their legal experiences, aggrieved workers developed a consciousness of 'informed disenchantment' (p. 783): having gained legal knowledge and access to legal institutions to fight for their rights, they were subsequently disappointed by the functioning of the court in delivering redress. The plaintiffs' previously high expectations of the legal system were undermined by their real experiences of it as involving complicated processes and being more favourable to their employers (p. 804). Xin He, Lungang Wang and Yang Su (2013) also utilise the idea of legal consciousness to explain collective actions of wage claimants to demand compensation, such as occupying government offices or threatening suicide. He and colleagues argue that wage claimants' 'cultural perception of justice' (2013, p. 709), which embodies the notion that one should be fairly paid for one's work, drives them to take disruptive actions. This research takes into account the role of the state's laws and regulations as well as other sets of norms and values in conceptualising individuals' legal consciousness. These studies offer valuable insights into the social (in)significance of law in a post-socialist context, yet they still leave unaddressed the complex, rather than contradictory, nature of the relationship between law and other sets of norms and values in shaping the form of consciousness. This book suggests that the relationship between law and morality in post-socialist regimes is complex and mutually reinforcing. It extends the analytical focus beyond instrumental and strategic approaches to state law and policy, that is, whether and how workers succeed or fail in deploying state laws to seek redress and pursue their causes. In this study, workers' acts of resistance, such as strikes and lodgement of letters, present the appropriate settings through which to unpack practices and ideas about law. In looking at workers' verbal and written accounts, I highlight the importance of understanding workers' interpretations of their workplace experiences prior to their actions and to certain events surrounding labour disputes. These experiences include workers' interactions with shop floor managers, supervisors, and their fellow workers; the emergence of workplace grievances; and other experiences (e.g., their past engagement with legal aid and law enforcement institutions) that motivated workers to seek justice or prevented them from doing so. These experiences are crucial to our understanding of how law penetrates workplace relationships and how it enables and/or constrains workers' contestation of managerial power. The analysis also fleshes out different values that shape workers' claims-making, and in turn shed light on the socio-cultural contexts shaping the constructions of workplace (in)justice in Vietnam.

The Field Research

This research employs qualitative case-study analysis of documentary evidence and fieldwork, conducted from December 2014 to April 2015, and from December 2015 to February 2016. The field site is Đồng Nai Province, one of the top regions of rapid industrial development in the south of Vietnam. The Đồng Nai Labour Federation, which is the provincial branch of the VGCL, is well reputed for its emphasis on promoting legal education to factory workers. The Legal Aid Centre (LAC), affiliated with the provincial labour union, has been in operation for more than two decades and has become a model for legal aid activities in other industrial hubs. Đồng Nai is also an industrial hub that, together with Hồ Chí Minh City and Bình Dương Province, accounts for the highest incidence of strikes and labour disputes in Vietnam since the early wave of foreign investment in the 1990s. From 2009 to 2014, strikes in these localities account for 60–70 per cent of strikes happening over the country (VGCL 2015, p. 1). In Đồng Nai, the number of strikes per year climbed steadily from 1995 to 2005, peaking at 185 in 2008, then dropping to 36 in 2014 (Đồng Nai Labour Federation 2014. See also Table 1.1 for national and provincial figures). In this province, I concentrated on three areas: Biên Hòa city, Nhơn Trạch, and Trảng Bom Districts, which have the largest

Table 1.1 Number of strikes in Đồng Nai, Hồ Chí Minh City, and Bình Dương compared to total strikes nationwide from 2009 to 2014

Year	*Đồng Nai (A)*	*Hồ Chí Minh City (B)*	*Bình Dương (C)*	*Nationwide*	*Percentage of (A), (B) and (C)*
2009	42	70	71	342	53.6
2010	147	62	131	507	67
2011	168	201	328	993	70.1
2012	47	109	234	601	64.8
2013	39	97	103	384	62.3
2014	36	81	71	293	64.1

Adopted from VGCL (2015)

numbers of enterprises and have been fraught with strikes. Labour relations and labour dispute mediation in these areas are overseen by the upper-level unions, which are VGCL branches at district levels and within industrial zones. Around 50–60 per cent of strikes in these areas have occurred in January–February, when workers expect a wage rise and year-end bonus from the company management.

I obtained most of my data by conducting semi-structured in-depth interviews with migrant factory workers, who make up around 60–70 per cent of factory workers in the province. It was much easier to approach migrant workers, as they live in concentrated rental areas, whereas local workers, already residents, are scattered throughout the province. A yet more substantial reason for focusing on migrant workers is that the added financial burden of living away from home may influence the way they articulate their demands and grievances.[8] I should note that my interest in migrant workers does not stem from any evidence that they have organised for collective actions through native-place networks, nor that they are often the most vocal informal strike leaders (Pringle and Clarke 2011; Trần 2013). The focus of this research is not on how workers organise, but on how they draw upon law and other discourse and practice to justify their grievances and actions.

The way I designed interview questions was informed by Ewick and Silbey's approach (1998), which aims to explore how legal language and experiences permeate people's everyday experiences. Ewick and Silbey explain that in designing their method, they 'did not want [their] questions to imply or enforce a conventional definition of law and legality,' nor 'ask people about their legal problems or needs' (1998, p. 24). They therefore directed their interviewees to start with a depiction of casual events and stories about their neighbourhood, work, and family, and then asked more structured questions as interviewees mentioned particularly telling stories or legal matters. I found this a very fruitful way to unearth the relevance of law in social and often taken-for-granted contexts.

In a similar way, I did not frame my interview questions around legal terms, such as '(collective) disputes (*tranh chấp (tập thể)*),' or 'rights and interests,' but tried to elicit and analyse whether and how interviewees refer to these terms in their response to my questions. My approach is slightly different from Ewick and Silbey's in that most of my questions centre on workers' concerns and experiences at work, although I allowed interviewees to freely talk and elaborate on their other family and social concerns in their responses. In general, I found it useful to frame questions around common language, using terms like 'strikes' (*đình công*), 'grievances' (*bức xúc*), and 'problems' (*vấn đề*). In trying to ascertain how workers understand justice, I also did not use the word 'fair' or 'just' (*công bằng*), or the opposite word 'unfair' (*bất công*), in asking questions. Interviewees' responses to my general questions about details and past events at work have sufficed to elicit their views and experiences of (in)justice. Compared to a direct observation of strikes, which are unpredictable and might be deemed politically sensitive, this method of interviewing workers in a commonplace setting allowed me to contextualise and appreciate workers' situations without risking harm to them for their participation in the project.[9]

My research participants, however, are also different from those of Ewick and Silbey. These authors make it clear that they are interested in exploring the voices of a diverse group of people rather than just those who 'lodge their complaints, voice their grievances, seek their rights, or demand justice' (Ewick and Silbey 1998, p. 20). My research, in contrast, takes interest in those who have expressed dissatisfaction. My interview questions therefore were more structured around workplace complaints and grievances, but I usually asked in general terms and allowed workers to talk freely and at times digress from the questions. In analysing the interview transcripts and notes, I was able to see whether and how aspects of labour law arise in their interactions with and perceptions of the unions, their management and state authorities, as well as their justifications for silence or resistance.

Unknown to the area and not having previous contacts with workers, I first approached an acquaintance from the local Youth Union in Nhơn Trạch District who knows the locations of workers' residences. I then approached potential participants by accompanying her to workers' rental areas on Sundays, bearing in mind the names of a few companies where strikes had occurred.[10] The rental areas are located in small alleys, about ten minutes by motorbike to get to from the main roads. There are usually 15–20 units in each of these rental areas, which sometimes have an entry gate and a board of regulations (regarding tenants' behaviour) hung up by the landlords near the gate. Most of the units that I visited have a half storey upstairs and can accommodate a family of four including children. The living area where I sat and talked to the workers, which is about nine square metres, is also an area for dining and sleeping. Even on Sundays, it was sometimes difficult to meet workers, since they were often working overtime. When they were at home, workers would often have their doors open, with their children playing and running around. They would often be engaged in chatting with their neighbours or cooking meals together. Later on in the field trip, I approached friends, acquaintances, and relatives of core workers[11] (*công nhân nòng cốt*), who helped with the recruitment process but did not intervene during the interviews. There were refusals from potential participants, mainly because workers are hesitant to talk about their workplace conditions to outsiders. Thirty ordinary workers, ranging in age from 25 to 55 years, agreed to participate in the research. They worked across six different companies belonging to the food, wood manufacturing, and footwear and garment industries. In the remainder of the book, very limited information about each company will be disclosed, so as to protect the identity of research participants. All interviews with workers were conducted either at their rental units, workers' social gathering place near their units, or in cafés.

Another important research participant group was the core workers who received legal training from an Oxfam-funded project. These workers are different from other workers in that they are knowledgeable about labour law and have more contacts with union officials at district and provincial levels as a result of their legal training. I approached these workers through the lawyer from the LAC. My interviews with them were structured around issues similar to those discussed with ordinary factory workers. In addition, I asked general questions about their opinions and evaluations of labour law, policies, and disputes, and more specific, detailed questions about the role of the state and union in protecting workers' interests. I had several follow-up interviews and conversations with them during the fieldwork. There were in total 14 participants, including five women, in this group. The small number of female compared to male core workers is due to the nature of legal aid commitments and funding. Briefly, the time demanded of legal aid prevents female workers with family commitments from actively engaging with this activity, and, therefore, only a small number of them were known to me during my field trip.

Other data used in the book were obtained from interviews with union officials in upper-level unions, which are local branches of the VGCL, labour mediators in the city/district labour bureaus, officials of the industrial zone authority (IZA), and the labour lawyer. All these interviewees are key parties overseeing labour relations, legal aid activities, and settling labour disputes in the province. Lastly, I interviewed a manager and a human resource manager in two strike-affected foreign-owned companies, to learn how they understand and evaluate the current Labour Code as a factor that stirs up or contains labour disputes in their companies. I obtained access to these two interviewees through the IZA. It was important to approach workers and their managers through two separate channels, so as to protect workers' identities and ensure that their sharing of information with an outsider was not known to the managers.

Other sources for the book include workers' complaint and petition letters, obtained from union offices in Đồng Nai Province and from workers themselves, with one letter published in the national labour newspaper, *Labour* (*Lao Động*). Within these letters I am interested in whether or not workers draw on the language of the Labour Code and associated policies and regulations in describing their grievances and justifying their actions. A close reading of these written accounts complements the verbal narratives as they provide powerful testimonies of the way workers depict their experiences on the shop floor and articulate a sense of (in)injustice. Other sources used for this research include policy decisions and official guidelines relating to labour relations, labour disputes, and strikes in the field site province, as well as news articles published online in national and provincial newspapers focusing on labour issues.

Chapter Outline

The book is structured as follows. Chapter 2 discusses key aspects of Vietnam's labour law regime, including the Labour Code, the government's annual minimum wage adjustment, the union's legal aid activities, and union and state discourse about strikes. Chapters 3, 4, 5, and 6 are dedicated to analysing verbal and written accounts of three forms of workers' resistance. Chapter 3 draws on interviews discussing workers' grievances in strike-affected enterprises in Đồng Nai Province, with an in-depth focus on a food processing company. The recurrence of strikes in the case-study area from 2010 to 2014 enables an exploration of the link between the local state's strike settlement measures and workers' acts of resistance. I posit that the regulatory effects (or failures) of strike settlement and prevention partially do contribute to the recurrence of strikes. But the more important contributing factor lies in the state's and management's failure to meet what workers understand to be their moral obligation to award the workers a fair payment for their labour.

Chapter 4 analyses workers' letters lodged at the upper-level union offices in 2013 and 2014 and a grievance letter that made news headlines. The chapter examines the extent to which the language and values embodied in labour law shape and construct workers' accounts of their experiences on the shop floor and the contexts in the lead-up to their writing. These letters are telling not just because of the channels and audience to which they are directed but also because they reveal important perceptions of labour rights and the fusion of legality and morality in workers' pursuit of justice.

Chapter 5 looks at the legal aid project and explores the views and activities of core workers involved. It sketches out the key functions of the LAC and how messages about workers' capability to defend their rights and interests are circulated through the provincial labour news. The second part is about core workers' interactions with ordinary workers, specifically concerning their beliefs and attitudes towards the role of law and legal aid in advancing labour rights. Chapter 6 explores three stories of core workers' involvement in letter writing and mobilisation against unfair practices at their company. Individually, two of these workers also brought their management to the union office and to the court. Drawing from interviews and core workers' letters, I demonstrate whether and how their understandings of workplace grievances and ideals of justice differ from ordinary workers mentioned in the previous chapters. The remainder of Chap. 6 will follow up on the resolution processes and outcomes after workers lodged their letters. The aim is to grasp the dynamics of their legal consciousness through the course and resolution of their petitioning process. The final chapter (Chap. 7) revisits the link between law, morality, and justice in post-socialist regimes and the debate on rights consciousness. It also reflects upon the nature of law and popular resistance in authoritarian regimes, and evaluates the role of law in generating social change and advancing social justice.

Notes

1. Foreign enterprises account for 2.7 per cent of all enterprises in Vietnam in 2015, dropping from 3.9 per cent in 2000 (General Statistics Office 2017a). However, registered foreign capital has increased over the year, jumping from US $6.84 million to $24.1 million from 2005 to 2015, despite suffering a significant fall after 2008 following the aftermath of the Asian Financial Crisis (General Statistics Office 2017b). The total disbursed foreign capital has seen a more stabilising trend since 2008, ranging from US $10 to $14 million each year.
2. Government of Vietnam (2009). Decree 13/NQ-CP on the directions and measures to attract and manage foreign direct investment in the future.

3. See Chan and Norlund (1998) for a comprehensive discussion of Chinese and Vietnamese labour regimes.
4. James Scott's moral economy framework (1976), which traces the values that shape social relationships and inform understandings of justice in pre-capitalist peasant society, has been referred to occasionally in analyses of labour resistance in China and Vietnam. For Scott, subsistence needs are a fundamental right of agrarian societies and infringement of this right has been a major cause of peasant resistance in times of crisis (Scott 1976, pp. 6–10). Having their subsistence needs fulfilled becomes a benchmark for peasants to judge whether the state and landlords are treating them in an ethical or exploitative manner.
5. I use the term 'capitalist' here to refer to a model of development in which the state allows and facilitates the growth of private capital. I note, however, that Vietnam in particular still holds on to socialist ideology. The proclaimed 'socialist-oriented market economy' (*kinh tế thị trường định hướng xã hội chủ nghĩa*) is a 'multi-sectoral commodity economy that functions according to market principles and follows the management of the State under the leadership of the Communist Party' (Central Committee of the CPV 2011).
6. In Vietnam, the saying 'the king's edict stops at the village gates' (*phép vua thua lệ làng*) (Wells-Dang 2014, p. 162) is often quoted by legal scholars to illustrate the dominance of local social values over new state laws, which are seen as transplants of global standards.
7. An offshoot of the law and society movement in the USA, socio-legal research has moved beyond legal studies of texts and formal law-making processes and shed light on the relevance of law in individuals' pursuit of justice and social movements (Merry 1990; Ewick and Silbey 1992; McCann 1994; McCann and March 1996). This law and society intellectual movement emerged in the 1970s and originally centred on illuminating the gap between 'law in the books' and 'law in action' and uses 'methods of behavioral science' to examine how law matters in people's approach to social problems (Liu 2015, p. 3).
8. Other sources have also stressed the socio-economic disadvantages of migrant workers compared to local workers, which are mainly due to the household registration system (*hộ khẩu*) in Vietnam that ties a citizen's one and only legal residence status to their household (Hoang 2011). Migrant workers thus face difficulty in accessing social services, such as public healthcare, childcare, and children's schooling, at their destination provinces.
9. My involvement in a strike that is deemed politically sensitive, if by chance discovered by the state's civil security forces, might have caused trouble for the workers with whom I talked.

10. Information on strikes, including the company's name, the reasons and resolutions, the number of workers involved, the duration of strikes, was obtained from the upper-level and provincial unions.
11. As will be discussed shortly, these core workers received training about the Labour Code and other labour laws and policies and were introduced to me by the Legal Aid Centre, which belongs to the provincial Labour Federation. Here I wish to reiterate John Gilliom's note in his study on American welfare mothers, which emphasises the importance of obtaining 'the level of trust necessary to undertake meaningful interviews' (2001, p. 46) rather than the scientific representation of the sample. Interviews with mothers receiving welfare in his research were indeed conducted by two women who share the same social status and locality with his research participants (p. 45).

References

Becker, J. (2014). *Social Ties, Resources and Migrant Labor Contention in Contemporary China: From Peasants to Protesters*. Lanham: Lexington Books.

Chan, A. & Norlund, I. (1998). Vietnamese and Chinese Labour Regimes: On the Road to Divergence. *The China Journal*, 40, 173–197.

Chan, A. & Siu, K. (2012). Chinese Migrant Workers: Factors Constraining the Emergence of Class Consciousness. In Carrillo, B. & Goodman, D. S. (eds.). *China's Peasants and Workers: Changing Class Identities*. London: Edward Elgar.

Chan, A. (2001). *China's Workers under Assault: The Exploitation of Labor in a Globalizing Economy*. Armonk, NY: M.E. Sharpe.

Chan, C. K-C. (2008). *The Challenge of Labour in China: Strikes and the Changing Labour Regime in Global Factories*. Unpublished PhD thesis. University of Warwick, Coventry.

Chen, F. (2000). Subsistence Crises, Managerial Corruption and Labour Protests in China. *The China Journal*, 44, 41–63.

Cotterrell, R. (2006). *Law, Culture and Society: Legal Ideas in the Mirror of Social Theory*. Hampshire & Burlington: Ashgate.

Do, Q. C. & van den Broek, D. (2013). Wildcat strikes: A catalyst for union reform in Vietnam?. *Journal of Industrial Relations*, 55 (5), 783–799.

Đồng Nai Labour Federation (2014). *Report on the work of taking care of material and mental lives for workers and the situation of strikes and work stoppages*.

Elfstrom, M. & Kuruvilla, S. (2014). The Changing Nature of Labour Unrest in China. *ILR Review*, 67 (2), 453–480.

Engel, D. (1998). How Does the Law Matter in the Constitution of Legal Consciousness?. In B. J. Garth & A. Sarat (eds.), *How Does the Law Matter?* Illinois: Northwestern University Press.

Ewick, P. & Silbey, S. (1992). Conformity, Contestation and Resistance: An Account of Legal Consciousness. *New England Law Review*, 26, 731–749.

Ewick, P. & Silbey, S. (1998). *The Common Place of Law: Stories from Everyday Life. Chicago: University of Chicago Press.*

Felstiner, W., Abel, R. & Sarat, A. (1980/1981). The Emergence and Transformation of Disputes: Naming, Blaming, Claiming…. *Law and Society Review*, 15 (3/4), 631–654.

Friedman, E. & Lee, C. K. (2010). Remaking the World of Chinese Labour: A 30-Year Retrospective. *British Journal of Industrial Relations*, 48 (3), 507–533.

Friedman, E. (2014). *Insurgency Trap: Labor Politics in Post-Socialist China*. Ithaca: ILR Press.

Gallagher, M. (2006). Mobilizing the Law in China: 'Informed Disenchantment' and the Development of Legal Consciousness. *Law & Society Review*, 40 (4), 783–816.

General Statistics Office (2017a). *Vietnamese Business in the First 15 Years of the Decade (2000–2014)*. Statistics Publishing House.

General Statistics Office (2017b). Foreign Direct Investment licensed in the period 1988–2016. https://www.gso.gov.vn/default.aspx?tabid=716. Accessed 2nd February 2018.

Gillespie, J. & Nicholson, P. (eds.) (2005). *Asian Socialism and Legal Change: The Dynamics of Vietnamese and Chinese Reform*. Canberra: ANU E Press & Asia Pacific Press.

Gilliom, J. (2001). *Overseers of the Poor: Surveillance, Resistance, and the Limits of Privacy*. Chicago & London: The University of Chicago Press

Government of Vietnam (2009). *Decree 13/NQ-CP on the directions and measures for attracting and managing foreign direct investment in the future.*

He, X. & Feng, Y. (2016). Mismatched Discourses in the Petition Offices of Chinese Courts. *Law & Social Inquiry*, 41 (1), 212–241.

He, X., Wang, L. & Su, Y. (2013). Above the Roof, Beneath the Law: Perceived Justice behind Disruptive Tactics of Migrant Wage Claimants in China. *Law & Society Review*, 47 (4), 703–738.

Hoang, L. A. (2011). Gendered Networks and Migration Decision-making in Northern Vietnam. *Social & Cultural Geography*, 12 (5), 419–434.

Hui, E. S-I. & Chan, C. K-C. (2012). The 'Harmonious Society' as a Hegemonic Project: Labour Conflicts and Changing Labour Policies in China. *Labour, Capital and Society*, 44 (2), 153–183.

Hurst, W. & O'Brien, K. J. (2002). China's Contentious Pensioners. *The China Quarterly*, 170, 345–360.

Knutsen, H. M. & Hansson, E. (2010). Theoretical Approaches to Changing Labour Regimes in Transition Economies. In A. C. Bergene, S. B. Endresen & H. M. Knutsen (eds.). *Missing Links in Labour Geography*. England: Ashgate Publishing Limited.

Koh, D. (2007). Modern Law, Traditional Ethics, and Contemporary Political Legitimacy in Vietnam. In S. Balmé & M. Sidel (eds.), *Vietnam's New Order: International Perspectives on the State and Reform in Vietnam*. New York: Palgrave Macmillan.

Lee, C. K. & Hsing, Y-T. (2010). Social Activism in China: Agency and Possibilities. In Y-T. Hsing & C. K. Lee (eds.). *Reclaiming Chinese Society: The New Social Activism*. London: Routledge.

Lee, C. K. (2007). *Against the Law: Labor Protests in China's Rustbelt and Sunbelt*. Berkeley, Los Angeles & London: University of California Press.

Liu, S. (2015). Law's Social Forms: A Powerless Approach to the Sociology of Law. *Law & Social Inquiry*, 40 (1), 1–28.

Lorentzen, P. & Scoggins, S. (2015). Understanding China's Rising Rights Consciousness. *The China Quarterly*, 223, 638–657.

Marshall, A-M. (2003). Injustice Frames, Legality, and the Everyday Construction of Sexual Harassment. *Law and Social Inquiry*, 28 (3), 659–690.

Marshall, A-M. (2005). Idle Rights: Employees' Rights Consciousness and the Construction of Sexual Harassment Policies. *Law & Society Review*, 39 (1), 83–124.

McCann, M. & March, T. (1996). Law and Everyday Forms of Resistance: A Socio-Political Assessment. *Studies in Law, Politics, and Society*, 15, 207–236.

McCann, M. (1994). *Rights at Work: Pay Equity Reform and the Politics of Legal Mobilization*. Chicago & London: The University of Chicago Press.

Merry, S. E. (1990). *Getting Justice and Getting Even: Legal Consciousness among Working-Class Americans*. Chicago & London: The University of Chicago Press.

Nghiem, L. H. (2006). *Work Culture, Gender and Class in Vietnam: Ethnographies of Three Garment Workshops in Ha Noi*. Unpublished PhD thesis. University of Amsterdam, Amsterdam.

O'Brien, K. & Li, L. (2006). *Rightful Resistance in Rural China*. Cambridge: Cambridge University Press.

Pham, D. N. (2005). Confucianism and the Conception of the Law in Vietnam. In J. Gillespie & P. Nicholson (eds.). *Asian Socialism and Legal Change: The Dynamics of Vietnamese and Chinese Reform*. Canberra: ANU E Press & Asia Pacific Press.

Pringle, T. & Clarke, S. (2011). *The Challenge of Transition: Trade Unions in Russia, China and Vietnam*. Basingstoke: Palgrave.

Pun, N. & Smith, C. (2007). Putting Transnational Labour Process in its Place: the Dormitory Labour Regime in Post-Socialist China. *Work, Employment and Society*, 21 (1), 27–45.

Pun, N. (2005). *Made in China: Women Factory Workers in a Global Workplace*. Durham and London: Duke University Press.

Pun, N. (2016). *Migrant Labor in China: Post-Socialist Transformations.* Cambridge: Polity Press.

Quan, K. (2015). One Step Forward: Collective Bargaining Experiments in China and Vietnam. In A. Chan (ed.). *Chinese Workers in Comparative Perspective.* Ithaca: ILR Press.

Quinn, Beth A. (2000) The Paradox of Complaining: Law, Humor, and Harassment in the Everyday Work World. *Law & Social Inquiry*, 25 (4), 1151–1185.

Sarat, A. (1990). …The Law is All Over: Power, Resistance and the Legal Consciousness of the Welfare Poor. *Yale Journal of Law and the Humanities*, 2 (2), 343–379.

Scott, J. (1976). *The Moral Economy of the Peasant: Rebellion and Subsistence in Southeast Asia.* New Haven and London: Yale University Press.

Steinberg, M. W. (2010). Marx, Formal Subsumption and the Law. *Theory and Society*, 39 (2), 173–202.

The Central Committee of the Communist Party of Vietnam (2011). *Political Report at the 11th National Congress.*

Tran, A. (2007). Alternative to the 'Race to the Bottom' in Vietnam: Minimum Wage Strikes in Vietnam and their Aftermath. *Labor Studies Journal*, 32 (4), 430–451.

Trần, N. A. (2013). *Ties that Bind: Cultural Identity, Class, and Law in Vietnam's Labor Resistance.* Ithaca: Cornell Southeast Asia Program Publications.

Vietnam General Confederation of Labour (2015). *Report on the situation of labour disputes and strikes from 2009–2014.*

Walder, A. (1986). *Communist Neo-Traditionalism: Work and Authority in Chinese Industry.* Berkeley, Los Angeles & London: University of California Press.

Wells-Dang, A. (2014). The Political Influence of Civil Society in Vietnam. In London, J. (ed.). *Politics in Contemporary Vietnam: Party, State and Authority Relations.* Hampshire, England & New York: Palgrave Macmillan.

Wong, L. (2011). Chinese Migrant Workers: Rights Attainment Deficits, Rights Consciousness and Personal Strategies. *The China Quarterly*, 208, 870–892.

Yang, L. & van der Wal, Z. (2014). Rule of Morality vs. Rule of Law?. *Public Integrity*, 16 (2), 187–206.

CHAPTER 2

Labour Law and the State's Management of Labour Relations in Vietnam

This chapter provides background information about the labour law regime, needed for an understanding of the relationship between law and labour resistance in Vietnam. It first outlines the development and significance of the Vietnamese Labour Code in the regulation of industrial relations in Vietnam. Second, it discusses key aspects of the Labour Code that concern key workers' rights and benefits, workplace relationships, and the types and resolution of labour disputes. The next section addresses the state's approach towards law and labour regulation over the past few decades, taking the example of strike settlement and strike prevention in the field site of Đồng Nai Province. The last section outlines the development of legal aid by the Vietnam General Confederation of Labour (VGCL) and its objectives in relation to workers' rights protection.

The Vietnamese Labour Code

The introduction of the Labour Code in Vietnam sits within the broader context of the state's passage of new laws that are compatible with and aimed at furthering the development of a market economy. Following market-oriented economic reforms known as *đổi mới* (renovation), the Communist Party of Vietnam (CPV) introduced the 'law-based State' doctrine which emphasises the role of 'stable, authoritative and compulsory law' (Gillespie 2007, p. 845) in governing a modern industrial society. Post-reform legal institutions serve to replace the pre-reform socialist

T. P. Nguyen, *Workplace Justice*, Critical Studies of the Asia-Pacific,
https://doi.org/10.1007/978-981-13-3116-9_2

ideal of moral rules grounded in the Party's mandates and policies, and confer on state officials a 'management tool' to balance social relationships (Gillespie 2007, 2011, p. 248). The new labour legislation adheres to the state's rhetoric of ruling society by law and lays the ground for regulating labour relations according to market principles.

The Vietnamese Labour Code was first passed in 1994 and most recently amended in 2012. The enactment of the Code marks a shift from the pre-reform socialist labour regime, wherein management and workers were state employees and were assumed by the state to have no conflicting interests, to a market labour regime understood as involving differences and potentially conflicts between the interests of employees and management (Do 2011). The Labour Code establishes a contractual labour regime, and designates both rights and obligations of employers and employees upon entering a contractual relationship. The Code also lays the ground for new practices in labour relations, such as the tripartite negotiation of minimum wages at the national level and collective bargaining between employers and employees in workplaces. In so doing, it sets out a new role for the VGCL and its affiliated bodies to represent employees in bargaining with management and ensure the enforcement of their lawful rights and interests.

The Drafting Committee of the 1994 Labour Code included officials from the Ministry of Labour, Invalids and Social Affairs (MOLISA), the Minister of Justice, and the VGCL. Employer representatives were not involved in the drafting process and were a weak voice during consultation. The marginal role of employer representatives at the time can be explained by the immaturity of business associations and the non-existence of the tripartite mechanism in labour-related decision-making (Do 2016). With the development of the private sector and their associational power, the Vietnam Chamber of Commerce and Industry (VCCI), as business representative, became part of the Drafting Committee of the 2006 Amendment Law (Do 2016).

The drafting process also involved consultation with the International Labour Organization (ILO) and resulted in the ratification of 12 ILO conventions. The ratified conventions concern the minimum age for work, night work, underground work for women, weekly days off, labour inspection, and occupational health and safety (ILO n.d.-a, -b). Conventions in relation to freedom of association, collective bargaining, discrimination, child labour, social security, wages, and conditions of work were not ratified (ILO n.d.-b). However, as will be indicated later in the chapter, concepts and principles from some of these conventions were adopted in clauses of the Labour Code, such as those on collective bargaining (*thương lượng tập thể*) and the requirement that minimum wage must satisfy employees' and their families' living needs. Recently, some proposals concerning labour law amendments in Vietnam are brokered as part of US-Vietnam bilateral agreement, following these countries' participation in Trans-Pacific Partnership (TPP).[1] A significant proposal concerns the right of employees to form a grassroots trade union that can operate independently of the VGCL.[2] Yet, the US withdrawal from the TPP in 2017 has nullified the proposed changes and consequently weakened the commitment to grant freedom of association to the Vietnamese workforce.

Articles 4 to 8 of the Labour Code 2012 set out key objectives of the state with regard to labour relations, the rights and obligations of employers and employees, and prohibited acts in labour relations. Some of the state's objectives are (1) to guarantee 'legitimate rights and interests' (*quyền và lợi ích chính đáng*) of employers and encourage agreements providing them with more favourable conditions than those compulsory in the law; (2) to guarantee the rights and interests of employers, and democratic, fair, and civilised labour management in accordance with labour laws; (3) to guide employees and employers to have dialogue and bargain collectively to develop harmonious, stable, and advanced labour relations; and (4) to ensure gender equality and stipulate policies to protect female workers.[3] Following these objectives, prohibited acts on the employers' part include discrimination on the basis of gender, race, or marital status; discrimination on the basis of establishing or joining trade union activities; maltreatment or sexual harassment of a worker; the use of forced labour; and the use of false promises or false advertisement.[4]

Employees are entitled to the following rights: (1) to work and freely choose their work and occupation; (2) to receive a wage commensurate with the skills and knowledge agreed with the employer, and other welfare benefits; (3) to work in a safe and healthy environment; (4) to unilaterally terminate the employment contract in accordance with labour law; (5) to request and participate in dialogue with the employer, and implement regulations on democracy and consultation in the workplace to protect their lawful rights and interests; (6) to establish and join a trade union, and participate in trade union activities; and (7) to strike.[5] The first four categories apply to individual employees, while the remaining three indicate a collective right. There are, however, institutional and legal constraints upon the latter collective rights, especially the right to strike, which will be discussed later. In return, employees are obliged to abide by employment contracts, comply with labour discipline rules and regulations, follow lawful orders of the management, and comply with regulations on social and health insurance.

Labour Contracts

There are three types of employment contract, based on the duration of employment: an indefinite term contract, a definite term contract for the duration of 12 to 36 months, and a contract for seasonal work or a specific task with a duration of less than 12 months.[6] The terms and conditions within a labour contract are established on the basis of employer and employee negotiation and on existing wages and workplace regulations. There are additional conditions under which short-term contracts may be renewed and employees' entitlement to permanent employment is ensured. In particular:

> When an employment contract expires and the employee continues to work, during a period of 30 days from the date of expiry of the contract, the two parties must sign a new employment contract. If no new contract is entered into, the definite term contract shall become an indefinite term one, and the seasonal contract shall become a definite term one within a period of 24 months.
>
> Where the two parties conclude a new contract with a definite term, it shall be the one and only additional definite term employment contract to be signed; after that, if the employee continues to work, an indefinite term contract shall be signed.[7]

Both employers and employees have the right to unilaterally terminate labour contracts under specified circumstances provided that they give notice to the other parties at least three days in advance, depending on the type of contract.[8] In particular, an employee can unilaterally terminate a contract: when certain conditions relating to their work differ from those agreed in the contract; if they are not paid in full or on time; if they face maltreatment and sexual harassment; and when they are unable to fulfil their work due to pregnancy, ill health, and personal problems.[9] An employer may terminate employment in certain circumstances when an employee repeatedly fails to perform their work; when an employee fails to present themselves at work after the expiry of the suspension of the contract; when an employee is unable to work after having received treatment of sickness and accident; and when natural disaster and fire cause the business to scale down.[10]

Employers must not unilaterally terminate a contract when an employee is being treated for illness and accidents, or is on annual leave or other leave permitted by the employer, or when a female employee is pregnant, getting married, on maternity leave, or nursing small children.[11]

Wages and Other Benefits

Chapter VI of the Labour Code defines a wage as an amount of money paid to an employee to perform work as agreed by an employer and employee, according to the nature of the work or position.[12] The employer must ensure that an employee's wage is not lower than the government's minimum wage and the wage will be paid based on labour productivity, the quality of work performed, and must not discriminate between the gender of the worker.[13] The minimum wage is 'the lowest payment for an employee who performs the simplest work in normal working conditions and must ensure the minimum living needs of the employee and his/her family.'[14] Although the Vietnamese government has not ratified the ILO's minimum wage convention, it has incorporated the convention's key feature, the guarantee of employees' livelihoods, into the Code.

Despite the stipulation of the minimum wage in the earliest 1994 version, substantial debates on it did not start until the peak of foreign investment and labour tensions in Vietnam in 2005. Factory workers across industrial regions, especially in foreign direct investment (FDI) sectors, went on numerous strikes to protest against the state's failure to adjust the minimum wage from 1999 to 2005 (Trần 2013, p. 197). Adding to such failure was weak economic management, which led to a two-digit inflation rate after 2007. Following the strikes, the state put in place annual adjustments of the minimum wage, which is also the legal wage that domestic private and FDI enterprises are obliged to pay employees. The annual minimum wage rise was introduced in 2007 and formalised nationally in 2013 with the establishment of the National Wage Council.[15]

The minimum wage varies across four different regions. Each of the four regions includes different provinces, cities, and lower-level municipalities, classified mainly according to their average living costs. The minimum wage in 2015 for region I, which is the highest of all the four regions, is 3.1 million dong (around US $142.2) a month, an increase from 2.7 million dong (around US $123.8) in 2014.[16] Key urban and industrial areas in my field site, Đồng Nai Province (including Biên Hòa, Nhơn Trạch, Vĩnh Cửu, Trảng Bom, and Long Thành), have a region I minimum wage rate, while the remaining rural areas have region II and III rates.[17] In practice, according to VGCL surveys in 2013 and 2014, the minimum wage can satisfy only 70 per cent of the minimum living needs of workers in industrial areas, which falls far short of the legal condition assuring the decent livelihood of employees and their families (Lao Động 31 July 2014).

Apart from the obligation to pay workers the legal wage, the Labour Code stipulates that a company must also develop the wage scale and wage table to be used for wage negotiations on entering into labour contracts and wage payment. The wage scale and wage table must (1) result from the employer's consultation with the workers' representatives, (2) be made available to employees, and (3) be registered with the local labour bureau or relevant authority of industrial zones where the enterprise's office is located.[18]

The most recent guidelines for designing wage tables are in the Government Decree 49/2013. Briefly, the table consists of varying wage levels for employees, from technicians and supervisors, to workers on the shop floor. The aim is to encourage employees to improve their skills or work capacity and reward them accordingly.[19] The difference between two consecutive wage levels must be at least 5 per cent.[20] A company must make known the wage table to employees and register its wage table with the local relevant authority where the company is based.[21] Such a wage table is to ensure fairness in the company's wage rises, with senior workers deemed deserving to be paid a higher rate than junior workers and newcomers. In addition, work that requires skill training, including training provided by the employer, must be paid with a wage at least 7 per cent higher than the national minimum wage. Work undertaken in hazardous and poisonous environments must be paid for at a rate at least 5 per cent higher than the national minimum.[22]

The basic wage, which must be equal to or above the minimum wage, is the standard against which contributions to social, medical, and unemployment insurance are calculated. The *actual* wage paid each month depends on the company's form of payment: whether by the hour, piece rate, or task completion.[23] The piece rate is calculated according to an employee's quantity and quality of production, while task payment is based on quality and the completion of the allocated workload in a certain time.

Employees' extra benefits, as well as other issues related to working conditions,[24] are to be determined through workplace dialogue and collective bargaining between employees, employees' representatives, and employers. A collective bargaining agreement is then established, which 'must not be against the law and must provide for terms and conditions for workers which are more favourable than those provided by law.'[25] An enterprise-level collective bargaining agreement can have a duration of one to three years, and must be submitted to the labour management authority at the city or provincial level. The collective bargaining agreement is obligatory by law and its enforcement shall be monitored by parties in the employment relationship. Besides this agreement, other forms of financial aid and bonuses are determined on the basis of business profits and employees' work performance, as a result of employers' consultation with employees' representatives.[26]

Working Hours and Overtime

Article 104 stipulates that normal working hours shall not exceed eight hours per day or 48 hours per week. An employee who works consecutively for eight hours is to have a rest break of at least 30 minutes, which shall be included in the working hours, and at least 45 minutes break for night-time work. According to Article 110, an employee is further entitled to periods of leave of at least 24 consecutive hours. The employer is responsible for ensuring that on average the employee has at least four leave days per month.

The number of overtime working hours of an employee shall not exceed 50 per cent of the normal working hours in 1 day, 30 hours a month, and 200 hours a year (except for special cases regulated by the government when 300 hours a year is permitted).[27] In regard to the overtime rate, the Labour Code specifies:

> An employee who performs overtime work shall be paid a wage calculated based on wage unit for piece work or piece rate, or the wage of his/her current work as follows:

- On regular days, at least equal to 150 per cent
- On the weekly day off, at least equal to 200 per cent
- On public holidays and paid leave days, at least 300 per cent.[28]

Additional guidelines on premium overtime rates are also given for employees performing night work and overtime night work. The Code also stipulates that employee's consent must be obtained for overtime work.

There are also provisions for rest time during working hours and between shifts, weekly breaks, and annual leave. Employees are entitled to paid leave on six public holidays.

Labour Discipline Regulations

Chapter VIII of the Labour Code outlines employers' and employees' obligations with regard to workplace discipline. An employer with at least 10 employees is required to have workplace regulations in writing, which must not be contrary to the Labour Code and relevant legal provisions.[29] Similar to other work-related documents, workplace discipline must result from the employers' consultation with the employees' representative, must be registered with the labour authority, and must be displayed within the enterprise.[30] In short, an employer can impose disciplinary measures on employees who are deemed to breach workplace regulations with regard to production, business assets, and equipment, provided that the employer demonstrates evidence about the employee's mistake and an employee is entitled to defend his/her behaviour in the settlement of disciplinary measures.[31]

Discipline can take the form of reprimanding, deferment of any wage increase for a maximum of six months, demotion, or dismissal.[32] Article 126 specifies that dismissal may be imposed when an employee commits an act of theft, embezzlement, or takes illicit drugs; causes threats to the assets or interests of the employer; or has been absent from work for 5 accumulated days in one month or 20 accumulated days in one year without legitimate reason. There are circumstances in which an employee is exempt from disciplinary measures, including when he/she is on leave due to illness and other types of leave, with the employer's consent in advance. A female employee who is pregnant, on maternity leave, or breast-feeding children under 12 months old is also exempt from discipline.[33]

Separate Provisions for Female Workers

The main purpose of having separate provisions for female workers is to promote gender equality in the workplace. These provisions take into account female workers' well-being and their child-bearing and child-rearing duties. Employers, therefore, are obliged to implement workplace policies and provide female employees with flexible working arrangements to fulfil these objectives.

Separate provisions for female employees include maternity leave, rest time, and measures to protect the well-being of pregnant employees. Female employees in general are entitled to an extra 30 minutes break during their menstruation period.[34] Female employees who are in the later stage of their pregnancy or are nursing a child under 12 months of age are not required to do night work or overtime and may be transferred to lighter tasks, or have their daily working hours reduced by one hour while receiving the full wage; and, as stated earlier, they are exempt from any labour disciplinary measures.[35] They can take maternity leave for up to six months and receive 100 per cent of the average wage for the full six months.[36] Further details of maternity benefits are provided in the Law on Social Insurance.

Trade Unions

This brief section in the Labour Code outlines key activities of unions at the grassroots level, that is, unions established within the business and under jurisdiction of VGCL branches at either the city or the district level. Article 188 specifies that grassroots trade unions:

> represent and protect the lawful and legitimate rights and interests of trade union members and workers; participate in negotiating, signing, and monitoring the implementation of collective bargaining agreements, [...], participate in resolving labour disputes; conduct social dialogue and cooperation with employers to build harmonious, stable and progressive labour relations in the enterprise, agency or organisation.[37]

Employers are responsible for supporting trade union activities and are prohibited from preventing or making it difficult for workers to form, join, or operate a trade union, or to take other coercive or discriminatory measures against workers and unionists.[38] Upper-level trade unions, which are local branches of the VGCL established at district levels and in industrial zones, also support grassroots trade unions in their operation, as well as educate and improve employees' understanding of labour and trade union laws.[39] Further guidelines on trade union's operation and activities are given in the Law on Trade Union.

The Resolution of Labour Disputes

There are separate provisions for the resolution of individual and collective labour disputes, and for different types of collective disputes.[40] Dispute resolution shall involve the representatives of each party, and be initiated through direct negotiation by the two parties. When one of the parties refuses to negotiate, the negotiation is unsuccessful, or the agreement reached is reneged by one party, the other party can request a resolution by an authoritative agency or individual.

A notable feature of formal labour dispute mechanisms in Vietnam is the distinction between rights-based and interests-based collective disputes. A collective labour dispute over 'rights' *(quyền)* is a dispute between a workers' collective and the employer arising out of different interpretations and implementation of labour laws, collective bargaining agreements, internal work regulations, and other lawful regulations and agreements.[41] This type of dispute is firstly to be resolved by the labour mediator, who works in the labour bureau or labour management authority at the district levels.[42] In case mediation fails or a successful mediation is not enforced, a disputing party can request a resolution by the People's Committee at the district level, and finally, the People's Court.[43] A collective labour dispute concerning 'interests' *(lợi ích)* is a dispute arising out of the request of the worker's collective for the establishment of new working conditions different to or additional to those set out in labour laws and other lawful regulations and agreements.[44] This will also go through a similar stage of mediation, before being resolved through the Labour Arbitration Council, established at the provincial level and made up of representatives from the state's labour authority, unions, and employers' organisations.[45]

As mentioned earlier, Vietnamese employees have the right to strike under particular stipulated conditions. A strike is 'a temporary, voluntary and organised stoppage of work by the worker's collective in order to achieve demands in the process of labour dispute resolution.'[46] Before the 2012 amendment to the Labour Code, employees could legally go on strike over both rights- and interests-based disputes. However, with the 2012 amendment, a strike must stem from an interest-based collective labour dispute,[47] following a failed or unenforced arbitration outcome by the Labour Arbitration Council. A strike must be organised by the company union or, in places where the company union has not been established, the upper-level union.[48] A decision to go on strike must receive approval from at least 50 per cent of employees whose opinions are solicited, and details and plans about the strike need to be notified to the employer and the provincial-level union and labour authority.[49] Strikes that violate this legal procedure are to be resolved on an ad hoc basis by the labour authority, unions, and relevant state agencies at the district levels. The next section will touch on this ad hoc measure and discuss the state's ambivalent approach towards law and labour relations.

Alternative Measures of Labour Dispute Resolution

As the formal system of dispute resolution is complex and exists in a formalistic manner, the government and union have put in place two alternative avenues. The first avenue is undertaken by the Labour Inspectorate, which belongs to the MOLISA at the city/provincial levels. Decree 119/2014/ND-CP in 2014 gives details on two types of complaints accepted in this avenue, which are 'complaining' and 'denunciation.' 'Complaining' is defined as 'an act in which an employee,[50] intern, apprentice, following the procedures outlined in this Decree, request the person in charge of resolving complaints on labour to reconsider the employer's decisions or conduct when he/she judges that those decisions and conduct contravene labour laws and violate their lawful rights and interests.'[51] As the first step, an employee must direct the complaints to his/her employer, who has a maximum of 30 days to resolve them.[52] If the resolution is not satisfactory or the time limit has passed, an employee can bring his/her complaints to the chief labour inspector and expect the resolution within 45 days.[53]

Denunciation is defined as 'an act in which employees [...] report to the authority about legal violations by individuals, organisations and agencies [...] that bring harm to, or threaten to harm the State's interests, or lawful rights and interests of citizens or other organisations.'[54] The chief labour inspector shall investigate and resolve the denunciation within 60 days.[55] The resolutions of complaints and denunciations are legally enforceable.

The second avenue for workers and employees to voice their complaints is the provincial and upper-level unions. The Examination Committee of the unions is charged with receiving and processing complaints. I will provide further detail about the process of complaint handling in Chap. 4. Unlike the first administrative avenue, an employee opting to take this path is not required to first direct his/her complaints to an employer, and can thus expect the resolution within 10 days.

The State's Approach to Labour Law and Labour Relations: The Case of Strike Settlement and Strike Prevention Measures

The transition to a market-based labour regime, following the late 1980s economic reform, has caught the Vietnamese state in a paradoxical position regarding its stance on labour issues. On the one hand, it continues to hail the working class as the vanguard of revolution and the path to socialism. Key measures to develop a strong working class and enhance its contribution to the economy, as outlined in Decree 20-NQ/TW (Central Committee of CPV 2008b), include skill development, amendments of labour laws and policies and monitoring of their enforcement, and taking care of workers' mental and physical lives. Different state agencies, unions, socio-political organisations, and employers are responsible for executing those measures. On the other hand, the government also highlights the importance of attracting foreign investment to foster industrial development (Government of Vietnam 2009; Nicholson 2002). This positioning has posed a dilemma for the state and VGCL when it comes to the mediation and management of labour disputes. The ongoing objective of developing 'harmonious and stable labour relations,' which originated from the Labour Code 1994, represents the rhetorical effort to justify the regulatory capacity of the state to strengthen the labour law regime and preserve industrial order.

The escalation of collective labour disputes, mostly in the form of factory strikes, has highlighted this dilemma and posed a particular political challenge, given the state's concern with stability. Between 1995 and 2012, when the Labour Code took effect, there were 5000 strikes across the nation (Lao Động 26 July 2013). Labour disputes put pressure on the state and VGCL to stand by workers, whom they claim to represent, and yet, they also affect the positive image of the state towards current and potential foreign investors, whose capital has been crucial to the country's economic progress. State authorities have put the blame on foreign investors and managers for failing to comply with labour laws, which in turn implies that workers' demands are lawful and legitimate (Siu and Chan 2015). However, at the same time, the state also rules all strikes illegal as they go against the procedures for resolving collective labour disputes. The rhetorical approach of the state towards legal compliance and labour disputes exemplifies the dilemma it has faced, and continues to face, in sustaining its relationship and image with both workers and managers over the last two decades.

The state's approach to law and labour relations in the past decade can be traced back to Directive 22-CT/TW (Central Committee of the CPV 2008a), which also mandates the practices of the VGCL and local authorities in charge of labour issues. The Directive first acknowledges the ongoing problem of collective labour disputes, which contravene legal procedures and in turn affect social order and industrial activities. It suggests that the major causes of labour disputes are employers' limited enforcement of the Labour Code and their lack of commitment to employees' lawful rights and interests. The Directive thus demands that different state bodies enhance the implementation of labour law in businesses and, in particular, that unions increase workers' legal understanding. It lays the foundation for the passage of the government's national plan to develop 'stable labour relations in enterprises,' whereby 'the interests of all parties are in harmony; the mental and physical lives of employees are improved; [...] labour disputes and strikes are reduced; and strikes that violate legal procedures are prevented' (Government of Vietnam 2014a, b).

Directive 22 additionally promotes existing practices outside the scope of the Labour Code that (mainly) serve the goal of sustaining growth and stability. One of those practices is the ad hoc measure of strike settlement established at the city or province level. This local approach to settling strikes emerged in the mid-1990s in key industrial provinces and cities and has been deemed effective by local governments as a way of quelling strikes and promptly restoring stability (Do 2011). From the state's perspective, strike settlement and strike prevention measures complement the existing system of law enforcement, including labour inspection, and can be substituted for the formal mechanism of labour dispute resolution. The Directive's guidelines around strike settlement and prevention still incorporate terms and regulations set out in the Labour Code, in order to ensure that the behaviour of both company management and workers accords with legal rule. The resolution of strikes therefore becomes an avenue for the unions and labour authorities to communicate the Labour

Code to employment parties and foster their understanding in the interest of harmony and industrial stability.

Đồng Nai Province is a good example of this practice. As a pioneer in the wave of industrialisation and foreign investment in the south, this province has also been among the regions experiencing a record number of collective labour disputes. Prior to 2008, the main responsibility for settling strikes rested with labour mediators from the Department of Labour in coordination with relevant unions and authorities. After 2008, as labour mediators were overloaded with the escalating number and complexity of strikes, this responsibility was shifted to governments at city/district levels (Interview, 18 December 2014). In 2009, the People's Committee issued decision 22/QD-UBND, which established a collaborative scheme to resolve labour disputes. The decision indicated clearly that it targeted disputes that do not comply with the formal procedures designated in the Labour Code and effectively includes strikes and work stoppages. The rationale for this decision reflects the limitations of the mechanism set out in the Code and the need to preserve stability. As stated in a report by the Department of Labour, Invalids, and Social Affairs (DOLISA) (2011), the mechanism which separates disputes on rights from disputes on interests 'has failed to reflect social realities, making it difficult for responsible stakeholders to execute their functions.' In addition, 'the time limit for resolving disputes, which is five days for disputes on rights, and seven days for disputes on interests, causes delays,' and affects the recovery to normal production activities (DOLISA 2011).

Following the provincial decision 22/QD-UBND, strike action teams were established at the city/district level, headed by the Chair of the People's Committee at this level. Strike action teams include upper-level union, officials from the IZA, and mediators from the labour bureau within the administrative area. In reality, the Chair of the People's Committee usually delegates his/her role to an upper-level union official, who takes the lead in the bargaining process. The engagement of labour mediators and IZA officials in strike settlement varies between lower-level cities and municipalities, depending on bureaucratic arrangements. For instance, the labour mediator and the upper-level unions share equal responsibilities in Trảng Bom District; in other places, the labour mediators mainly work as note-takers during the resolution meetings. Such variation does not affect the working principles of the action teams in these places.

When arriving at the strike scene, the action team first gathers workers together and solicits their reasons for striking. The action team then can opt for either of the two approaches: having a closed meeting with management without the workers' presence; or requesting management and workers to have a dialogue, with the strike action team in attendance, in the company yard or kitchen area. Most of the time, state security officers also make their presence known to ensure that there is no disturbance, damage, or violence, rather than to suppress the striking workers.

In taking the first approach, after receiving a list of workers' problems and demands, the action team brings them to a closed meeting with management, classifying them into rights and interests. Regardless of whether workers explicitly draw on legal principles in making their demands, strike settlers examine and find a resolution to them based on labour law and policy. With regard to rights, the management is asked to review their conduct and policies in accordance with state law and policy. With regard to interests, the team will bargain with management on behalf of workers, bearing in mind the company's rate of production and its losses or profits. If necessary, the action team will ask a small group of workers' representatives to join the meeting. These are often leaders of production teams or assembly lines. If required, these people can convey resolutions to the rest of the workers as soon as an outcome from the meeting has been reached, in order to quickly calm the crowd. Company management is required to issue a final announcement to workers at the end of the bargaining process (Interview, 15 December 2014; 18 December 2014; 20 January 2015).

Alternatively, the action team can ask workers and management whether they would like to hold a direct dialogue, which normally takes place in the kitchen area or in an open area outside. Interviewed officials referred to Government Decree 60/2013/ND-CP as the recent policy guideline and considered themselves as mediators and facilitators of the conversations. The action team can then explain and give advice about legal and policy issues, the main purpose being to enhance a mutual understanding between the two sides, which in turn helps reduce the occurrences of labour disputes. Decree 60 also stipulates how and how often communication should take place between employers and employees, and aims to promote a form of grassroots democracy in the enterprises.[56]

Promoting legality in labour relations seems to be the main principle of strike settlement. For instance, one union official said:

> We explain to workers about the legal regulations, company regulations, and collective agreements. We offer our opinions and analyse what is right or wrong in order for the two sides [workers and employers] to compromise bit by bit and reach a consensus. (Interview, 23 December 2014)

During our conversations, labour mediators and IZA officials frequently mentioned the law and referred to the legality of disputing parties' actions. They considered legal compliance as a goal and focused on persuading management to change company policies in accordance with labour laws. While these officials tended to work more with management, union officials that I interviewed often claimed to take the lead in dealing with workers, such as explaining what counts as lawful demands and actions, and mobilising them to get back to work.

Officials in the strike action team also make use of other persuasive tactics to put an end to strikes. In his recent dissertation, Ha Do found that local strike action teams in the south have taken an approach similar to the party campaign of 'mass mobilisation,' as expressed through 'soft' measures such as verbally mobilising (*vận động*) and persuading (*thuyết phục*) workers to get back to work (Do 2016, p. 219). The action teams also seek to promote empathy and understanding between management and workers to mediate their conflicts, instead of issuing administrative fines to law-violating businesses or suppressing workers. Soft measures were also found in my conversations with officials of the strike action teams. In recalling their experiences in strike settlement, they mentioned such things as '[asking workers to] share the difficulties with the company' or '[asking management to] consider giving more to senior workers for their long-term service.' It is thus evident that strike settlement measures are a combination of law-based and extra-legal verbal tactics by the state and unions, designed to ease workplace tensions. Whether these measures are effective in promoting legal compliance and enhancing the image of the state in the eyes of workers and management will be further examined in Chap. 3.

Since 2009, in addition to strike settlement, the province has also put in place strike prevention measures to monitor businesses' compliance with labour laws. These measures can be broken down into two main tasks: advising business of the need for an annual wage adjustment and year-end bonus payment, and coordinating with management and company unions to resolve early signs of unrest. The unions and authorities are aware of the sensitivity of the January–February period before the Lunar

New Year holidays, when a large number of strikes occur. Following the national government's annual wage rise, which normally takes effect at the start of the year, workers are inclined to expect some sort of announcement from the company on its new wage policy, together with the year-end bonus. With this in mind, the provincial labour federation, upper-level unions, and municipal labour bureaus have coordinated to visit businesses at this time of year, to remind them of these matters. Particular attention is paid to businesses that are prone to labour disputes. One union official said about the task:

> If the enterprises have not made wage adjustments following the government's minimum wage decision, nor decided on the year-end bonus, our team reminds them to do so as soon as possible and gives them a 'due' date. We then request them to report these matters, once decided on, to upper-level unions and relevant state bodies. (Interview, 14 January 2015)

I consider these strike settlement and strike prevention measures as forms of 'regulatory conversations,' defined as 'forms of interpersonal communications' between the regulators and regulated, which take place in 'formal and informal settings' (Black 2002, pp. 170–171). Strike settlement and prevention functions as a quasi-regulatory practice, whereby the state and union officials, in attempting to broker an agreement, seek to influence the behaviours of disputing parties in line with state laws and policies. These measures allow state authorities and union officials to mould the behaviour of management and workers, without resorting to stringent legal measures that might damage the state's image in the eyes of both parties.

In 2015, the government amended and tightened the regulation on strike resolution. Decree 5/2015 rules that when an illegal strike breaks out, the employer is required to immediately report to the district government and upper-level unions.[57] After relevant bodies have investigated the situation, the city or provincial government shall issue an announcement regarding the strike's illegality. Thus, the local government now takes over the role of the local court to rule over the lawfulness of strikes, and employers can have the unlawful strike verdict issued within a day when they can proceed with the calculation of damages and costs incurred from it. The Decree also reinstates Article 218 of the Labour Code that employees shall receive no wage during the time of strike engagement.[58]

The Union's Legal Aid Activities

Free legal aid for employees is not a central pillar of national law and policy promoting legal aid activities (which mainly target the poor, people of ethnic minorities, people of the revolution, the elderly and disabled). The Vietnamese state's initiative in providing legal aid can be traced back to Resolution 03/NQ-HNTW issued by the Central Committee of the CPV in 1997. The Resolution incorporates legal consultation for state agencies and citizens, especially the poor, into the broader justice reform project. It laid the ground for subsequent decrees providing guidelines for the organisation and operation of legal consultation activities and legal aid centres.

The VGCL issued its first guidelines for the union's legal aid activities in 2004, following the state's emphasis on promoting legal compliance in labour relations. The objectives of legal aid provision are to guarantee the legal and legitimate rights and interests of union members and employees, and contribute to enhancing their legal understanding and awareness of the need for legal compliance.[59] The unions at different levels can establish either legal aid centres, offices, or groups to carry out their legal aid activities, which focus on labour and union laws. In addition, the centres can expand the scope of their activities by providing and charging for legal services in other civil, criminal, and administrative areas.[60] Throughout their operations, legal aid agencies have the right to request relevant authorities to provide information related to issues under question. They can suggest that unions request the authorities to resolve issues related to the rights and interests of union members and employees.[61] In reality, Legal Aid Centres (LACs) of provincial-level unions in key industrial areas had been in operation well before the VGCL's decision. For example, LACs in Hồ Chí Minh City and Đồng Nai Province were established in the early 1990s. Recent improvements in legal aid activities have followed the prime minister's Decision 31/2009/QĐ-TTg to approve a plan to promulgate and promote laws to employees and employers in the period 2009–2012.

The VGCL decision also specifies the rights and obligations of legal aid recipients. In particular, they have the right to (1) request legal aid, or delegate such a request to other people; (2) be informed about the outcomes of consultation; (3) have the contents of legal advice or consultation kept confidential at their request; and (4) make complaints and denunciations regarding legal advisers' behaviour.[62] For their part, recipients are responsible for (1) proving that they are eligible for legal aid by providing essential identification; (2) providing sufficient and correct information or documentation; and (3) following the rules and regulations of the legal aid organisations.[63]

According to the VGCL's Decree 4/NQ-TLD in 2010, there were 47 legal aid centres and offices, and 569 legal aid groups in operation across Vietnam. This Decree reiterates the significance of improving the activities of legal aid 'as a way to allow trade unions to carry out their functions of representing and protecting the lawful rights and interests of employees.'[64] Further targets and objectives were issued and revamped in 2014, focusing on legal aid at non-state enterprises. Decree 04b/NQ-TLD of 2014 highlights the need for greater cooperation between different levels of the trade union in carrying out legal education and mobilisation. Importantly, it also mentions the longer-term impact of legal aid in providing employees and workers an opportunity to 'do research and learn about laws themselves, and defend their lawful rights and interests.'[65]

Most recently, *Lao Động*, the national newspaper for employees, has organised three 'Festivals of legal consultation for employees'[66] at three different tourist attraction sites in Hồ Chí Minh City, Bình Dương, and Đồng Nai Provinces. The newspaper, in liaison with the local-level unions, offers free tickets of entry to thousands of workers across these provinces, who had the opportunity to receive legal advice from labour lawyers and, through small plays performed by some volunteer workers, learn about the legal nature of commonly tricky situations at work (Lao Động 1 November 2015; 10 January 2016a; 20 March 2016b). The festivals were broadcast live on local television channels. The festival organisers also popularise the activities of legal aid centres affiliated with provincial-level unions and the contacts provided by the newspaper for legal consultation.

This chapter has outlined key provisions of the Labour Code, state policy approaches, and measures aimed at supplementing the Code and enhancing labour relations, including an example of strike settlement measures in the case-study province, and legal aid activities for workers. The four chapters that follow will present workers' narratives and evaluate whether and how these aspects of law contribute to workers' pursuit of justice and acts of resistance.

Notes

1. US-Viet Nam Plan for the Enhancement of Trade and Labour Relations (2016). Retrieved from https://ustr.gov/sites/default/files/TPP-Final-Text-Labour-US-VN-Plan-for-Enhancement-of-Trade-and-Labour-Relations.pdf. The Trans-Pacific Partnership is a trade agreement between 12 countries spanning the American and Asia-Pacific regions.
2. Still, any grassroots trade unions that would be formed have to register themselves with the VGCL or a competent government body.
3. Art 4, Labour Code.
4. Art 8.
5. Art 5.
6. Art 22.1.
7. Art 22.2.
8. Arts 37-38.
9. Art 37.1.
10. Art 38.1.
11. Art 39.
12. Art 90.1.
13. Art 90.2-3.
14. Art 91.
15. State-led wage bargaining has taken place annually since 2007, with the consultation of the MOLISA, the VGCL, and representatives of the business community. In 2013, the National Wage Council (NWC) was established to formalise the tripartite bargaining for wage adjustment (Decree 49/2013, Art 3-5). Its core function is to consult the government about adjusting and announcing the regional minimum wages. The official launch of the NWC is an institutionalised effort to reform the wage system, allowing space for the Ministry of Labour, the employers' and employees' representatives to deliberate on minimum wage. The council is composed of 15 members who reach a decision by votes: five officials from MOLISA, five members from the employers' representative organisation, led by the Vietnam Chamber of Commerce and Industry (VCCI), and five officials from the VGCL.
16. Art 3, Decree 103/2014/ND-CP on regulations of the regional minimum wages for employees working in enterprises, cooperatives, group work, farms, households, as individuals, and in organizations and agencies that employ labour according to the labour contract; Art 3, Decree 182/2013/ND-CP on regulations of the regional minimum wages for employees working in enterprises, cooperatives, group work, farms, households, as individuals, and in organizations and agencies that employ labour according to the labour contract.

17. Appendix of the list of areas for the implementation of the regional minimum wages from 1 January 2015, Decree 103/2014/ND-CP.
18. Art 93, Labour Code.
19. Art 7.2, Decree 49/2013/ND-CP on detailed regulations of implementing some clauses of the Labour Code on wages.
20. Art 7.2, Decree 49/2013/ND-CP.
21. Art 7.6, Decree 49/2013/ND-CP.
22. Art 7.3, Decree 49/2013/ND-CP.
23. Art 94, Labour Code.
24. These issues include necessary steps taken to ensure occupational health and safety. To help improve employees' general well-being and prevent occupational diseases and accidents, employers are responsible for organising periodic health checks, depending on the physical status and working environment of employees (Article 152).
25. Art 73, Labour Code.
26. Art 102.
27. Art 106.
28. Art 97.
29. Art 119.1-2.
30. Art 119.3-4 and Art 120.
31. Art 123.
32. Art 125.
33. Art 123.4-5.
34. Art 155.5.
35. Art 155.1-4.
36. Art 157.
37. In reality, most grassroots trade unionists take up their positions without employees' votes and are usually people holding managerial and supervisory posts.
38. Art 189 and Art 190, Labour Code.
39. Art 188.1.
40. Chapter XIV, Labour Code.
41. Art 3.
42. Art 201.
43. Art 204.2a-3 and Art 205.
44. Art 3.
45. Art 204.2b-3 and Art 206.
46. Art 209.1.
47. Art 209.2.
48. Art 210.
49. Art 211-213.

50. The Decree uses the term 'employee' in a broad sense; it does not make specific mention of 'the collective of employees,' or whether it shall apply to individual and/or collective types of complaints.
51. Art 3.1, Decree 119/2014/ND-CP.
52. Art 15.1 and Art 19, Decree 119/2014/ND-CP.
53. Art 15.2 and Art 27, Decree 119/2014/ND-CP.
54. Art 3.4, Decree 119/2014/ND-CP.
55. Art 39, Decree 119/2014/ND-CP and Art 21, Law on Denunciations (No. 3/2011/QH13).
56. Art 10–12, Decree 60/2013/ND-CP on detailed regulations of Clause 3, Article 63 of the Labour Code on grassroots democracy mechanism at workplaces. In particular, periodic dialogues between employers and employees' representatives should take place every three months, and outcomes from these dialogues must be made known to employees. Employer is also responsible for organising the annual convention with the participation of a proposed number of employee delegates every year.
57. Art 35.1, Decree 5/2015/ND-CP.
58. Art 218.2 states that employees shall not be paid during the time they participate in strikes, *unless* otherwise agreed by employer and employees.
59. Art 1, Decision 785/2004/QD-TLD on the organisation and activities of the union's legal aid.
60. Art 9, Decision 785/2004/QD-TLD.
61. Art 13, Decision 785/2004/QD-TLD.
62. Art 15, Decision 785/2004/QD-TLD.
63. Art 16, Decision 785/2004/QD-TLD.
64. Preamble, Decree 4/NQ-TLD on reforming and enhancing the quality of legal aid activities of the union organisation in the new era.
65. Section III.1, Decree 04b/NQ-TLD on enhancing the effectiveness of legal communication and education for workers and employees in the new era.
66. *Ngày hội tư vấn pháp luật lao động*. The term '*ngày hội*' (festival) in Vietnam is sometimes used to refer to a large information or educational session that allows participants to raise questions and queries with the service providers or advertisers, rather than an event of entertainment or recreational nature.

References

Black, J. (2002). Regulatory Conversations. *Journal of Law and Society*, 29 (1), 163–196.

Department of Labour, Invalids and Social Affairs (2011). Report on the situation of labour disputes, strikes and measures to prevent and resolve labour disputes and strikes in Đồng Nai.

Do, H. H. (2016). *The Dynamics of Legal Transplantation Regulating Industrial Conflicts in Post-Đổi Mới Vietnam*. Unpublished PhD thesis. The University of Melbourne, Melbourne.

Do, Q. C. (2011). *Understanding Industrial Relations Transformation in Vietnam: A Multi-Dimensional Analysis*. Unpublished PhD thesis. The University of Sydney, Sydney.

Gillespie, J. (2007). Rethinking the Role of Judicial Independence in Socialist-Transforming East Asia. *The International and Comparative Law Quarterly*, 56 (4), 837–869.

Gillespie, J. (2011). Exploring the Limits of the Judicialization of Urban Land Disputes in Vietnam. *Law and Society Review*, 45 (2), 241–275.

Government of Vietnam (2009). Decree 13/NQ-CP on the directions and measures for attracting and managing foreign direct investment in the future.

Government of Vietnam (2013a). Decree 182/2013/ND-CP on regulations of the regional minimum wages for employees working in enterprises, cooperatives, group work, farms, households, as individuals, and in organizations and agencies that employ labour according to the labour contract.

Government of Vietnam (2013b). Decree 49/2013/ND-CP on detailed regulations of implementing some articles of the Labour Code on wages.

Government of Vietnam (2013c). Decree 60/2013/ND-CP on detailed regulations of Clause 3, Article 63 of the Labour Code on grassroots democracy mechanism at workplaces.

Government of Vietnam (2014a). Decree 103/2014/ND-CP on regulations of the regional minimum wages for employees working in enterprises, cooperatives, group work, farms, households, as individuals, and in organizations and agencies that employ labour according to the labour contract.

Government of Vietnam (2014b). Decree 119/2014/ND-CP on detailed regulations of some articles relating to complaints and denunciations of the Labour Code, Law on Apprenticeship, and Law on Vietnamese employees working overseas.

Government of Vietnam (2015). Decree 05/2015/ND-CP on detailed regulations and implementation guidelines relating to some contents of the Labour Code, Hà Nội.

International Labour Organization, n.d.-a, Ratifications for Vietnam. https://www.ilo.org/dyn/normlex/en/f?p=NORMLEXPUB:11200:0::NO::P11200_COUNTRY_ID:103004. Accessed 24th June 2016.

International Labour Organization, n.d.-b, Up-to-date Conventions and Protocols not ratified by Vietnam. https://www.ilo.org/dyn/normlex/en/f?p=1000:11210:0::NO:11210:P11210_COUNTRY_ID:103004. Accessed 24th June 2016.

Lao Động (1/11/2015). Sáng nay, báo Lao Động tổ chức Ngày hội tư vấn, giải đáp pháp luật cho người lao động. https://laodong.vn/cong-doan/sang-nay-bao-lao-dong-to-chuc-ngay-hoi-tu-van-giai-dap-phap-luat-cho-nguoi-lao-dong-392395.bld. Accessed 19th December 2017.

Lao Động (10/1/2016a). Ngày 10.1, Báo Lao Động tổ chức ngày hội tư vấn và giải đáp pháp luật cho NLĐ: Công nhân lao động hiểu luật để tư bảo vệ mình. https://laodong.vn/cong-doan/ngay-101-bao-lao-dong-to-chuc-ngay-hoi-tu-van-va-giai-dap-phap-luat-cho-nld-cong-nhan-lao-dong-hieu-luat-de-tu-bao-ve-minh-414139.bld. Accessed 19th December 2017.

Lao Động (20/3/2016b). Ngày hội tư vấn, giải đáp pháp luật cho người lao động tại Đồng Nai. https://laodong.vn/cong-doan/ngay-hoi-tu-van-giai-dap-phap-luat-cho-nguoi-lao-dong-tai-dong-nai-530743.bld. Accessed 19th December 2017.

Lao Động (26/7/2013). Vì sao hơn 5.000 cuộc đình công không do công đoàn lãnh đạo. https://laodong.vn/cong-doan/vi-sao-hon-5000-cuoc-dinh-cong-khong-do-cong-doan-lanh-dao-129494.bld. Accessed 24th June 2016.

Lao Động (31/7/2014). Chủ tịch Tổng LĐLĐVN Đặng Ngọc Tùng: Lương tối thiểu vùng I năm 2015 cần đạt 3,4 triệu đồng/người/tháng. http://laodong.com.vn/cong-doan/chu-tich-tong-ldldvn-dang-ngoc-tung-luong-toi-thieu-vung-i-nam-2015-can-dat-34-trieu-dongnguoithang-229651.bld. Accessed 24th June 2016.

National Assembly of Vietnam 1994 & 2012, *Bộ Luật Lao Động [Labour Code]*.

Nicholson, P. (2002). Vietnam's Labour Market: Transition and the Role of Law. In S. Cooney, T. Lindsey, R. Mitchell & Y. Zhu (eds.). *Law and Labour Market Regulation in East Asia*. London & New York: Routledge.

Prime Minister of Vietnam (2009). Decision 31/2009/QĐ-TTg on approving the plan of propagating and communicating law for employees and employers in enterprises from 2009–2012.

Siu, K. & Chan, A. (2015). Strike Wave in Vietnam, 2006–2011. *Journal of Contemporary Asia*, 45 (1), 71–91.

The Central Committee of the Communist Party of Vietnam (1997). Resolution 03/NQ-HNTW at the 3rd National Convention on promoting citizens' right to autonomy and continuing to develop the transparent and strong state of the Socialist Republic of Vietnam.

The Central Committee of the Communist Party of Vietnam (2008a). Directive 22-CT/TW on intensifying leadership and guidance on developing harmonious, stable and progressive labour relations.

The Central Committee of the Communist Party of Vietnam (2008b). Resolution 20-NQ/TW at the 6th National Convention on continuing to develop Vietnamese working class in the modernisation and industrialisation era.

The People's Committee of Đồng Nai province (2009). Decision 22/2009/QD-UBND issuing cooperative mechanism for resolving collective labour disputes that do not follow the legal procedures and paperwork at enterprises in Đồng Nai.

Trần, A. N. (2013). *Ties that Bind: Cultural Identity, Class, and Law in Vietnam's Labor Resistance*. Ithaca: Cornell Southeast Asia Program Publications.
Vietnam General Confederation of Labour (2004). Decision 785/2004/QD-TLD on the organisation and activities of the union' legal aid.
Vietnam General Confederation of Labour (2010). Decree 04/NQ-TLD on reforming and enhancing the quality of legal aid activities of the union organisation in the new era.
Vietnam General Confederation of Labour (2014). Decree 04b/NQ-TLĐ on enhancing the effectiveness of legal communication and education for workers and employees in the new era.

CHAPTER 3

On the Shop Floor

This chapter examines how workers in strike-affected companies in Đồng Nai Province justify their grievances and includes an in-depth discussion of one company case study. Going on strike is so far the most common form of resistance taken by Vietnamese workers. Almost all strikes in Vietnam today contravene procedures outlined in the Labour Code, as they do not strictly stem from disputes about 'interests' (*lợi ích*) as opposed to 'rights' (*quyền*), occur without union leadership, and bypass the process of mediation and arbitration. For these reasons, the state and unions in Vietnam have deemed all strikes illegal; yet, at the same time, they attribute the reasons for strikes to businesses' violation of labour law (Siu and Chan 2015; Trần 2013). While the form of strikes has remained unchanged over the past two decades, their causes have shifted from workers' demands for rights to demands for interests since 2006 (Clarke, Lee and Do 2007). In its recent report, the Vietnam General Confederation of Labour (VGCL) observes that, from 2010 to 2014, strikes mainly stemmed from collective disputes based on interests or on both rights and interests, while strikes before 2009 occurred mainly due to businesses' violations of labour law (VGCL 2015).

Existing works on labour resistance in Vietnam show that factory workers have employed their understanding of the Labour Code to mobilise fellow workers and justify their demands in strike actions (Kerkvliet 2011; Trần 2013; Siu and Chan 2015). For example, Trần writes about how, in a well-known strike of workers in Hue Phong Leather Shoe Factory in

T. P. Nguyen, *Workplace Justice*, Critical Studies of the Asia-Pacific,
https://doi.org/10.1007/978-981-13-3116-9_3

2006, two female workers coordinated with each other and mobilised their fellows both inside and outside the factory to take action (Trần 2013, p. 240). These women took advantage of their knowledge of the Labour Code and their social and productive networks to pressure management to comply with the minimum wage and social insurance scheme. This well-known case study suggests that despite the complicated legal process that deters workers from taking legal actions, the Labour Code sets out legal entitlements which workers draw on in their collective actions against management's conduct (Kerkvliet 2011; Trần 2013). Further evidence can also be found in Vietnam's main labour newspaper, *Lao Động*, in their coverage of strikes where workers 'demand their rights and interests' (*đòi quyền lợi*) (Lao Động 2011–2014).

Still, these studies tend to focus on the causal processes leading to strikes and take labour law into consideration when legal language and institutions are explicitly deployed before and during strikes. My analysis instead explores how varying aspects of labour law and workplace practices more broadly contribute to striking workers' motivations, demands, and justifications for their actions. As has been shown in socio-legal studies on employees' workplace grievances in the USA, employees' decisions to escalate or give up on their disputes are subject to numerous factors concerning their workplace experiences, with little influence from their awareness of rights endorsed in certain laws and policies (Albiston 2005; Quinn 2000; Marshall 2005). Even when legal language is not present in employees' articulations of their demands, it is still essential to examine the subtle effect that law might have in shaping their awareness, expectations, and understandings of workplace issues.

The rest of this chapter first outlines common causes of strikes in Đồng Nai Province from 2010 to 2014, as obtained from policy documents and interviews with state and union officials. The chapter then investigates the grievances and demands of workers interviewed in 2014 and 2015 who had been involved in strikes in six selected companies in Đồng Nai Province. The six selected companies are among 18 foreign-owned and private domestic companies in the province that were affected by strikes at least twice in the period of 2010–2014. An in-depth case study of one of the companies also includes an interview with the human resource manager to understand how aspects of the labour law regime are used or abused at the company.

Strikes in Đồng Nai Province, 2010–2014

Local upper-level unions have kept a good record of strikes taking place in the districts or industrial zones in which they are in charge. The tabulated annual reports that I obtained from these unions contain information about the time and duration of strikes, the workers' demands, the industrial sector of the affected enterprises, the number of workers involved in the strikes, and their outcomes. The level of detail in reporting the cause and resolution of strikes varies across unions. In Nhơn Trạch, I was given a note, hand-written by the union chairwoman, which only includes very brief reasons for strikes, such as 'wage' and 'bonus,' and no information concerning the resolution. It also referred to a few cases when 'strikes have been prevented.' The union in charge of Biên Hòa's industrial zones records more information about the causes and outcomes of strikes, including, for instance, the exact amount of wage rise or bonus demanded by workers. I obtained the most detail about strikes from the union office in Trảng Bom District, including both the union's tabulated reports and the individual documents produced by the labour mediator on the unfolding of strikes which indicate the actors and agencies involved in strike settlement. The most strike-affected companies belong to the footwear, garment, electronics, and wood manufacturing industries.

It is common for workers to raise several demands in a single strike, with single-demand strikes often being about wages or the year-end bonus. The following table summarises the number of workers' demands counted from the reports into the following main categories based on their frequency: wages, bonus, overtime, meal quality, managerial/supervisory treatment, and others (Table 3.1).

Table 3.1 Strike demands in industrial zones in Biên Hòa, Nhơn Trạch, and Trảng Bom, 2010–2014

	2010	*2011*	*2012*	*2013*	*2014*
Wages	83	113	14	28	36
Bonus	21	8	8	8	4
Overtime	11	7	5	2	2
Meal quality	18	14	5	2	2
Managerial/supervisory treatment	8	5	5	2	3
Others (such as workplace regulations, allowances, insurance benefits)	62	33	17	7	6
Total	**203**	**180**	**54**	**49**	**53**
Total number of strikes	*147*	*168*	*47*	*39*	*36*

As mentioned in Chap. 2, the period from late December to February is considered 'sensitive' (*nhạy cảm*) since workers expect a wage rise following the government's minimum wage adjustment, and a bonus before the holidays (Interview, 15 December 2014; 18 December 2014; 23 December 2014). To be clear, while the unions and labour mediators keep referring to the government's minimum wage decision to account for workers' demands, most of the demands as seen in the reports are concerned with workers seeking wages *higher* than the minimum wage, rather than a wage rise equal to the new minimum level.

Demands for a wage rise can be split into two sub-categories, based on their justifications. The first concerns the wage differentials between senior and junior workers, or between skilled and unskilled workers. The root cause for this, according to the labour lawyer, is companies' failure to establish or enforce the wage table, and consequently to deliver a legal and fair pay rise. The second sub-category comes from workers' comparison of wages between their company and others, or between the current and previous years. It appears that in strike-affected enterprises, two-way communication between workers and management is often non-existent; wage rises are decided by the top management without any engagement with workers.

The union reports have different ways of framing workers' demands. At times they convey a sense of sympathy with workers, suggesting, for instance that 'the wage level between senior and new workers is unfair,' and pointing out that 'demand for an allowance [is] because lives are difficult.' At other times, the wording is more favourable to management, suggesting that strikes took place despite the fact that the businesses had acted according to the law. The reports also provide subjective interpretations of workers' attitudes, noting, for example, that workers 'disagree,' 'did not accept,' or, in one case, 'envy' the wage levels between different workers.

None of the officials involved in strike settlement nor the annual reports on strikes attributed the reasons for strikes to workers' awareness of their rights or the Labour Code. Most officials put the blame on the workers, seeing them as gullible and over-demanding. The annual reports obtained from Đồng Nai Labour Federation and the Department of Labour, Invalids and Social Affairs also stated that the persistence of illegal strikes is mainly due to workers' unawareness of the Labour Code, and in particular the legal procedures for strikes. Only a third of the officials demonstrated sympathy for workers' strike actions, and even then cautioning that they should arise from 'legitimate and/or lawful rights and interests.' One labour mediator mentioned that the frequency of strikes in some companies is due to the management's 'broken promises' to the workers (Interview, 18 December 2014).

The year-end bonus, also colloquially known as the Tết bonus or 13th-month wage, is the third most common reason for striking, following wage demands and 'others' category. The bonus allows workers to buy goods to celebrate the Vietnamese Lunar New Year, the most important holiday in Vietnam, and thus has a cultural significance besides material benefits (Chae 2003). Bonus-related strikes occur when workers want to push for management's decision and announcement on the bonus, or when they are dissatisfied with the bonus issued. In the Labour Code, the bonus is not obligatory and dependent on business profits. However, if the bonus is specified and included in the company's collective bargaining agreement, which is a legal document, then the management is obliged to issue the bonus as designated in the agreement (Interview, 22 January 2015).

The third category of strike demands, concerning overtime, includes workers' complaints about excessive working hours and management's failure to pay the premium rates. The fourth category revolves around complaints about the poor quality of company-provided meals, and the workers' demand that the company increase their payment to meal suppliers. Lunches and meals between shifts in the factories are provided either by a canteen owned by the company or by a food supplier. In the broader context, there have been reports of workers' food poisoning and hospitalisation as a result of unsanitary and unsafe meals (Lao Động 17 June 2011b; 18 June 2012a; 2 October 2012b; Người Lao Động 21 March 2014b; 2 June 2014a).

The fifth category is specifically related to the treatment by and attitudes of managers and supervisors to workers. Sometimes the report specifies their nationality, such as the Korean or the Chinese; at other times, it also includes workers' demand to change managers and supervisors because of their rude treatment. The last category, 'others,' is concerned with managerial discipline and rules, such as unfair punishments, wage and bonus deductions; workers' demands for extra allowances, such as for transport; and management's failure to provide for healthcare benefits, maternity insurance, and other issues relating to workers' contracts and social insurance.

Regarding strike outcomes, previous research has suggested that most strikes in Vietnam have been effective in awarding workers with immediate gains, while not necessarily improving post-strike labour relations (Pringle and Clarke 2011, p. 70; Lee 2006). From my conversations with interviewed workers, after a strike has been settled in the workers' favour, the management may later retaliate against those deemed to be the strike instigators or put more pressure on workers' performance and productivity. The unions' strike records in the province demonstrate an 80 per cent win (or partial win) for the workers. These outcomes, however, are not legally binding and there are no administrative measures taken against management for failing to honour them. As will be illustrated in the in-depth case study, a successful strike, or a peaceful strike settlement, does not necessarily deliver workplace justice.

An Overview of Workers' Grievances and Reasons for Strikes

This section examines common grievances and reasons for strikes from my interviews with 24 workers in five different companies in the garment, footwear, and wood manufacturing sectors. It is beyond the scope of this study to discuss the differing labour processes of workers in these sectors. However, as will be shown in the following empirical discussion, responses from workers across these sectors carry common threads of judgements and concerns about what is fair and unfair at work. The garment, footwear, and wood manufacturing companies pay by the hour. The garment and footwear companies assign certain quotas per hour or day for workers to fulfil. Workers' monthly incomes in these sectors range from 4 million to more than 6 million Vietnam dong (approximately US $177 to US $266 in 2015). These are the final payments after the addition of the company's extra benefits such as diligence rewards and transport allowances, overtime payments, and the deduction of social insurance payments and union fees. They also receive a year-end bonus averaging one month's basic wage.

The most common statement from my interviews is concerned with the wage rise at the beginning of the year. Two-thirds of the workers mentioned that they normally received a new wage 'when the state raises wages every year.' Workers' experiences of the company's wage rise and the time at which it is implemented led them to refer to the state's move as a benchmark for the company decision. In this respect, the government's minimum wage adjustment, though not precisely articulated by the workers, has raised their expectations about a wage rise from the company each year, regardless of the extent of their legal knowledge. Still, two-thirds of the workers caution that an annual wage rise is also accompanied by an increase in rent and prices of other essential items, and thus does not necessarily make them better off.

Half of the workers who received a wage rise every year were not content, even though some did not express their dissatisfaction to unions or management. For instance, one of them said that 'Other companies raise wages twice a year, but not my company. Here they only raise wages according to the state, by the same amount to old and new workers' (Interview, 20 December 2014). Two issues can be inferred from this statement. First, as far as I understand, 'raising wages twice a year' refers to the government's annual minimum wage adjustment plus a company's wage rise according to its own wage table. As noted in Chap. 2, the wage table consists of varying wage levels for employees, from technicians and supervisors to workers on the shop floor. According to a labour lawyer, many companies pay workers in accordance with the adjusted minimum wage but do not take into account the wage table and thus fail to raise wages for senior people (Interview, 18 December 2014). The workers, though, may not interpret their problem in such a way, as none of the interviewed workers mentioned the wage table. Workers only specified to me, either in absolute or in percentage terms, the rates of a wage rise as announced or implemented by management.

The second issue reflected in this quote is that workers tend to compare their wages with those of other workers in different companies, especially when they believe they are worse off than others. Their comparison gives a sense of an unequal situation between workers in different companies, and conveys an expectation that they should receive remuneration similar to that of workers elsewhere. Even though workers do not talk about the wage rise or their degree of (dis)content explicitly in terms of legal language, their narratives imply an understanding of an uneven implementation of the Labour Code across different companies. The clearest reflection of uneven implementation of the legal requirement for an annual wage rise came in the account given by Mrs Tâm, who has worked for six years in a wood processing company:

> Here [in this district] the best place is company X. Let's assume that the state stipulates a wage rise [starting at] 300,000 up to 500,000 dong. That company gives a different wage rise to different people, say 300,000 for those who've worked one year, 400,000 to 450,000 for those who've worked two to three years, and then 500,000 for more senior people. Every other company has that kind of wage differential except for my company. (Interview, 20 December 2014)

Tâm only presented her observation and gave no explicit explanation for the differences between her company and others. Similar to other respondents, she did not complain or express her discontent, but conveyed a sense that her company's conduct falls short of desirable practice. There is, worse still, another problem with the wage rise implementation at Tâm's company:

> When the state raised wages once every year, the company also raised our wages, but the money did not all go to our basic wages. It was divided and then added up to other bits like allowances or diligence money. For instance, if the raise was 300,000 dong, then only half of it was added to our basic wage and the rest to allowances or hazard money. It is just this year that all the money will be added to our basic wage. (Interview, 20 December 2014)

Tâm understood that the receipt of other monetary rewards depends on the workers' position and their actual work performance. For instance, the receipt of hazard money is only paid to workers undertaking work in a hazardous environment and the diligence money is only paid in full when workers take no day off in a month. Had the wage rise been added to the basic wage, workers' monthly income would have been stable rather than being subjected to variation.[1] Here the fact that she did not express her discontent warrants some discussion. One possible reason, suggested in her last sentence, is that the company's conduct changed for the better that year. Second, when I asked whether her wage is sufficient to get by, she said yes, though with some reluctance, and added that this was 'because I do not overspend (*không xài quá*) and know how to save money (*biết tiết kiệm*)' (Interview, 20 December 2014). Therefore, although she expected to have received a higher income after six years at work, she considers her current income to be sufficient for her living standards. A male worker also showed the same attitude, saying that 'even though my wage is not so good compared to others, it is enough for me and my family' (Interview, 30 January 2015).

During our interview, Tâm also mentioned the case of a fellow worker, who once spoke up against management and then had to leave the company after a few days. Five other workers I interviewed in her company also recounted a similar situation, when their fellow workers were disciplined or dismissed after raising their grievances or concerns to the management and supervisors. It was only at the end of our interview that Tâm was straightforward: 'Sometimes I think I know that the company is doing wrong, but I don't dare speak up' (Interview, 20 December 2014). This example shows that workers' framing of their workplace conditions and (in)action is not based on their understanding of labour law but on their capacity to live on their current wages and their experience of seeing that workers who spoke out often jeopardised their positions.

With regard to overtime, interviewed workers knew the premium rates for overtime work, which suggests that they have some familiarity with the Labour Code. All respondents said that overtime was forced upon them, both with and without advanced notice from the supervisors. One-third of respondents 'hoped' or 'wanted' the company to organise overtime regularly so that they could earn more income and feel more relaxed in their spending. One worker said that regular overtime is a key factor in her decision to apply for her current job. Five workers complained about excessive overtime hours. Two of these were required to work throughout the night, a situation they described as 'too hard' or 'unbearable.' Interestingly, none of these workers had a clear idea of the number of hours they actually spent at work in a given week.

Only five workers referred to 'rights and interests' or 'shared rights and interests' (*quyền lợi chung*) when justifying previous strikes, which occurred because of low wages, the company's broken promises, and poor meal quality. And yet, as in the interviews with other workers, their justifications did not elaborate upon details of the Labour Code, but rather upon the expectation of care and consideration from management. A male worker, employed for ten years in a footwear company, put it like this:

> Recently, overtime has been compulsory. It used to be organised on Monday, Wednesday, and Friday, but recently it has also been added on Tuesday, Thursday and Saturday. [...] There is a limit to our endurance! Workers have family and children, and they have to take care of them. Since a strike broke out in December, the company has allowed workers to leave early but they still have to complete the quotas before leaving. (Interview, 28 December 2014)

Here, he referred to workers' family commitments to explain why overtime work, taking place from the late afternoon into the evening, pushed workers to go on strike. This implies an understanding that workers' rights and interests are tied to their familial duties, something that the management failed to take into account when demanding that workers do overtime. His exclamation about the limit of their endurance also speaks to workers' previous attempts to appeal to the supervisors and managers, as well as to the local labour inspectorate, to no avail. Such sentiments were also expressed in other workers' accounts, when they spoke of strikes as the inevitable outcome when they were too 'aggrieved' (*bức xúc*) and 'frustrated' (*tức quá*).

The outline of these narratives demonstrates that workers do not refer to law in framing their workplace grievances, and instead justify them in terms of certain expectations for moral and fair treatment on the part of management. Nonetheless, examples of workers' references to the government's wage rise or their entitlements to premium rates for overtime work illustrate that aspects of labour law still inform workers' understandings, though not in a direct or an explicit manner. The following in-depth discussion of a case study allows me to expand on the issues touched upon in this section and elaborate on the values and expectations implicit in workers' strikes and their accounts of strikes.

A Company Case Study

The company, which in 2014 had more than 600 employees, is a food processing company based in an area where labour disputes are common. According to a report obtained from the labour bureau, the average income of employees in 2014 ranged from 3.3 million dong to 4 million dong. Workers in this company are entitled to a transport allowance, responsibility money or hazard compensation, and a diligence reward.[2] The normal payment that workers receive every month includes the payment for their labour plus extra benefits, minus insurance money and union fees.

According to the strike record kept by the upper-level union, strikes broke out in this company four times between 2010 and 2014. The causes of three strikes were related to the year-end bonus. In the strike in 2014, workers demanded an increase in basic wages, an increase in the year-end bonus; a payment of a 200 per cent premium rate for Sunday work; that the company make known the wage rate for each production unit; and that no deduction of the diligence reward be made when days taken off counted towards annual leave. (The diligence reward, given to workers who work the full number of working days in a month, is not stipulated in the Labour Code, so employers are not obliged to pay it. However, many employers apply this as an incentive for full work attendance and enjoy much leeway in their practice. In some companies, for example, if a worker takes one day off for personal reasons or two days off for sickness in a month, he/she will have no diligence reward. In some others, in those same situations, the reward is reduced by 30 per cent.[3])

Workers' Main Grievances

While increased wages and bonuses are common demands in strike situations, in this company workers had further specific grievances related to company practice. They were discontented because although they registered their days off as paid annual leave, which is different from personal and sickness leave and should be exempt from any deduction, they still had their diligence reward cut off. But the company also does not apply premium overtime rates as defined in the Labour Code. Indeed, some workers were not really sure whether such a rate had been included in what they called productivity money (*tiền năng suất*). This ambiguity was also complicated by a variance in the number of standard working days a month, which was set at 26 or 28 for different groups of workers. Many workers were required to work up to two Sundays in a month, whereas the Labour Code stipulates that employers must allow for at least four rest days a month.

The most pressing concern for workers originated in the company's unclear wage policy, with wages being paid by piece rate. A piece rate policy is a notorious managerial strategy to exploit and discipline the workforce (Lee 1998; Friedman 2013). Having wages tied to a piece rate makes great demands on the worker in terms of speed and productivity. But this company has never disclosed what entailed a piece, nor the exact rate for each production unit to the workers. All interviewed workers, from various sections on the shop floor, complained that they had no idea of how their actual pay was calculated. Despite being able to estimate, or even ask their line/group leaders about the quantity they produced, they did not know what a unit of production was worth. Their payslip only indicated the total amount of money earned per month, without any specification as to how this amount is calculated. This lack of transparency in wage calculation has been the key reason for workers' grievances in the past and has caused a number of newly employed workers away from the company.

The information I obtained from the three female workers in this company contained particularly rich data, with much detail, and it was filled with emotion. As mentioned in Chap. 1, I believe that my gender and the workers' gender influenced the manner in which workers shared their stories. However, in this particular company, there is another substantial reason concerning working conditions that explains the difference between male and female workers' responses. The three female workers, in the food processing sections, were in conditions that were cold and at times unsanitary. The male workers who gave interviews were in the quality control and storage sections. Like the women, they worked long hours but they did not experience difficult conditions. As I understood from workers, the food processing sections are dominated by women, although the record I obtained from the labour bureau shows relatively equal numbers of male and female workers in this company.

In examining the values and practices that underpin workers' resistance, it is essential to take into account workers' general descriptions of experiences of injustice on the shop floor in addition to the reasons that they give for specific strike actions. Particularly in this case study, the two pressing problems concerning the piece rate and overtime rate have become an enduring part of workers' shop floor experiences, which, over time, have entrenched their frustration with the management and supervisors. Rather than being articulated solely as reasons for striking, these two grievances prevail throughout workers' stories about this workplace. As I will further explain later in the chapter, these grievances and reasons for striking are interwoven with each other and with workers' concerns about their livelihoods and their desire for fairness.

Besides sharing with me their own grievances, interviewees spoke of incidents when small groups of fewer than ten people immediately stopped work as a sign of protest right after receiving extremely low wages for their month's labour. Others burst into tears. There were many cases in which a worker, who had worked for a full month, received notably less money than one who had taken one or a few days off. In other instances, senior workers, who believed they worked harder and more productively, received a lesser amount than newcomers. These blatant inconsistencies have frustrated the workers for so long that they have begun to put up with them after all their failed attempts to speak up.

All interviewed workers in this company said that they had more than once voiced their queries and complaints relating to their wages to shop floor managers and supervisors. Their unresponsiveness to these queries and complaints has perpetuated and compounded the workers' frustration. A female worker named Hoa recalled that their manager had responded, but the reasons given were 'unacceptable' (Interview, 8 March 2015). She was told that 'new workers are paid by the hour, not by piece rate' (Interview, 8 March 2015), and 'this month's wage was lower because the orders were easier to complete.' These workers had also found that it was also of no use to voice their concerns to the company union, which was led by the group leader of the storage section and an administrative staffer. According to an interviewed worker, in 2014, the company union asked workers to fill in a form listing their concerns and requests. The most common requests were that the company make known the piece rate, and that it pay a premium rate for work on Sunday. However, there was subsequently no response, follow-up, or policy change in the company.

Subsistence, Fairness, and Reciprocity

Similar to other respondent workers, workers in this company noted that they were poorly paid when compared with workers in other companies. For instance, a male worker named Chiến complained that 'Other companies raise the basic wages every year. I've worked here for more than 10 years but our basic wage only increased recently' (Interview, 17 April 2015). Two female workers also said that 'Overall, working here is very hard, but our wage is very meagre. At other places people are paid double for Sunday work. Here, there is no extra rate and we don't feel at all motivated to work on Sunday' (Interview, 8 March 2015). In addition, they observed that workers in other companies with a similar length of work experience work for a smaller number of hours than they do, yet still receive the same income as theirs.

Workers' complaints about their wages and working conditions often contained references to 'my friends in other companies,' 'my wife in her company,' or even 'other workers/people' generally. With very limited time and opportunity to access the news and media, essential information about labour law was verbally circulated through workers' social networks, often facilitated by their living arrangements in rental areas. Workers saw better practices at other companies and wished for a similar experience at their workplace. Their comparison implies a desire for equal treatment and remuneration for all workers with comparable length of service.

However, unlike other interviewed workers, these workers also expressed a strong sense of unfairness in considering wage levels of different groups of workers within their own company. They reasoned that the income they received did not match up with their workload and seniority. For instance, two female workers said that their many years of experience meant that, with respect to their speed and productivity, they were highly competitive, and this should have earned them a higher income than they received (Interview, 8 March 2015). Other male workers also referred to their long service in the company as the reason for their dissatisfaction. As senior workers who had been employed for more than ten years, they said that it was 'mean' for them to receive wages that were little different from new or shorter-term workers' wages.

As they went on talking about their problems, these workers also expressed their feelings about their relationship with management. They talked of their long service to the company as a form of loyalty and bonding (*gắn bó*)—a close emotional and interpersonal connection—and felt bitter that this bond was not reciprocated by the management. Mrs Hoa put it this way, 'The company can make a profit thanks to workers' bonding. Why isn't there any compassion for senior workers? In fact, the senior workers are often those being oppressed (*đì*)'[4] (Interview, 8 March 2015). In her recounting, oppression manifests in forms such as discipline, punishment, surveillance, and blunt responses to workers' queries. In a more measured manner, Chiến highlighted that senior workers like him are only the minority; besides the monthly income, he also deserves to receive a higher year-end bonus:

> The company announced last year that workers employed for three to four years or longer would get a bonus of 1.3 month's wage, and those employed for less than that would get a bonus of one month's wage. It was quite *unfair* for those who had worked for 8, 9 or 10 years that they got the same bonus as people working for around half that time. You know, there are around 600 to 700 workers in the company but only 100 to 200 are long-time workers like my brother-in-law and me. The company does not give a higher reward to those who have committed to (*gắn bó*) the company for a long time. (Interview, 17 April 2015)

He further added that senior workers like him have seen their company go through several years of loss in the past until recently when it has recovered and started to make a profit. For all their service and contribution to the business, Hoa and Chiến expected reciprocation from the management, through being entitled to more empathetic treatment (with less personal oppression and less strict discipline) and higher wages. The employment relationship, in their view, should not be based on the labour contract and rigid rules, but should have space for fair treatment on the basis of loyalty. It is essential to emphasise that, in the broader context, affection, or sentiment (*tình cảm*), is a central element of social relationships in Vietnam and a moral touchstone of one's treatment of each other (Hoang 2015; Luong 2016). Any practice that fell short of workers' expectations, in this regard, was seen to constitute unfairness and further entrenched workers' resentment. In a comparative perspective, these sentiments are close to what Xin He and colleagues have termed the 'cultural perception of justice' (2013, p. 709) that they encountered in studying the values underpinning the wage claimants' collective actions in the Chinese construction industry.

Workers' repeated attempts to improve their condition resulted in further promises being made and broken by the company management. These promises were often made after workers went on strike or raised their queries about their income payment. For instance, Chiến recalled, 'After workers went on strike, the management promised and kept on promising. Well, they promised about the bonus and we got the bonus, but the piece rate has remained unclear for the past 10 years' (Interview, 17 April 2015). Sơn, Chiến's brother-in-law, added that the management had promised to fix the pay day, which they had done, and yet their promise to clarify the piece rate had never been honoured. On the one hand, workers' tendency to frame the management's communication as a promise implies an expectation of the management's moral integrity and of their being accountable for their own words. On the other hand, the fact that the management has kept their word when it comes to some issues, such as the bonus and pay day, could possibly explain why these workers continue to hold on to the other more significant major piece rate promise, only to be repeatedly let down.

Management's refusal to address workers' grievance has served to perpetuate its exploitation of workers. According to the Labour Code, workers are entitled to a one-hour break each working day. In this company, many workers have voluntarily given up most of their mid-day break:

'Instead of having a one-hour break, many workers eat their meals hurriedly in fifteen minutes and get back to work' (Interview, 14 February 2015). As can be seen from the aforementioned workers' accounts, there are two reasons for this. First, workers have held on to the (false) hope and expectation that their hard work will eventually be rewarded through management's recognition of their performance and long service. Second, and relatedly, their meagre average income leaves them with no choice but to put in more effort at work.

In our conversations, language that seems to derive from law has been adopted by workers to communicate their lay understanding of what is fair and unfair about management's conduct. In particular, workers referred to the legal terms, 'rights and interests' (*quyền lợi*), but it is necessary to establish what workers mean by these terms by considering the context in which they are spoken. While the Labour Code separates rights from interests, these two terms always go together in workers' justifications of their strike actions and work stoppages, as well as when they talk about having experienced unfair managerial practices or non-compliance in relation to workers' entitlements. In interviews, workers referred to rights and interests as inclusive of the need to sustain their livelihoods, as well as the earnings and rewards that they deserve for their labour and their 'bonding' to the company. Scholars taking an institutional perspective have shown that the legal separation between rights and interests mainly serves to constrain workers' strike actions (Trần 2013; Chan 2011). The analysis of workers' stories here reveals that this separation also fails to reflect workers' desire for fairness. For instance, interviewed workers evoked their struggle with everyday expenses when they recalled previous instances when the company failed to pay wages on time, causing them to stop work and demand their 'rights and interests.' Though we can easily assume that workers use the language of law to legitimate their claims, what they actually mean in these circumstances has to do with their living needs: paying for rent, food, children's schooling, sending money to their family back in the rural hometown, and sometimes saving for their new houses. In summing up their lives at the time as 'insecure' (*không ổn định*), these workers effectively linked their grievances and demands to management's failure to ensure their livelihoods.

Thus far we see that workers have framed their grievances in moral terms, complaining about management's broken promises, verbal abuse, and their meanness in treating long-serving and hardworking labourers. One of the key concerns in these narratives is reciprocity, a value that falls beyond the provisions of the Labour Code. Another is with livelihoods. In fact, there is a provision in the Labour Code that reflects workers' desire for a stable income that meets basic needs. Article 91 on the minimum wage stipulates that such a wage must meet the minimum living needs of employees and their families. Even though the government's adjusted minimum wages have fallen short of this provision (Trần 2013; Lao Động 2 August 2014a), it is a legal provision which, the VGCL has argued, should be honoured as a commitment of the state to Vietnamese employees. This argument was documented in a range of news outlets, which target both the general public and the employees and factory workers; at the time the National Wage Council convened to deliberate on the new minimum wage levels (e.g., Lao Động 31 July 2014b; Người Lao Động 3 August 2014c; Tuổi Trẻ 4 August 2014).

The norm of subsistence is an example of an existing moral value that overlaps with values embedded in state law. As suggested in the preceding paragraph, it is possible that workers' expressions of (un)fairness, couched in lay language, involve an understanding about the minimum wage that they understand from the Labour Code. However, it is just as likely that the norm of subsistence, widespread in Vietnamese society, has influenced both the drafting of the Labour Code and, separately, workers' understandings of labour relations.[5]

In addition to their views of management, morality also plays out strongly in workers' perceptions of the role of the state. First of all, it is essential to acknowledge that workers in this case study went on strike to appeal to the state and upper-level union officials only after they had exhausted avenues of direct communication with their supervisors and management. The intervention of the upper-level union, as part of the strike action team, gave workers an opportunity to voice their grievances and have them addressed. Raising their demands and queries to the upper-level union during strike settlement represented an act of resistance against the supervisors and/or managers who had rebutted them and told them to 'shut up' in response to their complaints and queries. Mrs Hoa boldly stated that 'Whenever the authorities or unions asked us anything, we told them all that we know. We had to speak up to let them know that we are not stupid nor dumb' (Interview, 8 March 2015). She could be referring to both the unions/authorities and the company management who have previously ignored their voices.

From an institutional perspective, the establishment of the ad hoc measure of strike settlement in Vietnam could work against the state's objective of preventing strikes, as it gives workers hope of achieving their claims and subsequently leads them to continue resorting to strikes when workplace problems arise (Lee 2006; Do 2011). This proposition applies to a certain extent in this case study, as interviewed workers admitted that the union's intervention allowed workers to voice and successfully claim their demands for the year-end bonus. Yet, as discussed earlier, the year-end bonus is only the tip of the iceberg; it is the piece rate and low income that have troubled workers for many years. As the intervention has failed to address their most pressing concerns, the claim that strike settlement begets further resistance does not adequately explain the intent of workers in this case study to repeatedly go on strike.

The case-study workers' appeal to the state and official unions was mainly based on sympathy and sentiment and was also linked to subsistence ethics, albeit in an indirect manner. In my interviews with the workers, discussion about the state and official unions was only initiated when I asked workers more specifically about the course of events during previous strikes; general questions about their workplace grievances and hardships would not lead to such discussions. Hoa said with emotion, 'We didn't ask for too much. We only pleaded (*xin*) with them [the state and unions] to show compassion for workers, and give us a little bit more if possible' (Interview, 8 March 2015). If the compassion she expected from management arose from her bonding and contribution to the business, in this case it was premised on the perceptions of her and her fellow workers as subjects in need of assistance from the state. Her plea gives the sense that workers had exhausted all their justifications and reasoning, and thus could only rely on the very basic moral foundations of interpersonal relationships and livelihoods to seek a resolution to their problems. In describing the strike resolution, interviewed workers expressed their trust in the role of the state and upper-level unions in facilitating a decision from the management that somehow responds to workers' claims. Mr Lê's wife insisted: 'It is only when we saw the notice put up by the [upper-level] union that we accepted the resolution and got back to work' (Interview, 14 February 2015).

The way in which workers look upon the state for assistance warrants further discussion of the Vietnamese state's continued socialist ideology and its projection of the political connection between the working class and the Communist Party of Vietnam (CPV). The explanation that workers' (repeated) attempts at striking are a partial result of the strike settlement measures fails to capture the morality and expectations underpinning their actions. These strikes stem directly from workers' struggles with their livelihoods and are likely also to be influenced by the state's and the VGCL's rhetoric. In the decades since *đổi mới*, the state has maintained its vision of building socialism in the spirit of the slogan 'A rich people; a strong, democratic, equal and civilised society' (Central Committee of the CPV 2008a, b). This slogan is widely promoted through the Party's and the state officials' public speeches and statements, and through banners and posters in commemoration of national days. The core message of this slogan, which captures the state's vision of delivering welfare and social equality to its citizens, is reflected in interviewed workers' expressed desires and expectations for an income that meets their living needs and their appeal to the state for a solution to their problems.

Besides the aforementioned slogan, we can further understand workers' expectations of the state by examining the political rhetoric surrounding the Vietnamese working class. The Party's Directive 20/NQ-TW in 2008 affirms that the working class:

> is the vanguard in the task of building socialism; a leading force in the modernisation and industrialisation of the country for the goal of a rich people, a strong, democratic, equal and civilised society; a core force in the alliance between the working class and the peasant class [...] under the leadership of the Communist Party. (Central Committee of the CPV 2008b)

Directive 20 confirms the political significance of the working class and outlines objectives, measures, and actions to promote the contribution of the working class to economic development and allow them to benefit from their contribution. It highlights that 'looking after the material and mental lives of workers' (*chăm lo đời sống vật chất, tinh thần cho công nhân*) is an important task in the broader goal of 'developing a strong working class' in modernisation and the industrialisation era (see also Lao Động 15 January 2011a). Further guidelines for the task put a stress on improving labour laws and policies that target workers' wages, insurance, and housing support. The state's and Party's discourse with regard to the working class echoes the promise of economic welfare imbued in the socialist social contract in Vietnam before the economic transition (Trần 2013). As a main institution overseeing labour issues, the unions have propagated the aforementioned welfare rhetoric in a range of their social activities and support to factory workers (for instance, see Đồng Nai Labour Federation 2014). The Vietnamese Constitution 2013 reinstates these sentiments, proclaiming a close connection between the working class and the ruling party: 'The Communist Party, the vanguard of the working class […], is a faithful representative of the interests of the working class, the toiling people and the whole nation' (Article 4).

As can be expected, the state's and the union's failure to adequately address workers' appeals and meet their moral obligations has stirred workers' distrust. As Hoa frankly put, while she has faith in the union's announcement about the strike settlement outcomes, her overall view of the union is not positive. She made a sharp assessment of its collusion with management:

> Apparently, the union officials know more than enough about our problems but do not solve them. For us, we know that nothing can exceed the power of money. When the union gets into the company, it is always that 'the money that comes ahead is the wise money' *(đồng tiền đi trước là đồng tiền khôn)*. The higher the position one has, the more money he/she is offered. Every step of the union at the company is all pre-arranged. We know this, but we have to speak up, otherwise they will think that workers are stupid. … Now that they use money, at least we have to use our words and our minds so that they listen. We have to speak up about our grievances so that the union might do something right for us. (Interview, 8 March 2015)

These words indicate the worker who experiences deep disenchantment and yet, at the same time, still has hope. On the one hand, this worker is frustrated that the state and unions have deliberately avoided addressing workers' problems; on the other hand, she does not give up hope that her voice shall at least be heard and workers' demands acted upon. Her statement about money and corruption, which is a popular statement among ordinary Vietnamese, effectively sums up the reason behind workers' persistent suffering. It questions the state's and the union officials' moral integrity in relation to workers' demands and illustrates the erosion of workers' trust in the delivery of what they would see as a fair resolution. In speaking up on behalf of her fellow workers, she demonstrates that workers are acutely aware of the perpetual unfairness they face. Regardless of that, they have refused to keep their silence, have 'risen up with one heart' (*đồng lòng đứng lên*), and persisted with solidarity in their resistance (Interview, 14 February 2015; 8 March 2015).

Apart from the moral narratives mentioned earlier, regulations and provisions derived from the Labour Code also emerge in the workers' responses, albeit to a limited degree. In recounting her conversation with the union officials, Thơ said: 'As the union explained to us, the 13th month wage is the ***right and interest of the company*** [sic]. The amount the company rewards workers depends on how much they [the company] earn' (Interview, 8 March 2015). This woman later demonstrated to me how she grasped a sense of her legal entitlements, in wondering why her management did not raise the bonus despite her observation that production had been good during the past year. While the strike action team purported to seek a compromise with workers by explaining that management is not obliged to meet demands for interests, it did not stop this worker from employing her understanding to justify her query and expectation of a bonus rise. Other workers also recalled how the union explained the Labour Code to them, yet none showed any appreciation of the union's functions in this matter. Thơ's query concerning the year-end bonus also resonates with responses of interviewed workers in the other strike-affected companies. Their lay understanding of the Labour Code's Article 103 on the bonus scheme has also come to them via the strike action teams or through their social networks.

Lê, a male core worker, expressed the same grievances and observations of management's conduct as other workers, but he had a different explanation as to why he was dissatisfied with the company's policies and the role of the state and the union. Lê is fully informed about the Labour Code and has experience with legal aid activities.[6] He told me that the upper-level union did not address workers' demand for transparent piece rates, as a union official explained to workers that the company paid wages according to ***task completion,*** rather than by piece. He claimed that, in saying this, the union official responded using the manager's reasoning without investigating workers' issues carefully, and that workers were paid a piece rate, which is quite different from a task completion payment.[7] Ultimately, he said, 'while the management agreed to the extra payment demanded for Sunday work, how could we workers know how much the right payment is when we don't know the piece rate?' (Interview, 5 February 2015). Thus, in his account, instead of properly implementing labour law in response to workers' demands, the union let workers down by speaking with the company management's rationale, words, and interests.

Lê recalled that, in 2014, a group of workers managed to compile and send a letter to management before the strike broke out. The letter contained five demands, which I list in the order recounted by this worker:

transparent calculation of piece rates, payment of the premium rate for Sunday work, a year-end bonus, an increase in meal portions, and a transport allowance. There are some discrepancies between his account and the official strike record. In particular, the most important demand from his perspective is listed last in the record. Furthermore, the official record of the strike outcomes claimed that workers' basic wages were increased by 14.8 per cent, which is also the rate at which the minimum wage rose in 2014. However, as mentioned earlier, the basic wage is the base for the calculation of social insurance contributions, rather than of the actual income that workers receive every month. This worker knows that an increase in the basic wage only leads to an increase in insurance payments; it does not otherwise necessarily alter workers' monthly income.

The other demands included in the letter, besides the piece rate and premium rate discussed earlier, warrant further consideration in the context of workers' livelihoods. Meal portions and transport allowances are extra benefits that are not compulsory for management, but they are crucial in the workers' struggle to meet their subsistence needs and reproduce their labour. From the officials' perspective, these demands can be readily classified as interest-based, which in turn suggests that company management has satisfied all their obligations to employees and inadvertently shifts the blame for labour disputes from management to workers. However, as seen from the workers' perspective, the failure to meet demands for meal and transport allowances boils down to the exploitation and underpayment that workers have constantly endured and this is a situation of rights infringement. These rights are broader than the lawful rights invoked in official discourse and granted in labour law; they include the right to subsistence, fair wages, and fair treatment. A close analysis of workers' demands in this case study demonstrates that official discourse, which maintains the legal separation of rights and interests, fails to take into account the desperate situation facing workers and in turn entrenches the gap between law and workplace justice. The official discourse does not provide for a mechanism to lift the workers from their daily struggle to make ends meet.

Strikes from the Human Resource Manager's Perspectives

This section examines the practice and implementation of labour law from the perspective of a human resource manager in the case-study company, whom I will refer to as Mr An.[8] In order to help me secure an interview, an officer at the Industrial Zone Authority (IZA) introduced me as a student intern of the People's Committee working on labour policies in the province. The interview took place at a guest room in the company during office hours. To the human resource manager, I was someone sent from the Authority and, therefore, sharing his views and information with me also meant sharing it, or a large part of it, with the Authority. This goes some way to explaining his complaints and expression of dissatisfaction in regard to labour issues (with a hope that these might be possibly seen to), as well as his evasive responses to questions relating to law and policy implementation. Had I contacted the manager in some other way, such as through the business association with which the company is affiliated, he would have possibly responded differently, as the business association would certainly share more common interests with its members and business partners. I anticipate that he would have been more vehement in stating his complaints, which were not just restricted to the minimum wage policy and strike settlement practices, but also included other aspects of law and policy enforcement.

Unsurprisingly, An did not even recognise workers' claims and evaded questions about legal matters. He mentioned workers' 'rights and interests' *(quyền lợi)* as a general and collective term, and emphasised that workers' demands must be lawful and appropriate following the state's regulations. For instance, demands for extra benefits, he said, are excessive because they are not stipulated within the law. His concern about the legality of workers' demands effectively de-legitimised those that fall within the 'benefit' category but might be a part of workers' concern for their livelihood. In my interview, An explained that the company pays by task completion, and that the payment is calculated according to the workload assigned for a certain number of hours and already includes premium overtime rates. He ambiguously claimed that workers are committed to working overtime on a voluntary basis. From the beginning of the interview, he effectively ruled out workers' struggles as illegitimate and illegal, by insisting that the company's policies and conduct are all in compliance with law.

In response to my broad question about his opinions on the implementation of labour law, he complained about the difficulties for the company that result from the timing of the annual wage adjustment (the minimum wage policy is issued in November and implemented in the following January). As he explained, the company is often busy with bonus calculations around January every year, and they place their orders based on the wage rates of the previous year. He thus used business interests and profits as justification for the company's failure to meet the labour law's objective of helping workers cope with rising living costs. Other than that, he did not explicitly comment on the Labour Code, but indicated his dissatisfaction with the fact that some aspects of it were not properly implemented.

An's dissatisfaction started with the process of strike settlement. He briefly recounted the causes and the resolution of previous strikes:

> We understand workers' expectation at the end of the year for the 13th month bonus. So we decided on a bonus worth half a month's wage. Workers demanded more, and they stopped working for a few days. The state officials then came down but didn't ease the company's worry. Actually, they explained the company's situation to the workers but not thoroughly. In the end we had to increase the bonus to one month's wage. (Interview, 15 April 2015)

The first part of the quote gives a sense of An's understanding of and responsiveness to workers' wishes. It can be presumed that he has learnt from previous occurrences of bonus-related strikes that they should decide the bonus rates earlier rather than later. He then referred to the three-way dialogue between the strike settlers, workers, and managers, only to criticise the disappointing outcome brokered by the strike action team. In his view, the company's concession was not one based on law, but was forced upon them by the half-hearted approach of the state and union officials.

Given that strikes had previously been around the same issue, I enquired whether the company had any measures to help prevent subsequent strikes. This question was aimed at enabling me to see whether management was making any effort to enhance labour relations on the shop floor. However, the response was laying blame on the workers, and an articulation of the legal provision that makes their collective actions illegal:

> As I mentioned, strikes were spontaneous and didn't start with any procedure, so we couldn't prevent them. The company hopes that the state has some deterrent measures, so that workers follow the right procedures. These procedures include sending petitions to management, so we can respond. If workers are not satisfied with the response, they can decide to go on strike but have to inform management about the date and time of the strike. (Interview, 15 April 2015)

It can be seen from this response that An refers to law to defend the company against workers' claims of workplace injustices. Similar to the strike action teams, his complaints and explanations were centred on the spontaneity of workers' actions. In this regard, An and the strike action teams share convergent interests regarding the purpose of law, that is, to delegitimise and deter workers' attempts to raise their voices.

An also complained about payments for strike days. In principle, workers are not entitled to such payment if they participate in (legal) strikes. In practice, however, many waged workers in the province, including those I interviewed in this company and elsewhere, have demanded payment and consider it to be appropriate and normal. This manager was not at all happy about this:

> Workers demanded to be paid for strike days. The state didn't issue any statement to the effect that workers wouldn't be paid, so this didn't help the company. And what about the financial compensation for illegal strikes? You see, the procedures for bringing strike cases to the court are almost unworkable. (Interview, 15 April 2015)

It is clear from the interview that An has paid attention to clauses in the Labour Code that constrain workers' strike actions, and it is these aspects of labour law he expects the state (and workers) to uphold. In contrast, he had little appreciation of the role of the strike action team in strike settlement, arguing that upper-level unions and state authorities should do more to put in place stringent measures to regulate workers' behaviour.

In short, from this manager's perspective, labour law serves as a tool to help secure workers' obedience and deter their struggles. He referred to the existing provision on collective labour disputes in the Labour Code as a justification for blaming workers and the state for the rise and recurrence of labour tensions. Despite his dissatisfaction with the official unions' approach to strike resolution, his comments on law and labour disputes are quite similar to those of the labour authorities and union officials. The manager's view of law as a form of control and discipline results in the failure to deliver workplace justice to which workers aspire. As it happens, the persistence of strikes has not catalysed any reform in wage policy or labour relations within the company. Adding to this, the half-hearted resolution by the strike action team leaves intact the company's continuing strategy to exploit and underpay workers.

An Unusual Peace

If history had repeated itself, workers would have gone on strike in early 2015, well before the New Year holidays, to demand payment of a bonus. That no strike broke out was then referred to by both workers and An, the manager, as an unusual situation. Mrs Thơ explained: 'Last year wages were paid relatively promptly and the company situation looked relatively stable.' Mrs Hoa added that 'the company announced the bonus early so we were reassured' (Interview, 8 March 2015). Workers' confidence in the company's profit and, consequently, its capacity to sustain their livelihoods seem to be the main reasons that explain such temporary peace.

However, the lack of strike activity did not mean that workers were satisfied and complacent. Mrs Thơ raised a concern with me: 'Why was the bonus still the same as that in the previous year, while it was obvious that the company made a very good profit?' (Interview, 8 March 2015). At the time of this interview, the bonus had been paid to workers. In raising her concern, Thơ demonstrates her understanding that the more the company gains, the more it should reward its workers. Chiến made a different observation, noting that workers' incomes one month after the Lunar New Year's holidays were low, about 70 per cent of their usual average income. He also witnessed a small work stoppage and several people quitting the job. Therefore, despite the absence of a company-wide strike, workers' expressions of concern and their observations indicate their lingering grievances, grievances that can surface whenever there is a trigger.

Following the unusual peace in early 2015, two months after the New Year in 2015, workers were again on strike. The trigger, as could be expected, was the very low wages paid in the preceding month. The strike lasted for two and a half days, ending in an announcement with a long list of nine solutions from the management:

- The management will establish and make known the piece rates in the next few weeks.
- Overtime work is voluntary with employees' consent. The company will apply the rates according to the existing Labour Code: 150 per cent for week days, 200 per cent for Sundays, and 300 per cent for public holidays.
- The company will ensure that there are at least four days off within a month.

- The payslips will be made clear, including separate sections of payment.[9]
- The company will pay by the hour on the date [...] for all employees whose work was affected due to the gas leakage incident.
- The company union's executive committee will be re-elected.
- The management is obligated not to castigate or sack anyone, or transfer them to different positions. Workers will continue to stay in the same sections after production is resumed.
- The management is willing to receive employees' opinions to improve working conditions. The company will arrange an opinion box at the main office and all queries will be directed to the management.
- The company will pay for two days of strike.

In the end, following workers' frequent and persistent strikes, the company finally conceded its legal obligations and especially its commitments to improve labour relations. Indeed, with these resolutions, the management adequately addressed workers' demands in the hope of curtailing their future resistance. However, the future prospects for workers' wages and welfare are not clear, as the outcomes are not legally binding and their execution is contingent on business performance and management's goodwill.

In summary, labour tensions within the studied company have mainly revolved around lack of transparency with regard to wage payments, excessive overtime without workers' consent, and a failure to implement overtime rates. Facing discipline and ignorance by management on the shop floor, workers have taken their collective grievances beyond the company gates to make their voices heard. The struggles of workers here illuminate the complex relationship between labour law, workers' responses to injustice, and their justifications for those responses. The persistence of workers' low payment further demonstrates the state's failure to monitor the implementation of law, which in turn nullifies the role of law in protecting workers' rights and interests and erodes their faith in the legal institution. While workers have gained some successes and some compromises from their employers through strikes, this has not translated into employers meeting their legal and moral obligations in a fair and transparent manner.

Conclusion

The prevalence of factory strikes in selected companies in the covered period of 2010 to 2014 necessitates a detailed investigation into the grievances and problems that workers face on a more regular basis at work. As outlined at the start of this chapter, the main reasons for strikes nationwide since 2006 have shifted from workers' demands for rights to demands for interests. In Đồng Nai Province, union officials and labour authorities also recognise this shift, as they explain that strike demands tend to cluster around issues of bonuses, higher wages, and allowances rather than those stemming from the businesses' legal violations. Nonetheless, these official classifications miss important stories from the workers about workplace injustice.

Despite their sporadic references to the legal terms of rights and interests, interviewed workers do not perceive their demands in terms of legal rights granted in the Labour Code, or demonstrate frustration about the company's evasions of law. They instead invoke what they see as unequal situations of wage rise across different companies, the insufficiency of their incomes for meeting daily needs, the imbalance between poor wages and hard labour, workers' family commitments, and the lack of concern and compassion from management. On the one hand, workers' values and expectations concerning equality and subsistence can be traced back to the Party and state socialist rhetoric, the political connection between the Party and working class as stated in the Constitution, and the state's promises to take care of the working class' material and mental lives. On the other hand, reciprocal expectations and workers' justifications in relation to family commitments reflect prevalent norms in Vietnamese society. All these values and expectations have shaped workers' evaluations of their experiences on the shop floor and make them persist in their resistance.

The findings in this chapter challenge discussions of rights consciousness in post-socialist regimes where rights consciousness is often associated with citizens' legal knowledge and mobilisation. Workers in this chapter demonstrate different levels of legal understanding: from the many who explain their wages and entitlements in lay terms to the ones who make sense of them through language learnt from the Labour Code and associated regulations. Regardless of these variations, the way workers justify their actions in pursuit of 'rights and interests' is not limited to their knowledge of the Labour Code but is also drawn from their experiences of unfairness and struggles with everyday living. These workers exhibit consciousness of their basic social rights and a will to defend these rights without engaging with legal institutions.

However, it is important to acknowledge that workers' expressions of (in)justice are not all separate from law. Regulations with regard to the government's minimum wage, overtime rates, and bonus, couched in lay language, also appear to shape workers' expectations and understandings of managerial conduct. In addition, the letter of the law also provides for the guarantee of subsistence and is also likely to inform workers' appeals. These observations illustrate that values derived from both law and other norms within society shape workers' understandings and generate their resistance against unfair practices.

Notes

1. As far as I understand, if we consider this issue from the management's perspective, not adding all wage rises to the basic wage would reduce the legal amount of management's contribution to workers' social insurance. Tâm and other interviewed workers in this company did not explicitly perceive the problem as such but only showed concern with the income they receive.
2. The responsibility money (*tiền trách nhiệm*) is paid to workers in the storage section, the hazard compensation (*tiền độc hại*) is given to those working in the wastage and cleaning sections, and the diligence reward (*tiền chuyên cần*) is only paid in full to those who work the full number of working days in a month.
3. These details about the diligence reward and different implementation across companies were obtained from workers and strike records.
4. The word '*đì*' is a popular term used when one is discriminated against or is badly treated, yet I find that the translations of discrimination or maltreatment do not adequately capture the harsh situations that workers endured.
5. It is not possible to precisely trace whether these understandings come from the Labour Code or from workers' life experiences and social interactions.
6. I will come back to how this worker obtained his legal knowledge in Chap. 4.
7. If the company applies this type of payment, the payment will take effect when employees finish certain assigned tasks. With this type of payment and work organisation, more experienced and productive workers, who spend less time finishing the assigned work, are not paid more for each task, but can complete more tasks and therefore earn more money each month than others.
8. Scholars commonly focus on how the disadvantaged and marginalised make sense of and use law, and do not examine how it is viewed by those with

resources and in positions of power, such as Mr An. However, the literature on sexual harassment and employees' leave rights in the USA shows that management's strategies and interpretation of law are among the factors that shape the employees' inaction or reactions to their problems (Albiston 2005; Marshall 2003, 2005). My empirical examination of An's stance on labour law will similarly complement and enhance our understanding of the workers' experiences and their resistance.

9. The format of the new payslips was not mentioned in the announcement. However, as I understood from interviews with workers before this strike broke out, a clear payslip should have details of the amount of completed work and overtime payment.

References

Albiston, C. (2005). Bargaining in the Shadow of Social Institutions: Competing Discourses and Social Change in Workplace Mobilization of Civil Rights. *Law & Society Review*, 39 (1), 11–49.

Chae, S. (2003). *Spinning Work and Weaving Life: The Politics of Production in a Capitalistic Multinational Textile Factory in Vietnam.* Unpublished PhD thesis. City University of New York, New York.

Chan, A. (2011) (ed.). *Labour in Vietnam.* Singapore: Institute of Southeast Asia Studies.

Clarke, S., Lee, C-H. & Do, Q. C. (2007). From Rights to Interests: the Challenge of Industrial Relations in Vietnam. *Journal of Industrial Relations*, 49 (4), 545–568.

Do, Q. C. (2011). *Understanding Industrial Relations Transformation in Vietnam: A Multi-Dimensional Analysis.* Unpublished PhD thesis. The University of Sydney, Sydney.

Đồng Nai Labour Federation (2014). Report on the work of taking care of material and mental lives for workers and the situation of strikes and work stoppages.

Friedman, E. (2013). Insurgency and Institutionalization: the Polanyian Countermovement and Chinese Labor Politics. *Theory and Society*, 42, 295–327.

He, X., Wang, L. & Su, Y. (2013). Above the Roof, Beneath the Law: Perceived Justice behind Disruptive Tactics of Migrant Wage Claimants in China. *Law & Society Review*, 47 (4), 703–738.

Hiến Pháp nước Cộng Hòa Xã Hội Chủ Nghĩa Việt Nam 2013 [The Constitution of the Socialist Republic of Vietnam 2013].

Hoang, L. A. (2015). Vietnamese Migrant Networks in Taiwan: the Curse and Boon of Social Capital. *Ethnic and Racial Studies*, 39 (4), 690–707.

Kerkvliet, B. J. (2011). Workers' Protests in Contemporary Vietnam. In A. Chan (ed.). *Labour in Vietnam*. Singapore: Institute of Southeast Asia Studies.

Lao Động (15/1/2011a). Xây dựng giai cấp công nhân Việt Nam vững mạnh. http://laodong.com.vn/cong-doan/xay-dung-giai-cap-cong-nhan-viet-nam-vung-manh-14867.bld. Accessed 20th January 2017.

Lao Động (17/6/2011b). Đồng Nai: 120 công nhân bị ngộ độc tập thể. http://laodong.com.vn/cong-doan/dong-nai-120-cong-nhan-bi-ngo-doc-tap-the-53724.bld. Accessed 20th January 2017.

Lao Động (18/6/2012a). Nhọc nhằn bữa cơm công nhân. http://laodong.com.vn/phong-su/nhoc-nhan-bua-com-cong-nhan-69704.bld. Accessed 20th January 2017.

Lao Động (2/10/2012b). Chất lượng bữa ăn công nhân quá thấp. http://laodong.com.vn/cong-doan/chat-luong-bua-an-cong-nhan-qua-thap-86215.bld. Accessed 20th January 2017.

Lao Động (2/8/2014a). Vì sao phải điều chỉnh mức lương tối thiểu vùng I lên 3.4 triệu đồng?. http://laodong.com.vn/cong-doan/vi-sao-phai-dieu-chinh-muc-luong-toi-thieu-vung-i-len-34-trieu-dong-230519.bld. Accessed 24th June 2016.

Lao Động (31/7/2014b). Chủ tịch Tổng LĐLĐVN Đặng Ngọc Tùng: Lương tối thiểu vùng I năm 2015 cần đạt 3,4 triệu đồng/người/tháng. http://laodong.com.vn/cong-doan/chu-tich-tong-ldldvn-dang-ngoc-tung-luong-toi-thieu-vung-i-nam-2015-can-dat-34-trieu-dongnguoithang-229651.bld. Accessed 24th June 2016.

Lee, C. K. (1998). *Gender and the South China Miracle: Two Worlds of Factory Women*. Berkeley, Los Angeles & London: University of California Press.

Lee, C-H. (2006). Recent Industrial Relations Developments in China and Vietnam: The Transformation of Industrial Relations in East Asian Transition Economies. *Journal of Industrial Relations*, 48 (3), 415–429.

Luong, H. V. (2016). Social Relations, Regional Variation, and Economic Inequality in Contemporary Vietnam: A View from Two Vietnamese Rural Communities. In P. Taylor (ed.). *Connected and Disconnected in Viet Nam: Remaking Social Relations in a Post-socialist Nation*. Acton: ANU Press.

Marshall, A-M. (2003). Injustice Frames, Legality, and the Everyday Construction of Sexual Harassment. *Law and Social Inquiry*, 28 (3), 659–690.

Marshall, A-M. (2005). Idle Rights: Employees' Rights Consciousness and the Construction of Sexual Harassment Policies. *Law & Society Review*, 39 (1), 83–124.

Người Lao Động (2/6/2014a). Sau bữa trưa, gần 200 công nhân nhập viện do ngộ độc. http://nld.com.vn/thoi-su-trong-nuoc/sau-bua-trua-gan-200-cong-nhan-nhap-vien-do-ngo-doc-20140602172224017.htm. Accessed 20th January 2017.

Người Lao Động (21/3/2014b). Hơn 150 công nhân nhập viện, nghi ngộ độc thức ăn. http://nld.com.vn/suc-khoe/hon-150-cong-nhan-nhap-vien-nghi-ngo-doc-thuc-an-20140321085030245.htm. Accessed 20th January 2017.

Người Lao Động (3/8/2014c). Sống dưới mức tối thiểu. http://nld.com.vn/cong-doan/song-duoi-muc-toi-thieu-20140803230518361.htm. Accessed 1st May 2016.

Pringle, T. & Clarke, S. (2011). *The Challenge of Transition: Trade Unions in Russia, China and Vietnam*. Basingstoke: Palgrave.

Quinn, B. A. (2000). The Paradox of Complaining: Law, Humor, and Harassment in the Everyday Work World. *Law & Social Inquiry*, 25 (4), 1151–1185.

Siu, K. & Chan, A. (2015). Strike Wave in Vietnam, 2006–2011. *Journal of Contemporary Asia*, 45 (1), 71–91.

The Central Committee of the Communist Party of Vietnam (2008a). Directive 22-CT/TW on intensifying leadership and guidance on developing harmonious, stable and progressive labour relations.

The Central Committee of the Communist Party of Vietnam (2008b). Resolution 20-NQ/TW at the 6th National Convention on continuing to develop Vietnamese working class in the modernisation and industrialisation era.

Trần, A. N. (2013). *Ties that Bind: Cultural Identity, Class, and Law in Vietnam's Labor Resistance*. Ithaca: Cornell Southeast Asia Program Publications.

Tuổi Trẻ (4/8/2014). Lương tối thiểu phải bằng mức sống tối thiểu. http://tuoitre.vn/tin/2014/08/04/chinh-tri-xa-hoi/luong-toi-thieu-phai-bang-muc-song-toi-thieu/630244.html. Accessed 1st May 2016.

Vietnam General Confederation of Labour (2015). *Report on the situation of labour disputes and strikes from 2009–2014*.

CHAPTER 4

At Union Offices and to the News Headlines

This chapter examines how labour law shapes a further form of labour resistance in Vietnam: workers' lodgement of letters to union offices. Most scholarly attention has to date been concerned with factory strikes. Some works on labour in Vietnam have looked at workers' petition letters, banners, and posters, demonstrating the prevalence of legal terms in their protest language (Trần 2013; Kerkvliet 2011). However, as in their analysis of factory strikes, it is unclear as to what the law means to workers. Do workers refer to the labour law regime and/or the Labour Code in their complaint letters in order to condemn illegal practices and call for proper legal implementation, or are they attempting to convey a set of norms and expectations about workplace relations? My analysis seeks to explore the norms and values that inform workers' language and their justifications for appealing to the unions.

Workers' lodgement of letters of complaint concerning their workplaces with union offices is an action within a state-sanctioned channel, as upper-level unions are also responsible for monitoring businesses' legal conduct. This action nonetheless does not abide by the formal procedures set out in the Labour Code, since the unions are not recognised as a legal authority responsible for resolving labour disputes. Of course, workers' resistance can easily escalate and spill onto the streets if writing letters does not yield satisfactory outcomes. Yet the main question to be addressed is how letter writers frame their grievances and demands, and whether they

T. P. Nguyen, *Workplace Justice*, Critical Studies of the Asia-Pacific,
https://doi.org/10.1007/978-981-13-3116-9_4

invoke similar or different understandings of justice as compared to workers interviewed in the previous chapter.

The main source of data for this chapter is a set of workers' collective complaint letters sent to official unions: the provincial Labour Federation and three upper-level unions in Đồng Nai Province. By 'collective' I mean letters that contain grievances affecting a group of workers, since the scope of this study is concerned with collective disputes. At the union offices, I was referred to the Examination Office, whose staff of two to four officers take charge of receiving and processing workers' letters and noting resolution outcomes. My aim in analysing these letters is to explore whether the issues raised in them are the same as those raised by workers going on strike and to obtain more details about the way in which workplace grievances are framed. At the provincial union and two upper-level union offices, I was able to read and copy workers' letters lodged in 2013 and 2014,[1] totalling from about 40 to more than 60 at each office. At the fourth union office, after some difficulty in requesting access to the letters, I was given two letters relating to collective complaints (as I specified to the office earlier that I was interested in collective disputes). These letters had been transferred from the provincial Labour Federation.

I read through all the letters and selected those concerned with grievances that stem directly from workers' experiences on the shop floor. The fact that they stem from shop floor experiences is important as there are letters written by a group of workers who had already left the company and who were demanding their wages, allowances, or their social insurance notebooks[2] back. As these grievances emerged after workers have left the companies, they tell us little about the workers' situations and how they make sense of their situations before the writing of the letters. I finally managed to collect 21 letters in total,[3] and use textual analysis with close reading to shed light on the norms, values, practices, and discourse that underpin the language of the letters. I also include in my analysis one letter written by a worker named Nguyễn Thị Thắm in 2010. It was published in *Lao Động* (The Labour), the national labour newspaper, under the headline: 'A worker's letter full of grief' (1 June 2010a). Addressed to the VGCL Chairman Mr Đặng Ngọc Tùng, the writer clearly identified her work position and her company, a garment company named Hansoll located in Trảng Bom District. While *Lao Động* periodically publishes selective extracts of workers' verbal and written accounts of their labour disputes, Thắm's letter is the only one published in full between 2010 and 2014.

Citizens' written correspondences to government and state agencies provide valuable materials through which to explore the meanings of law, power, and justice. In her 1996 *Slavic Review* article, Sheila Fitzpatrick draws on Russian citizens' letters to the Soviet Union authorities in the 1930s to illuminate two main categories of writers based on the way they presented their complaints, denunciations, appeals, petitions, opinions, and confession.[4] One style of writer, the 'supplicant', tends to portray himself/herself as a victim of misconduct, showing deference to the regime, and requesting assistance and authoritative intervention on the basis of empathy or patron-client relationship (p. 103). The other style of writer, the 'citizen,' sees themselves as right-bearers, acting in the public interest of fairness and justice (p. 104). Nick Cheesman also uncovers similar patterns of language in Burmese citizens' letters, among the thousands sent to regional and national leaders and commissioning bodies in the 2000s and 2010s (2015, pp. 228–233). These scholars also note the fluid boundary between supplicatory expression and rights-based claim-making. Isabelle Thireau and Hua Linshan (2003), drawing from workers' letters sent to the Letters and Visits Office[5] in China in the late 1990s, go beyond the supplicant-citizen dichotomy, demonstrating that the invocation of state law and legal rights can serve to amplify ideals of justice underpinning long-standing social norms in Chinese society.

A closer analysis of citizens' letters, inspired by the socio-legal approach to rights and justice, provides a more nuanced perspective into the way law constitutes citizens' demands and claim-making. George Lovell's 2012 book *This is Not Civil Rights*, devoted to studying American citizens' letters during the Depression era, centres on the question of whether, and to what extent, state law permeates written communications between citizens and government officials. Lovell is less concerned with the letter writers' agency as manifest through their evocation of rights, and more about how language and categories derived from state law help these writers articulate their grievances, problems, and demands for redress. In particular, people often combine legal and non-legal language in their writing in order to make 'novel' and 'expansive' claims that go beyond what is deemed as legal and legitimate by government officials (Lovell 2012, pp. 28–31). These types of letters thus embody ordinary people's absorption of and resistance to law. Lovell's analytical approach allows for a comprehensive assessment of language and categories informed by state law, and not just rights, in ordinary people's expressions, as well as their consciousness of law and their entitlements.

Following this analytical approach, this chapter starts with a brief discussion of the complaint process handled by the union's examination committee. The second section analyses workers' letters based on the issues being raised and discusses their implications for our understanding of law, morality, and (in)justice.

The Union's Examination Committee

The unions in Đồng Nai have promoted themselves offering an avenue for aggrieved workers to have their problems addressed (Đồng Nai Labour Federation 2014, 2016). Complainants can send their letters to the examination committee of the upper-level union in charge of the industrial or district area where their company is based. Once the upper-level union receives a worker's letter, it is required to either verify the problem via the company union, or transfer the letter to the company union to resolve (VGCL 2014). In the first approach, after verifying the problems and if the company union is unable to reach a resolution on their own, the upper-level union will issue a letter inviting the complainants and the company management to the union's office for the negotiation and settlement of the reported issues. If the workers' complaints indicate a violation of labour laws and policies on the part of the company, the examination committee can forward a request to the labour inspectors of the provincial Department of Labour to check on the company's conduct. The maximum duration for this complaint processing is ten days from the date of receipt of the letter so as to serve the objectives of local government and unions in preventing workplace tensions from bursting out into spontaneous strikes.

In practice, workers' letters are often processed or transferred to relevant bodies in a very short time. I sighted two complaint letters of workers in the same company, signed by the writers on 4 and 6 January 2014. The upper-level union chairperson sent through the complaints and a notice to the company union on 9 January, requesting that the union and company management resolve the issue and report to the upper-level union by the following day. The company union and human resource manager compiled a report with their solutions on time, effectively complying with the upper-level union's request.

However, the promptness of letter handling does not necessarily favour aggrieved workers. As I understand from reading the unions' annual reports, a prompt and timely resolution of workers' collective grievances is one of the necessary measures to prevent strikes and maintain industrial stability. Another problem with the handling process is the anonymity of the letter writers. The Vietnam General Confederation of Labour (VGCL) amended the rules in 2014 so that the letters must now contain the date of writing, name, address, and signature(s) of the complainant(s). This is a notable change from the pre-2014 version of the rules, which allowed for letters to be sent anonymously, and means that anonymous letters are no longer eligible for processing. As of 2014, complainants' identities can be revealed to the company union and management, making it possible for them to be penalised for complaining about their bosses. Thus, while the official union has opened up an arena beyond the formal system of dispute resolution in the Labour Code in which workers can access and raise their complaints, this process of complaint handling might ultimately put workers at risk. Workers who sent their letters might not be aware of the process following their lodgement. As the data analysis will later demonstrate, their decision to send a letter often arises out of helplessness and desperation.

Sending complaints to the unions was not a favoured action with workers whom I interviewed. A third of them recalled the unions' participation in the settlement of strikes in their companies but made no mention of their intention to directly appeal to the unions in writing or to any past experiences of doing so. After some prompting that suggested the role of these unions in resolving workers' grievances, workers actually vocalised their disinterest or even distrust. Only one worker recalled that one of his fellow workers, on behalf of a production group, lodged a complaint letter to the upper-level union some years ago. Generally, the worker complained that their meals for overtime night shifts had been reduced in number and demanded that management provide the same number of meals as before. They succeeded in having this problem resolved. However, according to my respondent, that was the exception among many letters lodged by workers in that company. Considering the number of strikes in that company over many years, one can see that such an issue is trivial compared to other ongoing grievances such as excessive overtime and coercive treatment. When I asked my respondent whether his fellow worker, who wrote the complaint letter, is still working in the company, he said yes, and straight away explained that that was because the letter was anonymous. He sounded very certain that complainants who identified themselves would be called to the human resource office and disciplined or dismissed.

Workers' Letters to Union Offices

Some Notes on Data and Workers' Self-ascription

Among the 21 selected letters, 16 letters had no signature, though writers still identified themselves as 'workers in the company/section X.' In 2 out of those 16 letters, the writers explicitly stated that they refrained from revealing their names and staff numbers for fear of losing their jobs. Three letters were written and signed by one person on behalf of a group. Only two letters contained multiple signatures of 10 and 18 people respectively; the second also contained a list of complainants' names.

The letters included in this analysis vary according to what they are framed as and their style of writing. The first group of eight letters are entitled 'request letter' (*đơn đề nghị/kiến nghị*). All of them explicitly contain the writers' request for the union's and/or management's consideration of the issues raised in them. A second group of eight letters are titled 'complaint letter' (*đơn khiếu nại*), where three writers stated their intention to 'sue' (*kiện*) or 'complain about' (*khiếu nại*) supervisors or managers and the others talk at length about the issues of concern and request some intervention from the state and the union. The third group, four out of 21 letters, are entitled 'letter requesting resolution/assistance' (*đơn xin xem xét giải quyết/trợ giúp*), and only one is presented as a 'report letter' (*đơn trình*). While the writing style and structure of these letters are much the same across all types, as can be seen from their titles, not all of the letters are explicitly of a resistance nature. However, the language used throughout the texts adequately conveys workers' complaints or demands and their wishes to rectify existing problems. Even though some of the request letters do not lay any blame or make any accusations, they are presented in a manner that shows workers' disagreement and dissatisfaction with company management's decisions.

The letters are concerned with workers across 16 companies, with three of the companies having two letters raising similar issues. In the case of two of these companies, the letters were written on two consecutive dates; in the other case, they were written six months apart. All the companies belong to the footwear, garment, electronics, and wood manufacturing industries, or plastic, metal, and chemical production sectors.[6] The number of employees in these companies ranges from 170 to more than 18,000.

To whom the letters were directed is an important factor that shapes their style and language. Most of the letters appeal to the union and the state officials, those whom workers regard as having power and authority. These writers often tried to emphasise their helpless and despondent situations. The remaining three letters, titled 'request letter,' were directed at company management and concerned workers' demands for a higher wage rise. The language in these letters is more measured and assertive. They were sent to the union office to serve as evidence that workers had previously appealed to the management in vain. In one case, the letter has a signature of support by the company union's chairperson and gives a 'deadline' to the management for resolving workers' requests.[7]

Compared with most responses I obtained from interviews, the letters usually contained expressions of strong emotion and statements. The difference in style between the interviews and letters can be explained by the moment of articulation: while two-thirds of my interviews took place when workers' grievances and complaints had been dealt with, or when their workplace conditions had improved, the letters were written at a time when grievances and complaints were still unfolding or intensifying. Fifteen of the letters provide detailed stories and impassioned accounts of the complainants and their affected fellow workers, while the remaining six letters merely make brief complaints and requests. Additionally, while most interviewed workers were wary of speaking badly about their bosses, I found that half of the letters contained workers' explicit allegations about and personal attacks on supervisors' and management's behaviour.[8]

The translation of the letters into English was a fascinating but challenging experience for me as a native Vietnamese speaker. Many of them contain long sentences without breaks or commas, using colloquial and informal language and shorthand, and at times making vague references to the actors or subjects of particular actions. Such vagueness and disorganisation are understandable since most letters were likely written by people suffering from stress and distress. In my translation, I have refined the grammar of long sentences to make them easy to follow, but have kept intact the writers' rhetorical devices, such as rhetorical questions and exclamations. The meaning of some ambiguous references can be surmised from reading the surrounding text. I try to literally translate the lay language and common expressions when I am unable to find the English equivalent. While all efforts have been made to preserve the writers' original meaning, my translation may not have done justice to the feeling they put in the letters, especially through exclamatory and emphatic words.

The way in which writers address their letters to either state authorities, unions, or management, demonstrates a norm of deference typical in Vietnamese social hierarchies. All of the letters start with 'respectfully sent to' (*kính gửi*). In Vietnamese, the word 'respectfully' (*kính*) is normally used in writing when one wishes to formally address a person or people of an older generation, holding a more powerful position or having certain authority and influence. The letters that were directed to the state and unions refer to these bodies as 'the upper agencies and departments' (*ban ngành cấp trên*), 'the authoritative agencies' (*cơ quan có thẩm quyền*), or, in a more respectful way, 'the honourable office/agency' (*quý cấp/quý cơ quan*). The others simply make reference to management as 'the management board of company X.'

At the start of each letter, the writers generally refer to themselves as 'the collective of workers in plant, section, company X,' 'we workers,' 'workers, brothers and/or sisters,' or 'employees.' Their accounts feature their interactions with 'supervisors,' 'plant leaders,' 'group leaders,' 'human resource people,' 'managers,' and at times 'cadres.' Workers' use of the word 'cadres' *(cán bộ)* is interesting, since this word normally refers to public employees, officials, and authorities. In the workers' accounts, 'cadres' means people working in the office and occupying a managerial or administrative position in the company. Without detailed descriptions of workplace hierarchies, it is nevertheless clear that complainants, as manual labourers, regarded those in managerial and supervisory positions as belonging to a different group that is more privileged and powerful.

Workers see the company unions as being on the same side as those in managerial positions. This is not surprising as union positions are often filled by human resource staff, supervisors, and managers, who are unelected and unknown to the workers. The statement in one letter, 'I don't understand what our union is for,' suggests that the existence of the union is only symbolic. In other letters, the complainants express their disappointment about the union's blatant collusion with management and its failure to improve workers' conditions. These statements do not necessarily reflect workers' understandings of the company unions' legal functions, but rather imply their own views and expectations that a good union should be able to help them address their workplace problems.

Half of the complainants describe themselves as rule-abiding employees and workers. For instance, one letter starts with: 'We work full time and have not violated any rule or caused any physical damage to the company.' The writers of this letter refer to workers' good behaviour, hard work, and compliance with company regulations to lay the ground for further justification of their claims. A few other writers first refer to their long service and emotional attachment to the workplace as their second home, which they then contrast with the reality of discipline and exploitation they encountered.

One exceptional letter that made it into the press as news headlines (hereafter referred to as the 'published letter') starts with an emotional plea and the female writer's sense of helplessness:

> We workers here have so many grievances but we don't know how to find equality. I did ask for help from some social organisations but didn't get any response. After some time pondering and looking for your address, I decided to write this letter to you. No! I do not 'sue' the company; I only wish to raise my voice as an employee. … I hope you put yourself in our position as employees, sympathise with our fates as workers, and look at the environment in which Vietnamese citizens are working. (Lao Động 1 June 2010a)

Thắm, who wrote this letter, continued with great detail about how and why she decided to try this last resort, after almost giving up on her search for 'equality'—an issue that resurfaces at the end of the letter and forms a vital part of her claims. By positioning herself as one of the 'employees,' 'workers,' and 'citizens,' she asserts her legal and political identity in her relationship with management and the state. This not only justifies her appeal to the chairman but also appears to be aimed at evoking a duty of care from the leader of the trade union. I can see the paradoxical situation Thắm was in when she talks about her urge to solve workplace grievances and fight injustice yet insists that she refrains from 'suing' or challenging the company. Yet throughout the letter, she cannot help but accuse the managers and supervisors of perpetual exploitation and maltreatment of the workers, thus exposing the power structure that has pushed her to cry out in desperation, and ultimately bring home her argument and aspiration for a 'rightful struggle' (*đấu tranh đúng đắn*).

Working Hours and Overtime

> None of the workers wants to work [during the lunch break], but they have to, because they are afraid of being repressed. During normal working hours, they [the management and supervisors] squeeze as much labour out of us as they can, and then do not allow us to have a rest at noon. As a consequence, the health of us workers has deteriorated seriously.

This extract exemplifies a common type of grievance relating to overtime work. Related complaints, which appear in 10 letters, include reductions in workers' rest time, forced overtime, and the failure to pay extra for overtime work. These complainants depict the exhausting conditions in which they work and call for reasonable working hours on the shop floor. They particularly attack the coercive behaviour of management, frequently describing such behaviour as 'coercing' (*ép*) and 'forcing' (*bắt*) workers to work overtime. The aforementioned extract, which is similar to statements in three other letters, makes clear that long working hours affect workers' health and, consequently, the reproduction of their labour power. The other letters weave this issue into a broader picture of their working conditions as 'too stressful' (*áp lực quá*) or 'unbearable' (*không chịu nổi*). Two writers also attribute workers being worked too hard to management's material pursuits, their obsession with quotas, and ignorance of workers' well-being. Titled as 'request letters,' these two letters end with a clear statement that the coercion to work during lunch and break time must be stopped.

The following is an example of the workers' concerns about physical health, as well as about management discipline and their material pursuits:

> The vice-managers of many plants force workers to work during lunch break, giving the excuse that there are many too many orders and rush orders. *They are afraid of falling short of the quotas and are just aiming for personal achievements.* [...] What we really need is our health. We can't take a rest at noon when the machines are still running; as a consequence, we get exhausted in the afternoon. The problem has continued for quite a long time. Do the company management know about this? Or do they know the problem but intentionally ignore it because it is in their interests? [italics added]

This extract and the one that precedes it do not mention exactly how many hours workers have to work overtime. Yet the description of exhaustion and the impression that they give of the continuance of the problem suffice to describe the management's exploitative practices. The rhetorical question about the management's deliberate ignorance of the overtime problem skilfully amplifies the previous criticism of their self-interests and sums up the writers' claims about unfairness stemming from managerial immorality.

The writer in the following extract did not only speak up against long working hours but also contrasted it with the situation during slow periods. Different from the previous extracts, this one contains short statements in dot points describing several other workplace problems as 'unfair.' It reads:

> The company where we work has the following unfair policies:
>
> - When the company has rush orders, workers must work overtime from 7.00 to 20.00, including Saturday and Sunday.
> - When the company has no orders, it no longer needs workers and is ready to sack anyone anytime. Dismissed workers can only get one month's wage and no type of allowance.

While this extract contains more details about the dates and hours of work, it does not indicate whether workers here were aware of the legal overtime limits and legal rest time. The second point also makes no mention of the legal provisions regarding employment contracts or the lawfulness of management's decision; it instead evokes a sense of unfairness about receiving little compensation upon losing one's job. The phrase 'no longer needs workers' (*không cần công nhân nữa*) in Vietnamese conveys one's sorrowful feeling following unfair treatment. These two points raised by the writers convey an understanding that the demands and profit motives of companies, rather than any other type of care or obligation, determine the workers' plight. There is no clear request or statement at the end of this letter expressing how the workers would like these unfair policies to be rectified, just a general request for the union's timely 'consideration, intervention, and resolution.'

In one case, the writer not only points out the coercive manner of work but also the management's failure to pay for extra working time. He/she writes: 'For the past year, in the company and especially plant 2, the supervisors and plant managers have often forced workers to work before start time and during lunch break, but have not paid us extra money.' This note about underpayment demonstrates the worker's subjective view of what constitutes fair pay and fair work hours with no mention of legal provisions concerning overtime. This is one of the two letters that explicitly detail workers' dissatisfaction with the lack of extra pay within a broader complaint about coercive and exhausting work.

Of all ten letters considered in this sub-section, only two contain explicit reference to the Labour Code's provisions relating to working hours. In one of the latter cases, this was woven in with another criticism of the self-interestedness of the managers:

> As we know, according to the regulations, we work for eight hours a day and have one hour lunch break which is not counted towards our working hours. The current law also has rules for overtime. Yet due to many rush orders and their obsession with output, the plant managers forced us to work during break time, for 30 to 40 minutes.

The writer adds that: 'we think the company should be clear about law,' which suggests certain expectations about management's legal behaviour. Yet this is not followed by a call for an honouring of legal rights. Rather, a reference to law here serves to complement and emphasise the management's unethical behaviour. The other letter that contains reference to the Labour Code includes similar statements:

> From 2011 to 2013 we worked for the company for a period of 12 hours per day (72 hours per week), which was many hours. The company back then still allowed us some rest time. But since 2014 until now we haven't had any rest. If we continue to work like this, our health will not be maintained for more work in the long term. In this situation, does the company violate Article 106, section 2b of Chapter VII of the Labour Code?

This example is the only one of all the letters I collected at the union offices that poses an explicit and straightforward question about a legal term and the management's legal behaviour. Still, this letter starts with the workers' general account and their subjective view of working hours, which should accommodate some rest time. The question posed at the end calls for a consideration of workers' legal rights and a condemnation of violation, but the writer seems to put more stress on the company's unfair treatment that affects their physical well-being and labour productivity.

Workplace Discipline

As indicated in the letters, workers commonly experience three forms of discipline: threats of reprisal for speaking up about their own concerns and grievances, having to lie about their working conditions to customers and inspectors, and verbal abuse from line leaders and managers in response to workers' queries and requests. Workplace discipline is not presented as a problem requiring intervention in itself, but is coupled with grievances related to wage policy, overtime, and working hours. In the following example, the writer complains about the company's failure to raise wages before pointing out why workers were better off keeping their silence:

> Recently, on 1st January, the state issued a wage rise decision for workers. But the company gave the excuse that workers violated the workplace regulations and did not raise wages for us. We consider this conduct as *abusing* and *exploiting* workers' labour. Having known that, we did not dare to appeal because we were worried about being repressed in our job. [italics added]

The writer here combines his/her general understanding about state regulations and their personal moral judgements to express dissatisfaction about the company's decision. This reference to the state suggests a lay understanding about the annual minimum wage adjustment issued by the government, which normally takes effect at the start of a year. In writing to the union, these workers refused to submit to the threat of managerial retaliation but instead struggled to raise their voices to a third party and seek intervention. The availability of a complaint mechanism beyond the workplace and workers' perception of the role of stakeholders involved in such a mechanism, to be discussed further, can play a major role in their decision to escalate their grievances.

This letter is one of three letters that accuse management of exploitation (*bóc lột*). In Vietnamese, the word '*bóc lột*' is understood as outrageous extraction of others' labour and seizure of their products to accumulate greater wealth and power. Often used to talk about the relationship between landowners and peasants in feudalism, it implies the maintenance of a social hierarchy in which the exploiting/landowning classes (*giai cấp địa chủ/bóc lột*) shall always enjoy unfair benefits from the peasants and lower classes' labour, service, and obedience. When used in the contemporary context, for instance, as seen in the media, exploitation refers to labourers' and employees' excessive work while receiving unfairly low pay. It does not usually have any class connotations, nor does it imply a broad critique of capitalism. However, in Communist Party of Vietnam's (CPV's) documents, at least up until the 1990s, exploitation, along with other problems of coercion and injustice, is mentioned as an inherent problem of capitalism.[9] For instance, according to the 1991 Report for the Seventh National Party Congress, a socialist society is one in which people are 'liberated from coercion, exploitation and injustice.' Yet this statement about the socialist vision was dropped in the Report for the Tenth National Party Congress in 2006 and in the revised Fundamentals of the Party in 2011. The writer's usage of the term 'exploitation' in the letter does not carry the sense of excessive labour, immiseration, and injustice implicit in earlier socialist and popular discourse. However, when used alongside the other word 'abuse' (*lợi dụng*) and followed by the mention of threat, it conveys a sense of unfairness quite similar to that associated with criticism of the landowner-peasant relationship.

In four letters, workers had accumulated long-standing grievances, both individual and collective, to such an extent that they could not be condensed in a few pages. In these letters, complainants describe their frustration as being shared by all workers on the same production line or in the same group. The following extracts talking about conditions in one company lucidly illustrate the ongoing collective experience of dissatisfaction and feeling of powerlessness:

> Letter A: Many times we caught a fever and had to take leave to go to the doctor's. Yet after that, when we got back to work, the manager and line leader asked us to stand at the end of the line for the whole day and did not let us work as usual. … We were also given a discipline note. Don't you think that *we were pushed too hard*? Many times we went to the human resource office to talk about our problems but our complaints were in vain. [italics added]
>
> Letter B: We were so aggrieved when other workers were *unfairly* scolded and yet none of us dared to raise our voices. If we had, the managers would have put more pressure on us and would finally have sacked us. [italics added]

Besides a strong sense of sympathy towards the mistreatment of other workers, the writer also conveys a collective feeling of anxiety and frustration. The rhetorical question in particular conveys the extremity of endurance and an emotional appeal to sympathy for treatment that has gone beyond what is deemed as morally acceptable. I understand the 'pressure' in the second letter to be a reference not just to the physical strain of labouring and catching up with quotas, which existing ethnographic studies on labour relations in Vietnam have shown (Chae 2003; Nghiem 2006), but also to the mental strain resulting from arbitrary discipline. I also interpret this protest against others' suffering as embodying an urge to protect oneself against the same sort of mistreatment. Workers' exposure of such immoral conduct to a third party represents a reaction against the silencing of their voices on the shop floor and the wish to be able to stay in their job (and earn their living) without being destroyed emotionally.

Perhaps the most distressing embodiment of workers' hardship and demoralisation is captured in the following lines, which were extracted from two letters referring to the same company:

> Letter A: *In fact, this is not a company but a jail. In this situation how can we live?* The manager and group leader have coerced workers too much, especially with overtime. I myself have seen many people who work hectically but are still yelled at, to the point that they cry when they are alone. [italics added]
>
> Letter B: I want to sue the company for coercing and *exploiting* workers' labour. Workers have to work overtime beyond their health limits. Many workers are sick but they are not allowed to take leave. The Chinese treat workers *like slaves, or prisoners.* Our working hours are 12 hours a day, from 7.00 to 19.00, Monday to Friday, and to 18.30 and 17.00 on Saturday and Sunday. The company compels workers to work 30 days in a month, every month. Anyone who is absent from work will be fined 300,000 dong. [italics added]

These complainants want to draw attention to their overall extreme working environment, rather than the specific problem of excessive working hours. The analogy between the company and a jail, and between workers and prisoners, tells a disturbing story of subordination in which human dignity and the right to self-esteem are stripped away. Again, use of the rhetorical question in letter A again powerfully communicates a loss of personal freedom and choice. The letter then goes to the heart of the matter: working under exhausting orders and in a confined space, it is as if they are in a labour camp, treated as 'slaves' or 'prisoners' rather than dignified workers they see themselves to be. The outlining of their working hours, long days, every day of the week and month intensifies the image of maltreatment. Further, the imposition of a fine as a punishment for workers' absence from work leaves them no choice but to remain encased in this cycle of exhaustion. This worker perceives themselves to be in an inhumane situation.

The writer's mention of the Chinese (*người Trung Quốc*) in letter B warrants further consideration. It is possible that this writer's depiction of the 'slave-like' conditions of workers in this factory reflects nationalistic sentiments and resentment of the long history of China's domination and its political influence over Vietnam. In four other letters there were references to Japanese and Korean managers or supervisors. Compared to letters in which the managers' ethnicity is not mentioned (from which we can assume that the managers are Vietnamese), the depictions of managerial treatment in these four letters convey more deeply a sense of workers' demoralisation and inferior status. An ethnographic study conducted by Suhong Chae of a multi-national textile company in Hồ Chí Minh City in the early 2000s similarly found that tensions on the shop floor were entrenched along ethnic lines (in that case, between Vietnamese workers and Korean managers (Chae 2003)). And Chae's study found that the Korean managers often 'shouted' (*la*) rather than 'talked' to the workers (Chae 2003, p. 93), a behaviour that workers saw as rude and contemptuous. It is not possible to make a conclusive statement about the role of ethnic difference in the letters under examination here. However, one interpretation is that, in evoking the managers' ethnicity, the writers want to appeal to the sympathy of union officials who share the same bond of citizenship with them, bolstering their accusations of the managers' immorality.

The sharpest allegations about management conduct are seen in the published letter, in which the writer Thắm extends her creative and provocative use of words to describe how workers experience and perceive the law in their relationship with management.

> I have to bitterly say that the company management is 'grabbing money' and 'gluing people's mouths' to cover up what is called 'labour coercion and exploitation.' The lack of knowledge and understanding about the Labour Code has meant that employees' legitimate rights and interests are trussed up (*xiềng xích*). We work hard, yet our wage is meagre while there are too many 'laws.' The company asks workers to arrive early to attend a meeting 'before [the start] time.' Then when we finish late, we don't get any more money. Our lunch break of 1 hour is also 'cut at the head and cut at the tail' of 20 minutes [quotation marks in original]. (Lao Động, 1 June 2010a)

Workers in Thắm's company seem to face the same problems as the food processing workers discussed in Chap. 3: there is an imbalance between their hard labour and the incomes they receive. Instead of focusing her complaint on the wage payment, Thắm uses it as evidence to support her broader accusations of labour exploitation, which appear for the third and last time in this analysis of the letters. The extract, as well as other sections in the letter, documents a range of exploitative behaviour on the part of management, such as the failure to remunerate workers fairly and very intense work demands. There is also a legal dimension to it when she points at management's ignorance of labour law and the harm this causes to workers' rights and interests. However, here and in the rest of the letter, Thắm does not condemn the management's behaviour as illegal; she instead draws the audience's attention to other 'laws.'

The 'laws' to which she refers in the middle of the extract are the stringent and unfair company regulations that managers use to justify the harsh discipline and exploitation. They are not true laws, but rather the adoption of mechanisms that are seen to benefit the company. This 'law' is the 'jungle law' (*luật rừng*) that is so often referred to in the Vietnamese media. Such a negative depiction of law refers to unofficial, unreasonable, and even illegal rules, often imposed or exercised by businesses and creditors (e.g., see Dân Trí 14 February 2014; Người Lao Động 4 August 2014; Tuổi Trẻ 11 September 2014). When I lived in Vietnam, I often heard the term 'jungle law' from family members, relatives, and older acquaintances of older generations to refer to coercive actions exercised by the police, civil security forces, or gangsters. In Thắm's recounting, the many 'laws' are manifested in the arbitrary and humiliating actions of supervisors, line leaders, and managers with regard to working hours, cases of workers' sickness, and production quotas. Her reference to the Labour Code does not just support her accusations of unethical behaviour among managers but also hints at the Code's powerlessness to defend workers in the face of other so-called laws.

Apart from the ironic use of the term 'laws,' what is striking in her letter is the coupling of workplace discipline with other observations of treatment at work. Thắm's depiction of the favour enjoyed by some office workers in contrast to production workers, with respect to eating meals and using mobile phones, for example, acutely illustrates her yearning for 'equality,' stated at the start of the letter:

> There is a regulation that bans workers from bringing personal amenities such as bottles, umbrellas, hats and coats, into the plant. Workers have to turn off their mobiles when they are in the plant. The company hangs a notice board [...] which has the following sentence about conduct: 'No discrimination,' but, needless to say, the reality is different. The office staff can bring their personal amenities, drink water in glasses/bottles [while workers have to drink water by putting their mouths right under the taps], and use their mobiles regardless of whether it's for 'public' or 'private' matters. They can bring umbrellas and hats [on their walk to the canteen] and are 'served from head to toe' [quotation marks in original]. (Lao Động 1 June 2010a)

Here Thắm gives further details about what she means by the 'laws' issued by the company, which look good on a notice board but are empty in practice. She then bitterly contrasts the privileged situation of office staff with the conditions endured by workers, who have to walk to the canteen and crowd each other to have their meal portions distributed. Ultimately, she writes, workers must 'swallow their humiliation' (*nuối tủi nhục*) in the face of incessant work pressure, disrespect, and indignity (Lao Động 1 June 2010a).

Workers being forced to lie about their working conditions is detailed in four letters. Such discipline is a tactic on the part of managers and supervisors to cover up their unlawful conduct in the presence of customers and labour inspectors. I call this tactic a form of workplace discipline since it is portrayed by the writers as a measure that accompanies some threat of punishment to the workers in the case of non-conformity. The managerial practice of 'training' and arranging for workers to tell lies when interviewed by labour specialists and customers has been documented in an ethnographic research on garment workshops in Hà Nội in the early 2000s (Nghiem 2006). But this study does not provide detail about workers' own opinions of such practices. From my reading of the letters, workers seem to exhibit more acute feelings about management's misconduct in the presence of outsiders with whom the company has a stake. Workers' inability to speak in their own voices in such circumstances adds to their existing frustrations associated with work pressures and management's immoral behaviour.

Workers' observations about this form of discipline appear to be indirectly informed by law but are mostly couched in moralistic language. For instance, one of the letters reads:

> When we were asked questions by the customers or anyone else, the plant managers and supervisors ordered us to lie that we work no more than two hours per day for overtime shifts and we do not work on Sundays. Whoever spoke the truth would have their overtime increased to three hours a day and work all four Sundays, or get sacked.

According to the Labour Code, the maximum overtime per day must not exceed half of the normal working hours for each day. For instance, employees who have an eight-hour working day are not to be asked to do overtime for more than four hours. The employer must also obtain the employees' consent in advance to the overtime being required. In addition, employees are entitled to a minimum of four rest days in a month. While there is no explicit reference to these legal guidelines in the aforementioned extract, a general understanding of what constitutes appropriate working time appears through the writer's recounting of the management's verbal strategy. The writer knows that they are being asked to lie for the benefit of the company and questions the moral integrity of the managers and supervisors. In situating this extract within the whole letter, it seems to me that, ironically, the lies which workers were forced to tell also become the foundation for their complaints about working 12 hours a day and 30 days a month. In another letter, besides the complaint about the coercive working environment, a legal issue about previous consent to do overtime also appears in workers' accusations of managerial treatment:

> Although workers are very tired and aggrieved, they still have to work [during lunch time]. If anyone asks us or any customer investigates, we still have to say [that we work] voluntarily. Many times when there were meetings where unions and customers asked workers' opinions, we were ordered by the upper people to say as they wish rather than telling the truth. Anyone who speaks up their own opinion will be threatened, repressed and schemed to quit the job.

Ultimately, workers conform to this kind of tactic because they do not want to be without employment. If threats to subsistence were a major cause of popular resistance among peasants in the twentieth century (Scott 1976) and Chinese state workers bearing the brunt of economic reform in the twenty-first century (Chen 2000), in this case in Vietnam the fear of workers losing their income and falling below subsistence has ironically served to entrench managerial power and hindered workers' intent to resist. There are similarities regarding power and inequality between the workplace situations of these Vietnamese workers and employees facing violation of their leave rights in the USA, as described in Catherine Albiston's socio-legal study of the Family and Medical Leave Act (2005). Most employees in the USA study opted to avoid confrontation by either quitting or dropping their cases. In the Vietnamese context, managerial practices have served to generate both obedience and resistance. Workers constantly struggle to maintain their moral integrity and to continue in their job without being subjected to an exploitative relationship with management.

Decent and Fair Wages

Wages have been the most pressing issue in labour relations in Vietnam (Tran 2007; Siu and Chan 2015) and, as discussed earlier, the most common reason for factory strikes. It was expected that wage demands would make up the largest group in the collected letters, and yet they are actually only the third most common source of grievances. This is likely to be explained as wage-related grievances, as a pressing and immediate issue that is closely linked to workers' welfare, are often the subject of strikes and are taken to the streets by the workers in the hope of putting pressure on management and triggering their immediate response. In the letters, wage-related grievances include those relating to underpayment, withholding of wages, and companies' failure to raise wages. While the state and union officials tend to attribute wage-related demands to companies' non-compliance with labour law and the government's minimum wage policy, most complaint writers have different justifications for their demands. Based on their justifications, I classify workers' demands into two categories: for 'decent wages' and for 'fair wages.'

Demands for 'decent wages' are based upon workers' living needs. My conceptualisation here is drawn from the International Labour Organization (ILO)'s 'decent work agenda,' which advocates for an employee's income that ensures 'security in the workplace and social protection for their families' (ILO n.d.). An income earned from decent work should suffice to meet the living standards of employees and their families, and especially in developing countries, prevent them from falling below the poverty line (ILO 2012, p. 19). In Vietnam, a decent wage must be distinguished from the minimum wage, which, according to VGCL surveys, only satisfies 70 per cent of minimum living needs (cited in Lao Động 2 August 2014).

Five letters revolve around the demand and concern for a decent wage. For instance, in the following example, the complainants draw attention to the difficulty of maintaining workers' livelihoods on their low incomes and with the late payment of wages:

> We were paid by piece rate. On that date the company handed out an order. The quota given by the company was too high, while the rate per unit was low. The earnings would not have been sufficient for us to get by in our daily lives. We were also unable to complete that quota.
>
> Today 10/4/2014 is pay day, but the company informed us that the wages of 10 people with resignation letters would be withheld until 18/4/2014. In our lives, we brothers and sisters depend on the monthly incomes earned by our tears and sweat. Now that the company withholds our wages, how can we afford to pay for our rent, food, children's school fees …?

It is clear from this letter that the writer and his/her co-workers are internal migrants, moving from the countryside to industrial and urban areas. Most of these migrant workers live in private rental units, which are often in a squalid condition but cost a substantial proportion of their monthly income (Trần 2013). Information obtained from my interviewees and key informants suggests that the rent in Đồng Nai ranges from 800,000 dong to 1.2 million dong per month, taking up approximately 25–30 per cent of a worker's average income of 4 million dong. As in the extract, workers' reliance on their income from one month to another demonstrates their precarious living conditions and limited savings.

The way the workers frame their demands here echoes the ethics of subsistence that prevails in pre-capitalist peasant society (Scott 1976). Similar to peasants who rebelled against their landlords when their minimum livelihoods were threatened, factory workers write and lodge their complaints against management when their basic needs are not secured. Besides the explicit rhetorical question in the aforementioned extract, workers' living needs also manifest in references in other letters to the need for 'our rice and clothes' (*vì miếng cơm manh áo*), 'taking care of our family,' and 'a stable income.' Paradoxically, as shown in the preceding sub-section, the fact that basic needs are barely or not met can also, ultimately, account for workers' silence and conformity in the face of managerial discipline, demands, and threats.

The behaviour of all writers discussed so far in this chapter fits well with Felstiner, Abel, and Sarat's definition of 'blaming,' that is, a behaviour in which 'a person attributes an injury to the fault' of another individual or entity, and 'claiming' (1980/1981, pp. 634–635), when he or she voices it to the responsible entity and demands remedial actions. Whilst Felstiner and colleagues illustrate their concepts with an incident that involved injuries, the workers writing these letters faced threats to livelihood, physical harm to their well-being, and/or psychological pressure. The consequent blaming and claiming they engaged in did not involve reference to injury, but did refer to threats and harm to their livelihood.

'Fair wage' demands, the second category, appear in three letters.[10] In the broader context, while the notion of a decent wage is popular in Vietnamese official and public discourse, especially around the time of the government's minimum wage bargaining, there is hardly any mention or discussion of a fair wage. In my textual analysis of the complaint letters, I did not particularly search for the word 'fair,' 'equitable,' or 'just' *(công bằng)*, but found lines in which the writers mentioned, complained, or made claims about their wages. Workers' appeals for a fair wage are not explicit in the letters but can be surmised from their description of what they deem to be the opposite, which is unfair wages, and their reasoning that a higher wage (rise) is warranted. I therefore consider the notion of a 'fair wage' to be subjective and contingent on individual worker's perceptions of his/her working conditions.

The following extract exemplifies a demand for a fair wage. Here, complainants reason that they should be entitled to a wage rise due to the intensity of work: the more time and physical effort one spends on tasks, the higher wage one deserves. The writer highlights that workers' contribution to the business is no less important than office staff's and calls for their equal treatment:

> Now the company only raises wages of office staff but not of workers. Officers only take orders and monitor workers, while workers do physical labour and frequently work overtime. So why did they have their wages raised but not workers? [underlining in original]

In another letter, delivered in an even more assertive tone, the writer justifies the workers' demand for a wage rise by pointing to the skill difference between workers in two different sections. As stated in Article 5 of the Labour Code, workers have the right to receive a wage which is commensurate with their occupational skills and knowledge on the basis of an agreement reached with the employer. This article further implies employees' right to negotiate their wages with their employer. While the workers' demand in the following extract is sanctioned in the Labour Code, the writer opts not to highlight this, but instead presents another argument:

> The wage rise level of the project section is very low compared to that of the production section. The project section includes labourers who have been trained and have technical skills, but (now) receive the same wage as those in the production section. We find that the wage rise level is not reasonable.

Instead of relying on the Labour Code or contractual agreements, these workers leverage their subjective judgements to ask that the management should remunerate them fairly for their skill and labour, implying a sense of distributive justice. In making demands for fair payment, complainants position themselves and their fellow workers as parties in a bargaining situation with management. They therefore seek to either present persuasive or assertive statements, albeit somehow presenting their claims in a hesitant and rhetorical manner. The delivery of these letters is in stark contrast to pleas for a living wage delivered in a desperate and pitiful manner. Whilst the emergence of disputes described in Felstiner, Abel, and Sarat's original study is preceded by an injury or a harmful incident, the aforementioned disputes in relation to fair wages are not, but are instead foregrounded by judgements of perceived unfairness.

While earlier I distinguished between two types of wage-related demand, the following letter provides an illustration that the line between them is not so clear-cut. This letter contains a demand for a higher wage rise, but the justification is about essential aspects of workers' living needs. The writer in this case starts with a short, sharp statement: 'The company's decision on our wage rise and reward is not reasonable and we totally disagree,' before explaining at length about workers' dissatisfaction. Among three reasons centring on the company's profits, inflation, and a delay of the wage rise in the previous year, the second reason is given the most space and articulation by the writer:

> We think that we, as consumers, are more affected [than the business] by the rising inflation: for instance, while in early 2012, it cost 18,000 dong for 10 eggs, the price now has gone up to 30,000 to 35,000 dong.
>
> Inflation is the common market problem facing all enterprises and factories, but it does not mean that all of them have refused to raise wages or have cut employees' reward like our company. [...] We think that this year the company should give us a higher wage rise to compensate for inflation like other companies.

Similar to other pleas for a decent wage, the writer also points to the workers' living expenses but focuses on reasoning rather than invoking sentiment from the reader. In describing themselves as consumers and citing the price of eggs—a basic food item in almost all households—as an example, these workers emphasise their wishes for a wage rise that allows them to fulfil their everyday needs. In this instance, while a large part of the letter is framed as a form of collective bargaining and negotiation between workers and management, their argument boils down to a demand for a decent wage.

What is also interesting about this letter is the clearly articulated claim for a right to fairer remuneration. As a whole, this letter is a tactical combination of different manners and modes of reasoning: a wage bargain on the basis of consumption costs and fair reward, and a request for decent treatment based on mutual interests, their participation in the company being seen as making them part of a family.

> We always try our best to fulfil our task because at heart we think that by producing goods for the company, we also do good to ourselves. We consider the company like our family. Why don't we have the right to benefit from what the company has achieved?

The writer's demand effectively invokes the norm of reciprocal obligation, that is, 'an obligation to return a gift or service' (Scott 1976, p. 167) that one previously received. The norm of reciprocity is a crucial part of a range of social arrangements in twentieth-century Southeast Asia that determine how rural people treat each other and how they expect to be treated by their fellows or other patrons (Scott 1976). In contemporary Vietnamese society, it still prevails in interpersonal relations and kin networks, for instance, when an individual is expected or obliged to return a favour of a comparatively equivalent nature to the other person (Luong 2016). In practice, one's judgement of how the favour should be returned is subjective and non-quantifiable, but living up to such mutuality is an important consideration in interpersonal relationships, and in this case, between workers and employers. The material connections between workers and employers are skilfully intertwined with their emotional connections when the writer brings in the image of a family, the embodiment of the most precious relationship in the Vietnamese society.

Another exception to the aforementioned classification of wage demand is seen in the published letter. While raising the wage issue, the writer also weaves her complaint in with other workplace problems and, in particular, with a twisted rhetorical reference to 'law.'

> We don't know whether our wages and insurance are calculated correctly, but we only know that, after receiving wages, many workers quit their jobs. Some workers complain that wages are calculated incorrectly. The company issued a wage table that I myself have only just seen 'for the very first time' [quotation marks in original]. Workers cannot dispute it because they do not know what the wage table regulated by the State looks like. My cousin raised a question and received a cold answer: 'That is the company law.' Which law is it? (Lao Động 1 June 2010a)

The extract makes clear that workers are not knowledgeable about labour law, but hints at their curiosity to know what it is and how it works. Such law stands in contrast with another 'law,' which is associated with the language of management and its arbitrary treatment of workers. Understanding the labour laws would allow workers to determine what is right and wrong about their wage payment; and they know that company 'law' means nothing but injustice. As such, while the writer hints at the possibility that a working knowledge of labour law might give them a better chance to review the income they receive, she later makes void that possibility. The rhetorical question at the end strikingly conveys how lost she feels when the law that is supposed to protect her and her fellow workers is replaced with another law that perpetuates their desperation. The 'cold answer' that workers receive seems to put an end to all queries, as it shows that workers eventually lose out regardless of whether or not they know about law or resist on the basis of it.

Female Workers' Special Rights and Their Abuses

Four complaint letters were related specifically to female workers, who are legally entitled to special rights. As noted in Chap. 1, the Labour Code has a separate chapter that entitles these workers to rights such as maternity leave, nursing, and rest time. Article 154 stipulates that employers are obliged to promote gender equality in the workplace, from recruitment to employment and training. Article 155 includes the following further provisions for female workers who are in the later stage of their pregnancy or are nursing a child under 12 months of age:

- They are not required to do night work or overtime.
- They may transfer to lighter tasks, or have their daily working hours reduced by one hour while receiving the full wage.
- They are exempt from any labour disciplinary measures.

However, in practice, these entitlements are often neglected and abused by the management. The attention to women workers' parental duties in the making of the law ironically generates injustice in its implementation rather than promoting gender equality.

Two letters raise the problem of unfair dismissals of female workers. According to the Labour Code, labour contracts may be for either a definite or an indefinite term. Definite term contracts have a duration of 12–36 months and may be renewed once. If the workers are employed beyond two terms of up to 36 months, then the contract becomes an indefinite one. For instance, a worker entering a company with a one-year contract may then have his/her contract renewed for another year, and then, after the renewal, becomes 'indefinitely' employed. Article 155 specifies that the employer must not dismiss a female employee or unilaterally terminate her contract due to her marriage, pregnancy, maternity leave, or her nursing, unless the employer encounters exceptional circumstances and has to cease operating. However, workers' complaint letters in the two following companies indicate that female workers often find it difficult to move into the indefinite contracts to which they were legally entitled:

Letter A: Some female workers have been employed for two years and also paid for social insurance during this time. They have not violated any rule and they work hard. Yet when they get pregnant or when the company knows that they are nursing small children, the company immediately terminates their contracts. *This makes life very hard for many female workers*: they still have to pay their rent and take care of the kids without any job. [italics added]

Letter B: Some pregnant women worked for two years and were about to get their long-term contracts. When their pregnancy reached seven or eight months, the company ended their contracts, meaning that they will give birth without receiving any maternity benefits. [...] Meanwhile, the company is employing new workers every day. That conduct is *inhumane* and we workers are very angry. [italics added]

The failure to renew female workers' contracts exemplifies the breach of articles prohibiting discrimination against pregnant and nursing women; however, the writers consider the situations as ethically wrong rather than unlawful. As can be seen from these short extracts, the complainants employ certain knowledge about the contractual provisions to paint a larger picture about the fates of those who have unfairly lost their jobs while being pregnant. Compared to other writers discussed so far, whose grievances and judgements stem from lay morality and their subjective views of justice, these workers' judgements of management's conduct reflect labour law. This example suggests the blurred boundary between law and morality, when certain understandings and practices informed by law contribute to shaping workers' sense of unfairness and their moral call for the state's and union's intervention. Complaint writers also perceive female workers' mistreatment as a shared injustice that frustrates not just them but other workers in the same workplaces. The writers have effectively shifted female workers' problems from the individual to the collective on the ground of subsistence ethics.

In addition, two letters complain that female workers nursing small children are not allowed to have an extra hour break time. In one of these two letters, there is another complaint about the company's harsh control of toilet breaks, causing discomfort for all, but especially pregnant women workers. These complaints show that the parental duties of female workers have been denied or neglected due to the company management's efforts to maximise labour power.

Similar to previous studies on workers' complaint letters in China (Thireau and Hua 2003) and on their protest language (Pun 2016), my analysis reveals that writers who invoke law tend to do so not in order to construct a legal claim or argument but to amplify their own expressions of what is fair or socially acceptable. Chinese and Vietnamese workers invoke values and language embedded in socialist discourse, moral economy, and shared behavioural norms, in their respective settings. The way in which workers support their claims suggests broader understandings of workplace ethics that go beyond labour law that management, and indirectly the state, have abused or overlooked.

In addition to showing that workers' use of law is varied, my analysis suggests two further functions and effects of law. Firstly, law has become a moral resource for workers to evaluate workplace practices, when certain aspects of it are enacted in their lay language and articulations. The letters reveal that workers' general understanding of appropriate working hours, demands for a wage rise according to the state's policies, and their explanation of contractual entitlements are derived from relevant articles and terms in the Labour Code. Without the introduction of the Labour Code and its uneven or failed implementation across enterprises, these workers might have taken their exploitative and unfair situations for granted, rather than challenging or viewing them as problematic in their letters. It is therefore important to acknowledge that, despite the gap in its implementation, law still contributes to workers' moral reasoning about their grievances and demands. In this regard, and secondly, if we accept Albiston and Leachman's conceptualisation of social change as a process that involves the reconfiguration of 'social practices and interactions' (2015, p. 543), labour law in Vietnam has already contributed to this process.

The Letters' Final Requests and Demands for Rights

In their requests for complaint resolution at the end of the letters, only two writers make explicit reference to the Labour Code, with one of them demanding a proper enforcement of law and the other making a general appeal for help. The others convey their expectation that the unions and the state will carry out their moral obligations to workers and show compassion for their hardship. This expectation echoes the state's and the unions' propaganda and rhetoric that they strive to 'take care of' (*chăm lo*) workers' lives and more broadly reflects perceptions of a social contract:

> I want to ask the state departments: if your children also worked as factory workers and were exploited and mistreated like we were, then would your hearts feel sore and touched? I therefore beg you to come to our company

> and investigate the managers and line leaders who abused their power and position and treated their workers in a heartless way.

Most other complainants put their requests in less emotive language: 'We request the unions/authorities/state departments to protect and help us,' 'intervene in a timely manner,' or 'protect the rights and interests of employees.' Placing their faith in the power of a third party to intervene, that is, the union and the state authorities, enables workers to find some way to break free of the cycle of being coerced to work, forced to fabricate their working hours, and threatened with being sacked. With regard to letters that voice the threat of managerial retaliation or repression, the writers do not just ask for a solution to the complaints and frustration being raised, they also ask for protection against such threats. In doing so, complainants accept a paternalistic relationship with the state (Goluboff 1999, p. 738) and in turn hold the state accountable for their problems.

The published letter ends in a similarly touching voice, yet it also details workers' actions in the face of mistreatment and especially the writer's determination to seek justice.

> As it is so unfair, some workers stopped work but the company still refused to address their problem. These workers then decided to quit the company and accepted that they would lose some days' wages and even their social insurance booklet.[11]
>
> There are still many other injustices that we have to endure. We used to struggle and go on strike but nothing has changed. ... My heart is not at ease. I used to approach the *Đồng Nai* newspaper, *Người Lao Động* (The Labourer), and *Lao Động* for their legal assistance, but have not received any response. (Lao Động 1 June 2010a)

As can be seen from these paragraphs, workers' resistance against management includes work stoppage, strike action, and appeal to the media; among these actions, only the last suggests a possibility of employing legal procedure. It seems that when workers have exhausted actions that bypass or go outside the law, actions within the law then become a possible option, albeit one that has yet to be successful. Thắm again finds herself caught in a cycle of paradoxes: after withstanding all the company's 'laws' and almost giving up on her intention to know about the state law, she had no other choice but to reach out for the latter. Even so, her last resort does not necessarily denote a faith in legal justice. Rather, it is a means to regain workers' dignity and perhaps put her heart at ease. The unresponsiveness of the newspapers following Thắm's request for their legal assistance seems to be a blow to her hope for justice, before she tried out the last resort and appealed to the VGCL Chairman.

Thắm also raises a passionate and desperate demand for workers' rights in a much clearer way than all the other collected letters. The meaning of these rights should be analysed alongside the writer's portrayal of workers' experiences throughout the letter and her self-ascription at the start. Initially she refers to herself and her fellows as 'employees,' 'workers,' and 'citizens,' yet the feelings of resentment become so strong in the middle of the letter that she is led to wonder whether the company sees workers as 'human beings' at all. Her demands, therefore, are demands for the very basic human rights that constitute the core elements of social justice:

> I and other workers here hope that you understand that our rights to equality, our rights to be respected, and our rights to life (*quyền nhân sinh*) are being abused by the employer. We don't know what to do, to struggle or not to struggle. What would be a rightful struggle, who would we trust and rely on? (Lao Động 1 June 2010a)

The 'rights' that Thắm calls for are more basic and broader than the legal rights designated in the labour law regime. The first demand resonates with basic citizens' rights endorsed in the Vietnamese Constitution, that is, 'all citizens are equal before the law' and 'are free from discrimination in all aspects of political, economic, civil, cultural and social lives' (Chapter II, Article 16). Citizens' honour and dignity shall also be protected under the law and all citizens are obligated to respect the rights of other people (Chapter II, Articles 15 and 20). As a Vietnamese citizen, it is likely that she has learnt from these constitutional values to make sense of what happened on the shop floor as problematic infringements of workers' basic (citizenship) rights. Her first call for 'equality' (*bình đẳng*) is a call for fair treatment that should be exercised and enjoyed by all people, regardless of their positions in the company, and in all circumstances, from the break time to the daily production quotas. In my understanding, the right to equality accompanies the right to be respected, Thắm's second demand, which is a core principle of interpersonal relationships in Vietnamese society.[12]

Thắm's third demand, the right to life, is interesting, as the original phrase '*quyền nhân sinh*' is quite unpopular in Vietnamese official and lay languages. Part of the phrase used, '*nhân sinh*,' is nonetheless popular and means a human's life in general, or the way in which one lives. The ideal of the right to life, in my view, is closely related to the fundamental human rights that are universally recognised and endorsed in the Vietnamese Constitution (Chapter II). Put together, Thắm's demands can be seen to derive from different but interrelated understandings of rights. The rhetorical question about a rightful struggle that follows conveys Thắm's moral imperative to overcome existing sufferings and a feeling of hopelessness. The rightful struggle that she refers to may not be a struggle that the law allows, but an ongoing moral struggle to reach hearts and minds and regain social justice for workers.

The moral values implicit in Thắm's demands for equal treatment and respect also resonate with some basic principles of labour relations given in the Labour Code. As stated in Article 6, one of the employer's obligations is to 'respect the honour and dignity of employees.' Article 7 designates that labour relations shall be developed on the basis of 'voluntary commitment, good faith, equality, cooperation, and mutual respect of lawful rights and interests of all parties.' The rights-oriented language in this letter does not include reference to the Labour Code nor employees' statutory rights, yet it effectively covers the values embedded within the articles mentioned earlier. Her demands attest to an ideal of rights that is not (yet) explicitly granted within the Labour Code but is implicated in the principles governing employment relationships. Workers' aspirations for respectful treatment, equality, and dignity can also be seen in other letters, although they are couched mostly in lay expressions of (un)fairness rather than rights-based assertions.

Thắm's appeal for rights provides an illustration of '*popular* rights discourse,' a term suggested by George Lovell (2012, p. 201 [original emphasis]) in his revisiting of the socio-legal debate on American rights talk. The author calls for an exploration of rights beyond official discourse and legal institutions, which are the sites through which most scholars examine rights talk and its implications for political and social change. Popular rights discourse is found in lay citizens' claims and expressions of (in)justice, which reflect their experiences with everyday situations or absorption of different political rhetoric and normative ideas (Lovell 2012, pp. 201–202). To illustrate, in his book on American citizens' complaint letters to the Department of Justice in the late 1930s and 1940s, Lovell found that some writers' claims for rights deviate from rights recognised by government officials or endorsed through lawsuits. Those rights claims were constructed, for instance, from citizens' invocation of democratic values, or their experiences with welfare access and employment (Lovell 2012, pp. 111–116). Similarly, Thắm's rights claims clearly deviate from the official discourse on employees' rights as legal entitlements that are separate from interests. They are instead based on her experiences with maltreatment and discipline on the shop floor and are likely to have been influenced by both the Constitution and fundamental shared norms within Vietnamese society. They are heartfelt pleas for human respect and dignity.

The resolutions of issues raised within the letters and workers' situation afterwards are unable to be traced. Only Thắm's appeal can be followed up in any detail as the VGCL Chairman's response was published in *Lao Động* below Thắm's letter. In his response of consolation, the VGCL Chairman cited the state's slogan 'A rich people, a strong, democratic, equal and civilized nation,' and acknowledged that the impingement of workers' rights is 'unacceptable' (Lao Động 1 June 2010a). He hinted at his intention to work with the provincial and district-level unions to rectify the company's treatment of its workers. The Chairman also encouraged Thắm to consider nominating herself for a position within her company's union. *Lao Động* also reported the Chairman's visit to the company, accompanied by a team of local union officials, under the headline 'It is obligatory to respect workers' dignity' (22 June 2010b). In their visit, the Chairman and other officials talked to workers in the company regarding issues raised in Thắm's letter. There is no mention of Thắm herself in this reportage. The visiting team led by the Chairman found that the company management had complied with the law but 'at a minimum level and in a cosmetic manner' (Lao Động 22 June 2010b) and made further suggestions to the company to improve workers' conditions. The Chairman's intervention is a welcoming sign of workers' voices being heard and acted upon, even though it is still unclear what happened to Thắm after the publication of her letter.

Conclusion

This chapter has examined to what extent and how aggrieved workers turn to labour law in the writing of their letters lodged with union offices. The letters at first sight reveal that management's failure to properly implement labour law is a factor that contributes to workers' grievances and generates their resistance. The letters show that, in workers' experience on the shop floor, legal provisions supposed to protect their interests have been replaced with arbitrary rules that have perpetuated exploitation and silenced their voices. However, most letter writers do not judge managerial conduct nor frame workers' demands explicitly in terms of labour law, but rather through the lens of conscience and morality. Even workers who adopt language from the language of the Labour Code attempt to emphasise their expressions of immoral treatment rather than make a legal case. The way in which these claims are framed suggests that workers have a consciousness of workplace ethics that the state, union, and management have tended to abuse and overlook.

A close analysis of the letters also reveals that writers have employed and combined different narratives and rhetorical devices. Writers go from depicting workers' hardship and destitution in an emotional manner to bargaining and negotiating for a fair reward. These modes of narrative are underpinned and accompanied by different values concerning workers' relationship with the state and management: the moral economy value that workers' subsistence shall be guaranteed and reciprocal obligations shall be upheld, and the ideal of social equality. While the writers' expressions of these values lack reference to the Labour Code, we need to acknowledge that the law contains provisions and principles that reflect the same values, such as a guarantee of employees' and their families' minimum livelihoods based on the minimum wage, appropriate remuneration based on their skills and experiences, and employers' obligations to respect and honour employees' dignity. Workers' moral understandings of justice therefore resonate with the law rather than being opposed to or distinct from it.

The evidence and findings thus far highlight the eminence of longstanding social norms and arrangements in Vietnam while also underscoring the relevance of the country's relatively new labour law in shaping individuals' views of justice. Already, it shows, labour law has contributed to social change in Vietnam by informing workers' perceptions of workplace practices and their consequent acts of resistance. The next chapter moves on to examine a legal aid project and the media discourse around workers' legal awareness. This discussion then lays the ground for considering the extent to which law enables or constrains workers' acts of resistance.

Notes

1. The offices had not retained letters prior to 2013.
2. The social insurance notebook is a record of contribution towards employees' social insurance. It is issued by the state agency to employees, but retained by the employer during the course of employment. The employer's refusal to return the booklet to employees after they quit their jobs makes it difficult for them to apply for unemployment allowances and other social insurance benefits. A common reason for such refusal is the employer's failure to make a contribution towards the employee's social insurance fund (Author's personal correspondence with workers, 2014 and 2015).
3. In cases in which letters were transferred from the provincial union to the upper-level unions, and copies were kept by each union office, I have counted the letter only once.
4. Confession here is understood as 'a sincere and complete [...] explanation of one's convictions, thoughts and actions' (Dal 1881, cited in Fitzpatrick 1996, p. 82).
5. The local-level government bodies charged with receiving and handling citizens' complaints.
6. Only five of the complaint writers mentioned the type of work in which their company engages. I obtained these details by looking up the companies' names on the Internet and in the union's strike records (5 of these 16 companies have been subject to strikes).
7. In this case, a strike may have broken out following the company management's failure to address the workers' requests. The letter could have made its way to the union office after union officials, as part of the strike action team, came to the company to settle the strike.
8. Some of my observations here echo George Lovell's methodological notes on the use of letters vis-à-vis interviews for understanding ordinary people's use of law and legal consciousness. Lovell (2012, pp. 24–26) considers the letters as embodying 'everyday political encounters' in which ideas, understandings, and contestation of law unfold. He also notes that studying the letters helps overcome a practical problem in conducting interviews, that is, interviewees' concern and anxieties in talking to outsiders may generate less intense or less direct expressions of anger and resistance.
9. '*áp bức*' can be translated as either coercion or oppression, and '*bất công*' can be understood as injustice, inequality, or unfairness.
10. These are the three 'request letters' that I mentioned earlier when describing the letters.

11. A social insurance booklet is a record of employees' and employers' insurance contribution, which is issued by the state to individual employees but is kept by the employers during the course of employment.
12. This core principle of respect indeed applies in interpersonal relationships in all societies.

References

Albiston, C. (2005). Bargaining in the Shadow of Social Institutions: Competing Discourses and Social Change in Workplace Mobilization of Civil Rights. *Law & Society Review*, 39 (1), 11–49.

Albiston, C. R. & Leachman, G. M. (2015). Law as an Instrument of Social Change. In J.D. Wright. *International Encyclopedia of The Social & Behavioral Sciences* (2nd ed.). Oxford: Elsevier.

Chae, S. (2003). *Spinning Work and Weaving Life: The Politics of Production in a Capitalistic Multinational Textile Factory in Vietnam.* Unpublished PhD thesis. City University of New York, New York.

Cheesman, N. (2015). *Opposing the Rule of Law: How Myanmar Courts Make Law and Order.* Cambridge: Cambridge University Press.

Chen, F. (2000). Subsistence Crises, Managerial Corruption and Labour Protests in China. *The China Journal*, 44, 41–63.

Dân Trí (14/2/2014). Doanh nghiệp dùng 'luật rùng' quỵt lương, đòi công nhân trả lại thưởng Tết. http://dantri.com.vn/ban-doc/doanh-nghiep-dung-luat-rung-quyt-luong-doi-cong-nhan-tra-lai-thuong-tet-1392782780.htm. Accessed 20th January 2017.

Đồng Nai Labour Federation (2014). Report on the work of taking care of material and mental lives for workers and the situation of strikes and work stoppages.

Đồng Nai Labour Federation (2016). General report on union work in 2015, and tasks and directions in 2016.

Felstiner, W., Abel, R. & Sarat, A. (1980/1981). The Emergence and Transformation of Disputes: Naming, Blaming, Claiming…. *Law and Society Review*, 15 (3/4), 631–654.

Fitzpatrick, S. (1996). Supplicants and Citizens: Public Letter-Writing in Soviet Russia in the 1930s. *Slavic Review*, 55 (1), 103–104.

Goluboff, R. L. (1999). 'Won't You Please Help Me Get My Son Home?': Peonage, Patronage, and Protest in the World War II Urban South. *Law & Social Inquiry*, 24, 777–806.

Hiến Pháp nước Cộng Hòa Xã Hội Chủ Nghĩa Việt Nam [The Constitution of the Socialist Republic of Vietnam].

International Labor Organization (2012). *Decent Work: Country Profile – Philippines.* Geneva.

International Labor Organization (n.d.). Decent Work. http://www.ilo.org/global/topics/decent-work/lang%2D%2Den/index.htm. Accessed 24th June 2016.

Kerkvliet, B. J. (2011). Workers' Protests in Contemporary Vietnam. In A. Chan (ed.). *Labour in Vietnam*. Singapore: Institute of Southeast Asia Studies.

Lao Động (1/6/2010a). Lá thư đầy uất nghẹn của một công nhân [A Worker's Letter That Is Full of Grief]. http://laodong.com.vn/cong-doan/la-thu-day-uat-nghen-cua-mot-cong-nhan-25710.bld. Accessed 15th October 2015.

Lao Động (22/6/2010b). Phải tôn trọng nhân phẩm công nhân. http://laodong.com.vn/cong-doan/phai-ton-trong-nhan-pham-cong-nhan-49328.bld. Accessed 24th June 2016.

Lao Động (2/8/2014). Vì sao phải điều chỉnh mức lương tối thiểu vùng I lên 3.4 triệu đồng?. http://laodong.com.vn/cong-doan/vi-sao-phai-dieu-chinh-muc-luong-toi-thieu-vung-i-len-34-trieu-dong-230519.bld. Accessed 24th June 2016.

Lovell, G. (2012) *This is Not Civil Rights: Discovering Rights Talk in 1939 America*. Chicago: The University of Chicago Press.

Luong, H.V. (2016). Social Relations, Regional Variation, and Economic Inequality in Contemporary Vietnam: A View from Two Vietnamese Rural Communities. In P. Taylor (ed.). *Connected and Disconnected in Viet Nam: Remaking Social Relations in a Post-socialist Nation*. Acton: ANU Press.

Nghiem, L. H. (2006). *Work Culture, Gender and Class in Vietnam: Ethnographies of Three Garment Workshops in Ha Noi*. Unpublished PhD thesis. University of Amsterdam, Amsterdam.

Người Lao Động (4/8/2014). Giám đốc công ty dùng luật…rừng. https://nld.com.vn/thoi-su-trong-nuoc/giam-doc-cong-ty-dung-luat-rung-20140804215838639.htm. Accessed 20th January 2017.

Pun, N. (2016). *Migrant Labor in China: Post-Socialist Transformations*. Cambridge: Polity Press.

Scott, J. (1976). *The Moral Economy of the Peasant: Rebellion and Subsistence in Southeast Asia*. New Haven and London: Yale University Press.

Siu, K. & Chan, A. (2015). Strike Wave in Vietnam, 2006–2011. *Journal of Contemporary Asia*, 45 (1), 71–91.

The National Party's Congress VII (1991). The fundamentals of building the country in the path towards socialism.

Thireau, I. & Hua, L. (2003). The Moral Universe of Aggrieved Chinese Workers: Workers' Appeals to Arbitration Committees and Letters and Visits Offices. *The China Journal*, 50, 83–103.

Tran, A. (2007). Alternative to the 'Race to the Bottom' in Vietnam: Minimum Wage Strikes in Vietnam and their Aftermath. *Labor Studies Journal*, 32 (4), 430–451.

Trần, A. N. (2013). *Ties that Bind: Cultural Identity, Class, and Law in Vietnam's Labor Resistance*. Ithaca: Cornell Southeast Asia Program Publications.

Tuổi Trẻ (11/9/2014). 'Làm ăn' trong rừng luật. https://tuoitre.vn/lam-an-trong-rung-luat-644149.htm. Accessed 20th January 2017.

Vietnam General Confederation of Labour (2014). Decision 254/QD-TLD on Trade unions resolving and participating in the resolution of complaints and denunciations.

CHAPTER 5

'Defending Their Rights and Interests': Bringing Law to Workers' Residences

Earlier, in Chap. 2, I briefly mentioned the trade union's initiatives in promoting legal aid and legal education to factory workers, with the main aim being to enhance awareness of workers' rights and press for more protection. In her book *Ties That Bind* (2013), Angie Trần briefly discusses the union's provision of legal aid and social support in workers' residential areas near industrial zones and how this has contributed to workers' mobilisation (Trần 2013, p. 243). In Hồ Chí Minh City, for instance, official unions have established 'workers' self-managed units' (*tổ tự quản công nhân*), which pay periodic visits to workers' rental areas. While these visits give space for sharing and disseminating information about labour law, their main aim is to channel workers' grievances to the unions and identify and pre-empt the potential of underground labour activism. Trần finds that workers' self-managed units (mainly) serve the interests of the state and the management in containing labour activism and strikes, which, in her view, prevent a critical moment of workers' bonding and shared interests (p. 2). Trần still recognises the benefit of those self-managed units in bringing labour law closer to ordinary workers and helping them understand their legal rights. However, little is known about how legal education contributes to raising workers' consciousness of rights and how their consciousness influences the way in which they perceive justice and frame their workplace problems.

China scholars, in comparison, have debated at length the contribution of legal aid to labour resistance. Since the 1990s, the Chinese state

T. P. Nguyen, *Workplace Justice*, Critical Studies of the Asia-Pacific,
https://doi.org/10.1007/978-981-13-3116-9_5

has promoted rule of law rhetoric to employees and the broader populations (Gallagher 2017). Citizens' active engagement with the law through petitioning and litigation is attributable to the state's initiative to reform its justice system and enhance popular support for its legitimacy.[1] Legal aid to Chinese workers is often run by domestic and foreign-funded non-governmental organisations, which are diverse in their activities and in their relationships with the unions and the state.[2] Several researchers have recognised the role of legal aid in helping disadvantaged workers to understand their legal rights, the infringement of those rights by management, and/or seek their redress through the courts (Gallagher 2006; Friedman 2009; Becker 2014). Other scholars nonetheless caution that legal aid agencies are only reactive, that is, they function in response to violations of law, rather than proactively advancing workers' rights and interests beyond those granted by law (Chan and Siu 2012).

Indeed, the important and potential contribution of legal aid and labour organisations to labour resistance in China is their role in raising workers' rights consciousness. Eli Friedman, for instance, provides a good illustration of the dynamic process through which workers' consciousness develops through their interaction with activists in a foreign labour organisation. Drawing from the two case studies of workers' informal organisation in two factories, the author details how the workers learnt about their legal rights *and* 'international human and labor rights discourses' (Friedman 2009, p. 210) from the Guangdong Migrants' Association (a pseudonym), the migrant labour organisation. Subsequently, in their collective petitioning, while workers in one factory pressed for their legal demands, workers in the other case pressed for extra benefits and the setting up of an independent trade union. The workers' actions and later activism, Friedman claims, would not have been possible without the transmission of knowledge about workers' rights, both enshrined in the Labour Law and international labour rights discourse, and strategic support offered by the labour organisation. While Friedman wants to highlight the importance of external resources offered to disadvantaged workers, what is more valuable to me from his case study is the different notions of rights transmitted by the labour organisation and absorbed by activist workers. On the one hand, there are universal human and labour rights norms enshrined within international organisations' agreements and implemented by all countries bound by those agreements. On the other hand, there are legal rights granted by a state's legal regime that are generally narrower than those endorsed in international agreements. The

Chinese factory workers in Friedman's study seem to have learnt about both sets of rights and utilised them in their resistance.

In this chapter, I discuss in detail the legal aid project and related activities in Đồng Nai Province in which workers are both beneficiaries and active participants. Hundreds of factory workers were recruited and trained under this project, once funded by Oxfam Solidarity Belgium, and became the 'core workers.' The core workers are then able to employ their legal knowledge to provide legal assistance to ordinary factory workers in their residential areas, while, at the same time, engaging with law enforcement institutions to demand justice for themselves and their fellow workers. The following section provides background information on the Legal Aid Centre, the central actor running the Oxfam project, and a sketch of local media coverage on employees' legal mobilisation. I then outline the role of core workers and discuss the significance of this project in facilitating interactions amongst the workers and core workers' views about the labour law, especially with regard to its role in achieving workplace justice.

The Legal Aid Centre and News Coverage of Workers' Legal Mobilisation

The Legal Aid Centre (LAC) was established in 1993. It belongs to the Đồng Nai Labour Federation (DNLF) and has its own office located next to the DNLF. As of 2015, the centre had two lawyers, three legal counsellors, an accountant and a treasurer, and a few volunteer legal counsellors. Except for the accountant and treasurer, all staff and volunteers at the centre have a bachelor degree in law. The lawyers and most legal counsellors have had more than ten years of experience working in law-related professions. Despite its small capacity, the centre offers services to a range of groups: employees, both within and outside Đồng Nai Province, business people, and union officials. It advises on a range of different issues relating to labour, union, and civil laws. The LAC is mostly funded by the Labour Federation. The remainder of its funding comes from its legal service fees, collected from the centre's legal advisory service to businesses and other non-worker citizens, and project cooperation with foreign donors.

The LAC mostly deals with labour grievances of an individual nature, such as a company's illegal termination of contracts, workplace injuries, workers' unemployment benefits, and social insurance. Some of its services include legal consultation in person or by phone, helping workers to write petitions and complaint letters to relevant official bodies, and preparing lawsuits and representing workers in courts. LAC lawyers have been given media attention in the local labour newspaper for successfully representing workers in courts, helping them to win their cases, and are especially hailed for their dedication in pursuing cases that have gone on for several years. According to the centre's report (2013), from 2008 to 2013, 95 per cent of the 475 labour lawsuits it handled resulted in a worker's win. This high success rate of legal representation is one important factor that, as I will later discuss, shapes the core workers' belief in using the law as a means for demanding workplace justice.

Cases of LAC's legal assistance and employees' litigation successes have been reported in detail in Lao Động Đồng Nai (*Đồng Nai Labour News, hereafter LDDN*). The 55 articles published online from 2014 to 2016, in a section called 'Readers and the newsroom,' summarise employees' disadvantaged situations and maltreatment at work, how they learn of the LAC, mostly through social networks, and the process and outcomes of their petitioning and litigation. Seventy per cent of employees' grievances and problems published in these articles are related to employers' illegal termination of labour contracts, which usually occurs after employers transfer employees to a task that is not suitable to them and/or against their wishes. Other cases relate to the employers' delay in processing workers' social insurance benefits, occupational injuries, and delays in wage payment. About 70 per cent of employees featured in these articles are factory workers and low-skilled employees, the rest including office staff and those holding managerial positions.

The headlines of these articles can be categorised into three groups. The first group draws attention to employees' success in the courts and emphasises employers' legal obligation as part of the resolution. Some examples are 'Employer must compensate an employee for incorrect wage payment' (LDDN 8 July 2014c), and 'Illegally dismissing an employee, the company compensated 88 million dong' (LDDN 18 May 2016a). The second group emphasises the lengthy and enduring journey of employees in demanding redress, such as 'Worn out after four years of suing' (LDDN 12 April 2015b), 'Nearly three years of demanding allowance' (LDDN 26 May 2015c), or 'One lawsuit, four times of adjudication yet still no end in sight' (LDDN 28 September 2016b). The third group of titles depicts workers' difficult if not desperate situation as a result of employer's treatment, like 'The boss escaped, workers are miserable' (LDDN 14 May 2014b), 'Desperate after suddenly made redundant' (LDDN 27 January 2015d), or 'Workers anxious after being transferred to a different company' (LDDN 11 May 2014a).

In some articles, workers' legal awareness and subsequent pursuits of their rights are foregrounded by detailed recounting of managerial mistreatment and its consequences on their livelihoods. The following excerpt from one of the articles provides a good example:

> Leaving the hometown Nghệ An, Mrs Ngân went to Đồng Nai and applied to work in Company B (based in Biên Hòa industrial zone 1) in 2005. She had a labour contract of indefinite term and received a monthly wage of 2.9 million dong. During her time at work, she always fulfils all assigned tasks.
>
> In early 2013, Ngân was allowed to take leave for a month to go back to her hometown and renew her national identity card. In early March 2013, when she went back to work for a few days, the company informed her to quit. The given reason is that she took leave without the company's approval, failed to coordinate well in doing the job, and created tensions in labour relations.
>
> 'Before taking leave, I did ask the leader of my shift and got his/her approval. Besides, I haven't ever violated the company regulations. I explained all to the company but they did not agree. Afterwards, they called me in for a meeting and asked me to sign a document which says that I will comply with the company decision in order to receive my wage and other benefits. At that time, I think that, since the company no longer needs me, I just signed [the document] to get it over and then looked for a job elsewhere.'
>
> After leaving company B, Ngân applied for jobs everywhere but was turned down since she is now old. Since then, her life is very difficult as she has to pay for her rent, for childcare of her grandkid, and food for three people.
>
> 'Every month, I have to pay a rent of 1.2 million dong and spend 1 million on my grandkid's childcare. My wage is really low and not enough for feeding three people. My son just moved here from our hometown but hasn't managed to get a stable job to help me out. Sometimes I have to skip my meals and try to find some petty work to have money to buy milk for my grandkid.' Up until recently, she managed to get a security position in a company which pays a modest wage.
>
> Since she wasn't clear about the law, Ngân didn't know whether the company's decision to sack her is right or wrong. She also didn't know the

> rights and benefits that she could demand. Afterwards, an acquaintance referred her to the LAC for consultation. After receiving the centre staff's dedicated help, she gained enough confidence to lodge her case at the court and demand her rights and interests. 'Since I don't study much and my knowledge is limited, I followed the company's order to sign the document [from the meeting where the company decided to sack her]. Up until later, after receiving advice from the LAC, I understand that the company's termination of contract with me is against the legal regulation. For that reason, I will persist in my lawsuit all the way and hope to successfully demand my rights and interests.' (LDDN 27 January 2015d)

Following this worker's lodging of her case, the employer presented to the court different documents and reasons that explain their decision to dismiss Mrs Ngân, yet did *not* refer to the document signed by Ngân in her meeting with the employer. The labour lawyer, as quoted in the article, suggested that the company's dismissal has no ground and its reactions indicate that the case should be ruled in Ngân's favour. Overall, the quotation depicts the workers' engagement with law as a transformative learning process. The article ends with Ngân's demand for her reinstatement at her old job and other financial compensation, but the outcome of this case is unknown.

In 2015, the newspaper published a series of four articles entitled 'Protecting legal rights and interests of employees,' which outlines a selected number of employees' petitions and lawsuits against management (LDDN 3 September 2015e; 6 September 2015f; 8 September 2015g; 10 September 2015a). The introduction to the series draws attention to that fact that many employees' lack of legal knowledge put them at a disadvantage when faced with employers' varying excuses and tactics. The second article of the series focuses on employees' trust in justice and demonstrates how this trust helped two of them endure legal battles that dragged on for four or six years. The final article acknowledges the dedication, passion, and enthusiasm of LAC staff, including their time spent at weekends on organising legal aid sessions for migrant workers.

The LAC also provides assistance with workers' collective grievances that arise from business' implementation of laws and policies. In such instances, the lawyer explains to workers their entitlements according to state laws, and helps them write and bring their grievances to the official unions or the state's labour authority. When workers intend to go on strike, the lawyer explains the legal regulations in relation to strikes and directs them to lodge their complaints (Interview, 18 December 2014). Giving legal advice is apparently the only action taken by the lawyer and LAC staff who then have little influence on workers' subsequent actions. It is therefore difficult to empirically prove the relationship between the LAC's functions and aggrieved workers' engagement with law. Even though LAC staff have engaged, to some extent, in workers' complaint writing, it is impossible to trace and verify this from the previous complaint letters to union offices. My randomly recruited participants also did not know of the LAC. Coincidentally, when I conducted my second field trip in December 2015, I managed to collect details of a labour dispute case that had happened three weeks before then and had the LAC's involvement. This case also attracted a wide media coverage through which I obtained most of the information that follows.

In November 2015, more than 1800 workers at a Korean company named Yupoong protested against the company's termination of their contracts. The protest occurred two months after one of its workshops was accidentally burnt down (Lao Động, 10 November 2015). The damage meant that production in the adjacent workshop could not continue; consequently, the company decided to end contracts of workers in both of these workshops. Before issuing its decision, the management had sought official guidance from the Industrial Zone Authority (IZA) as to how to lawfully handle the problem. According to the Labour Code, an employer can unilaterally terminate employees' contracts in cases of fire or disasters, after he or she has exhausted other means to recover the damages. The termination of workers' contracts in Yupoong followed the legal procedures with advance notice, and the manager also announced that they would pay allowances, unpaid leave, and social insurance premiums for pregnant workers. Workers were angry and demanded that (1) the company pay a higher allowance to give them time to find a new job, or (2) they be allowed to stay home and receive no pay until the company fully recovered its production (Vietnam Television Online News, 13 November 2015).

Meanwhile, dismissed workers also sent many appeals to the state authorities. Two core workers[3] referred some complainants to the LAC, and a legal advisor helped them to write their letters to the Department of Labour (Tuổi Trẻ, 9 November 2015). With some help from a labour officer, I managed to obtain two letters at the department: one typed and one hand-written. The hand-written one was entitled 'Letter of plea' and the writer stated that they were representing all employees in the company.

The letter was filled with description of the desperation that workers felt after being unilaterally dismissed:

> We workers have contributed our sweat and labour to the company [and its affiliated branches in other industrial zones]. We have contributed to the company since we were young, for 10 to 13 years. Now when we are old, the company ends our contracts. Now where can we look for jobs, especially those of us who are above 40 years old?

The expressions here are similar to the verbal accounts of workers in the food processing company in Chap. 3. Workers' contribution to the business and their term of employment imply a kind of service and loyalty that deserves the employer's acknowledgement. They thus expect the management to uphold its reciprocal obligation simply by allowing workers to stay in the jobs. The termination of workers' contracts, therefore, was viewed by the workers as an unfair dismissal of their long service and an abandonment of the company's obligations to workers as they grow old. By posing the rhetorical question about their uncertainty to find jobs afterwards, workers indirectly hold the company accountable for their employment. Workers' appeal to the management for a guarantee of their employment in this case is based on the perceived injustice of a failure to return one's favour, underpinned by a norm of reciprocity.

As can be expected, the writers move on to describing workers' struggle to get by when their main source of income is lost:

> Meanwhile we are facing difficult situations: some have small children, some are pregnant, and some are widows taking care of several children. Now, even if the company re-employs us but pays with a new wage level,[4] it would not be enough for us to get by in our lives. [...]
>
> Now we are at a disadvantage and losing all our rights and interests. We ask the authorities to please save us so that we can have stable jobs and receive the wage level as per our previous long-term contracts.

The tone of this letter is similar to previous complaint letters when the writers cite their struggling living conditions and call upon the authorities for salvation. The writers' use of 'rights and interests' in this case is also the same as that of respondent workers covered in Chap. 3: the apparently legalistic terms are deployed to legitimate their demand for a fair wage and a decent job. In the last line, the mention of workers' long-term contracts can be interpreted either as workers' attempts to justify their legal employment status or as a rhetorical device to bolster their previous demand. My reading of the whole letter would suggest the latter.

The second typed letter is entitled 'Letter requesting urgent intervention' in the names of workers in the workshop that was not burnt down but whose production was adversely affected by the fire. The letter was not headed by any specific writer but contained numerous signatures and names at the bottom of the page. The letter at the start asserts the legal employment relationship and work positions of appealing workers: 'we have worked as short as 1 year and as long as 13 years; most of us have permanent contracts and the rest have definite contracts of 12 months. We are factory workers working in the following sections: preparation, cutting and control.'

Compared to the previous one, this letter clearly points out the inconsistency in the company's conduct:

> According to the official document number 1651/KCNDN-LD, [...] only workshop 1 halted production. In reality, other production processes still run as normal and machines in workshop 2 were still in good condition. Yet the company suspended our work [of workers in workshop 2] then took its orders to be assembled in other companies. ... This is not reasonable.
>
> Now we write this letter to request the Department of Labour to intervene in this matter so that the company will allocate work for us. Most of us are migrant workers from other provinces and now our living conditions are very tough.

In making an explicit reference to an official document that provides for the company's practice, the writer comes close to constructing a legal case for workers' demands. However, the reasoning that follows shifts towards the moral sphere, though expressed in a much more measured manner than previous workers' letters. While the LAC has claimed to help workers understand and express their grievances according to labour law, in this case it opted for an approach based on 'reason and sentiment' *(lý và tình)* (Gillespie 2011, p. 248). This is a popular approach in resolving civil conflicts in Vietnam, which combines an application of formal rules with other ethical considerations. By bringing in workers' desperate situation to the state's formal avenue of appeal, it seems that the legal advisor behind this letter believed that it might serve as a moral trigger for state intervention when a legal judgement might possibly fail.

Despite their differences, these two letters evoke the workers' right to a decent wage and communicate workers' living conditions in the hope of the authorities' intervention. This subsequently led to an extra-legal solution coordinated by provincial unions and authorities, after workers' appeals and their five-day strike failed to sway the management's decision. The official unions and the IZA tried and succeeded in mobilising nearby companies, which require similar manual skills as Yupoong, to employ the redundant workers. As an intermediary that helps channel workers' grievances and demands into the formally sanctioned bodies, the LAC has moved freely between legal and moral ways of framing assistance to their clients. Regardless of their approach, both the LAC and provincial union recognise the importance of legal education and mobilisation, delivered through the core worker project, to make known existing channels of support to the broader workers' community.

Core Worker Project

In line with the union's legal aid initiative, the LAC partnered with and obtained funding from Oxfam Solidarity Belgium in a project to enhance workers' legal awareness. The pilot project, entitled 'Mobile legal aid for migrant workers in Long Bình ward, Biên Hòa city,' was approved by the People's Committee. According to a participant worker, Oxfam conducted a survey on workers' legal knowledge around his neighbourhood areas some time before starting this project. Long Bình ward was the first location selected for a trial of the 'mobile legal consultation sessions' (*buổi tư vấn pháp luật lưu động*). These sessions are mobile in the sense they take place at, and move around, different workers' rental units. According to the project plan written in 2009, Long Bình ward was chosen as half of more than its 74,700 residents are migrant workers (LAC–Đồng Nai Labour Federation, 30 September 2009). Even though the project's main targets are migrant workers, the legal sessions are open to all interested local employees in the neighbourhood. The first nine sessions in this area are reported to have attracted more than 800 participants (LAC–Đồng Nai Labour Federation, 30 September 2009).

With very limited staff, the LAC decided to train a team of 'core workers' (*công nhân nòng cốt*), to help with organising and running legal sessions. The training comprised two parts: legal knowledge and social skills. The trainings took place either on Saturday evenings or on Sunday and lasted from one and a half up to three hours. The size of each session ranged from 20 up to 40 people. LAC staff and some officials at the provincial labour federation took charge of the legal knowledge training. In each session, the trainers spent about two-thirds of the time lecturing about several labour law topics, such as labour contracts, working hours, maternity benefits, social insurance, and labour disputes. The lectures were delivered in a simple and easy-to-understand manner so that core workers could emulate this approach in their future running of legal aid lessons. After the lecture was question-and-answer time, in which participants were given some problem-solving scenarios and activities. The training materials for these core workers, which they could take home, included shortened and simplified versions of the Labour Code and Law on Social Insurance. The second part of the training was related to social skills including public speaking, organisation of group activities, and facilitation of group discussion. These sessions were run by either union officials or invited speakers and professionals working in different domestic institutes and social organisations. It took a core worker from two to three months to complete the training before they were ready to become a speaker at the mobile legal aid sessions. Core workers then further consolidated their skills in the process of advising other workers, with assistance from the LAC staff and senior core workers.

The key feature that distinguishes this project from other legal aid activities in other industrial cities and provinces is that it is run by workers themselves. For instance, a differently run project in Hồ Chi Minh City, known as 'Legal assistance to migrant employees in Vietnam,' is a partnership between different non-governmental organisations, social institutes, universities, and the local Youth Union organisations.[5] There are also similar legal sessions organised periodically at the residential areas of migrant factory workers, covering not only labour laws but also migration law, family law, and civil law. However, the legal sessions and other social support activities are run by the aforementioned organisations and law students. As the LAC lawyer proclaimed in a conference, 'only workers can help and understand workers' (17 December 2015). As both core workers and beneficiaries of the project are workers, there is the assumption that they will share the same identity, interests, and values, and thereby can easily interact with each other. The aim of the core workers project, and other similar projects, is not only to enhance workers' legal knowledge, but also to establish networks of social and legal support among workers. Furthermore, in drawing attention to migrant workers' difficult lives as the project's background and justification, the project hinted at the indirect support of legal aid to improving workers' lives. All of these objectives, according to the LAC, are best accomplished by the workers themselves.

The next section draws on my interviews and conversations with the LAC lawyer and 14 core workers, five females and nine males, who have been involved in the core workers programme for at least four years. These core workers are all migrants, mostly from the northern and central provinces of Vietnam, who have lived in Đồng Nai from five to 15 years. All but one currently resides in Đồng Nai. The exception, a male core worker, is now living and working in Hồ Chí Minh City, but still maintains connections with the LAC and core worker group. Two female workers are in their 20s and one of the men is in his 50s. The others are all in their 30s or 40s. I did not want to intrude into my respondents' personal affairs and so did not ask them directly about their educational qualifications. However, sometimes core workers mentioned these details voluntarily in our interviews or conversations, and, in one case, through an article in *Đồng Nai Labour News*. Consequently, I know that three of them had some training in vocational schools or colleges, three had university degrees, and one had finished junior high school (grade 9). Regarding family status, six were married with children, one was expecting her first child, two were married but without children, two were single parents, and three were unmarried.

While my fieldwork, from December 2014 to April 2015, took place at a time when the major funding for this programme had ceased,[6] I still managed to contact and interview these core workers, thanks to their ongoing commitment to legal aid activities. I contacted three key core workers through the LAC lawyer, and they then introduced me to the others. All core workers were more open and enthusiastic about sharing their experiences than those interviewed workers who had no legal training. I often started my interviews with general questions about core workers' workplace experiences and their legal aid involvement. I believe that these experiences are crucial to shaping the way they perceive and make sense of the law. I generally framed my questions in broad terms, such as 'what is good about the core workers project?,' 'how do you feel about your work?,' 'what do you think is workers' most common grievance?,' 'what do you think about labour law, the state and unions?' Issues about law, justice, and moral norms often came up in their responses to my broad questions. To six of them who were not or no longer doing factory jobs, the interviews and further conversations were more about their legal aid involvement. Those six workers seemed more interested in talking about legal aid, their general opinions, and their observations in relation to the law and labour relations, rather than their own past workplace experiences.

The analysis of core workers' views and behaviour is inspired by the legal consciousness approach, the way in which people 'draw on legal discourse to construct their understanding of and relation to the social world' (Albiston 2006, p. 56), and 'make sense of the law and legal institutions' (Ewick and Silbey 1992, p. 734). Scholars taking this strand of socio-legal inquiry viewed consciousness as dynamic, multi-faceted, and subjected to change according to people's social experiences, relationships, and activities. This concept therefore is broader than the notion of rights consciousness widely seen in studies inspired by rightful resistance literature, since it also incorporates the social environments in which rights understandings and perceptions take root, develop, and change. This and the next chapter will grasp core workers' consciousness and action through their engagement with the law and its institutions and their own circumstances and experiences at work.

Most core workers recalled their experiences of starting in the project with joy. Back then, they had joined a mobile legal session run by LAC lawyers in their rental areas. The session included a short lesson about a section of the Labour Code, and question-and-answer time when the lawyers raised questions about legal knowledge and received questions from participant workers regarding their problems or queries about the law. Participants who responded correctly to the speakers' questions were rewarded with small gifts. Core workers delightedly recalled their active participation and the good number of gifts that they received. Active participants, including those who raised many questions or good questions to the speaker, were considered potential trainees for the legal aid project. The lawyers then asked for their contact numbers, before inviting them to join free training classes about labour laws and later the Oxfam project.

During the Oxfam-funded period, from 2009 to 2013, the number of core workers grew to 667.[7] They worked across four of the most populated industrial regions in the province, where labour disputes are also high: Biên Hòa, Trảng Bom, Nhơn Trạch, and Long Thành. Normally, three to four workers took charge of organising each mobile legal session. Once having selected a particular rental area of migrant workers, these core workers then contacted the landlords/landladies, as well as the state authorities at the grassroots level, for their permission and assistance to organise the sessions. Usually the landlords or the grassroots authority helped send a notice around the areas several days in advance. The sessions often took place on Saturday or Sunday evening after seven o'clock, as this is a convenient time for most workers and organisers could expect a good attendance. There were often four evening sessions running concurrently at four different consultation spots (*điểm tư vấn*), covering one or several topics in the Labour Code or Law on Social Insurance. Some examples of the topics are labour contracts, wages, working hours, unemployment benefits, and social insurance. The organisers would return after a week or so to cover other topics. During the peak period of 2011 and 2012, Oxfam organised up to 15 legal sessions each month. According to the LAC report, there were 510 sessions from 2009 to 2013, with the participation of more than 24,600 employees.

Before the sessions, all core worker organisers gathered at a nearby location after having parked their own motorbikes. They all got into a small van supplied by Oxfam, which carried separate boxes containing the public address systems, leaflets, and gifts for participants. The organisers were dropped off at their exact spots with the boxes and were driven back to their previous gathering location after the sessions finished.

Each session lasted from one to 1.5 hours, or even longer, and had the same format as previous sessions run by the lawyers. At the start of the legal session, a core worker will announce through the loudspeaker:

> Dear workers, brothers and sisters, we are the core workers from the LAC, based at Đồng Nai Labour Federation. Today we hold a legal aid session around this rental area so as to share knowledge about labour law and employees' rights and interests. We hope you all can spend a bit of your time joining and supporting our session.

Each session consisted of a short legal lesson of 15–20 minutes, followed by question-and-answer time. The lessons were more or less interactive depending on the speakers' speaking skills. The speakers were also willing to respond to questions on topics that were different from those being covered. The organisers then handed out leaflets related to the presented topics to participants at the end of the sessions.

The following is an example of the question-and-answer time, which I observed in March 2015.[8] A part of the session was about employees' unemployment benefits. Before raising the question, the speaker gave some brief information:

> If we[9] have contributed to the unemployment insurance for 12 to 36 months, we are entitled to unemployment allowance for a period of 3 months. On top of that, if we have contributed to the insurance for an extra year, we are entitled to an extra month of allowance, and so on. In short, another year, another month.

He then raised a question:

> Friends, do you know how much we are supposed to contribute and how much we claim? I repeat: What percentage of our wage do we contribute and claim? Whoever has a correct answer will receive a gift.

A female participant had a correct answer: an employee contributes 1 per cent of the monthly wage and can claim 60 per cent of his/her average wage in the six months prior to becoming unemployed. The speaker then raised another question: 'When claiming the unemployment allowance, which documents are we required to bring?' Another female participant gave a near-complete answer. The speaker corrected her, saying that required documents include the employee's national identity card, a copy of the labour contract, the letter of contract termination, and social insurance booklet. Both of these participants received a gift each.

There were variations in the attendance of workers in these legal sessions. From core workers' anecdotes, the numbers of participants for each session ranged from eight up to more than 30, though the organisers often aimed for 20 to 30. One group leader told me: 'The participation rate is not a big deal. We would still run the session even if only a few people showed up' (Interview, 7 May 2015). At times the number of participants went beyond expectation, while at other times, the organisers had to knock at workers' doors and encourage them to attend. Another core worker described a crowded session:

> While we organisers often take turns to speak, normally there is only one speaker at a time. But a few sessions I organised attracted so many people that three of us had to speak at the same time, each 'taking care of' one group of people. I feel like those participant workers were hungry for knowledge. (Interview, 30 January 2015)

Legal sessions often took place outdoors and therefore were also subject to weather conditions. Some core workers were willing to share their phone numbers to participants in case they needed any support regarding queries about the labour law or workplace grievances.

Each core worker was paid 200,000 dong for organising each legal session, and 50,000 dong for participating in the monthly meetings with the LAC and Oxfam staff. The meetings allowed core workers to get updates about labour laws and policies, share experiences among themselves, and raise any problems or difficulties in their activities to the staff. The financial assistance, or lack thereof, is a factor that explains core workers' levels of commitment, which became evident after Oxfam withdrew its funding in 2013.

Meanwhile, three worker-supporting spots (*điểm hỗ trợ công nhân*) were also set up in a convenient location close to workers' residential areas in three of the four aforementioned municipal regions. The spots provided social spaces for all workers, who could visit to socialise with each other, read books, and enquire about legal issues. They were often renovated from, or attached to, a ward-level community house, equipped with one or two desktops, and filled with books related to law and of general interest. They were open every week night and for a few daytime hours during weekends. Core workers who lived nearby took turns in manning the spot and received a small allowance for their time.

The Oxfam funding ceased at the end of 2013, when the responsibility to oversee core worker groups was also assigned from the LAC to upper-level unions where these core workers were based. Since then, only two groups in Trảng Bom and Biên Hòa have remained active, though with dwindling vigour and a serious decline in the number of core workers. Besides the funding problem, work and family commitments also constrain core workers from participating in the programme. As of early 2015, the number of core workers had shrunk significantly to fewer than 40. However, for the past two years, according to the LAC lawyer, the centre has still managed to coordinate dedicated core workers to organise 15 mobile legal sessions a year across the province, which are funded by the People's Committee. Remaining core workers also participate in social events organised by the provincial Labour Federation and legal consultation events organised by the national labour newspaper, *Labour*.

The Social Contexts of Legal Information Sharing

The main factor that allows for greater interaction between core workers and other workers and in turn contributes to the benefits of legal aid activities is the location where mobile legal sessions take place and where legal advice is given. Organising legal sessions within workers' residential areas allows core workers to openly address participants' grievances, alert them to legal violations, and share tactics to shield workers' rights and interests against potential managerial abuses. An experienced core worker commented that 'many participant workers in these sessions indeed want to raise their questions and queries rather than to listen to our legal lesson' (Interview, 7 May 2014). Another female core worker further suggested: 'Most workers nowadays can easily access legal information in the news and television, and thus can somehow understand what is right and wrong about management conduct. What we core workers can actually help them with at the legal session is, after listening to what they said about company's legal violation, give them advice, or consult further with the union officials in our monthly meetings' (Interview, 20 December 2015).

Core workers also offer legal advice in person (when workers in the same neighbourhood approach them at their rental units), by phone, or at worker-supporting spots. As of 2015, two of the interviewed core workers have recently moved to new houses out of the area, but they still pay visits to migrant workers' rental areas when convenient on the weekend. One of them said that he and his family had 'emotional ties' to the old place, where his relatives and friends are still living and where migrant workers are still in need of legal assistance. The creation of these spaces outside the company compounds, where core workers and workers in need can openly converse without any pressure or monitoring from the management, is integral to workers' awareness of their legal rights which can potentially enable further action against injustice.

The situation was different when the legal sessions were held under the company's oversight. According to two core workers, during the height of the project, they used to be invited to organise legal sessions in the factory compounds and company-provided dormitories, thanks to some coordination between the official unions and the company management. It is unclear why these companies were interested in educating workers about labour laws. What is clear is that there was some constraint on the content of the sessions imposed by the hosting businesses. One worker recalled:

> Before our sessions at the dormitories, the company people asked core workers to speak exclusively about what is written in the law. That means we were not able to give examples about legal violations, advise workers of how to deal with such situations, or show them some tricks to protect themselves, which we can do in our mobile sessions at workers' residences. And you know, during the question and answer times, participants kept silent and raised no questions or queries, as they were wary of the companies' surveillance. This is in contrast to the fact that we always receive questions and complaints, if not too many, when having our sessions at workers' residences. (Interview, 18 March 2015)

As all core workers assume that most companies violate and evade labour law, they interpreted the 'silence' as workers' wariness to speak up rather than the companies' legal compliance. While legal sessions organised by the company could attract hundreds of workers, they could not generate the meaningful impact on workers' awareness that occurred in much smaller sessions at workers' residences.

For example, a legal session at a workers' residence that I observed in March 2015 includes content that concerns the actual practices of labour law. The session covered labour contracts and unemployment benefits. After a brief overview of different contracts and their conditions, the speaker moved on to talk briefly about wage rises. This issue was not part of the planned topics, but I understood from him that it was an important concern of most workers and was worth mentioning.

> A company is supposed to raise wages for workers according to the government's minimum wage and its own wage table. This means that the longer one works, the higher one's wage is, in relative terms. Let's take the example that the government raises the minimum wage by 400,000 dong. If the company applies that amount to the new wage of all workers across the company, that is wrong. Instead, senior workers deserve a higher wage rise. The rates of wage rise should take in longer years of employment.

Instead of explaining to participants about the wage table, the speaker sent a simple message that senior workers legally deserve a higher rate of wage rise than newcomers. I was a bit surprised at the participants' silence after his explanation. As wages are a common source of grievance and are important to workers' livelihoods, I expected participants to raise some follow-up questions about their own company cases. The silence would normally imply either that they understood the lawful measure of wage rise or that all the company managements are compliant. However, from my conversations with ordinary respondent workers and from the core workers' accounts, the wage table is unknown to ordinary factory workers. I also doubt that companies are compliant, given the issue of wage differentials being a common reason for strikes and labour disputes. Following the participants' passive reaction, the speaker, without hesitation, continued with his prompt: 'You can now judge if your company issues the right amount of wage rise for you. Please feel free to see us if you encounter any problem.'

Later on, he went back to the topic of labour contracts. He gave examples about the company's illegal termination of contracts and advised, if not encouraged, participants to sue the management when faced with such situations. He also told them 'not to be afraid of doing so' and specified the compensation money that litigants can claim. His bold statement not only reminded workers of the law as a potential tool to act against injustice, but also made them feel confident about their action.

Also in that same session, the speaker reminded participants about the legal regulations regarding employees' behaviour at work. As he specified, 'The Labour Code ensures not only our rights and interests but also those of the company.'

> When we violate any rules, the company can sack us. For instance, if we have five days off without permission in a month, or 20 days a year, the company can sack us. Do any of you remember that provision?

One participant then asked: 'How about annual leave?'

The speaker responded: 'Of course you can take your annual leave. What I mentioned was leave without permission.' He then continued: 'Let's assume that we have had 19 days or 19 and a half day off so far in a year. If the company sacks us, it is wrong. Then we can sue the company. If we sue, we are sure to win.' The speaker would not have exhibited such confidence had he not previously learned about cases of workers' victory at the courts. During and after the legal sessions, core workers also mingled with participant workers and were willing to share their contacts, alongside the LAC contact, to participants at the legal sessions.

The speaker frequently used the pronoun '*chúng ta*' throughout the session. While Vietnamese pronouns '*chúng ta*' and '*chúng tôi*' refer to first-person plural and have the same English translation, their uses are slightly different. The pronoun 'we' is the translation of '*chúng tôi*,' or similar terms such as 'all of us' and 'some of us.' While '*chúng tôi*' refers to me and them, not you, '*chúng ta*' refers to me and you; in other words, the former is an exclusive 'we' and the latter is inclusive 'we.' This use of an inclusive pronoun illustrates a sense of shared identity between the speaker and the audience, an identity as workers together. He spoke of the potential problems and the actions of the audience as collective ones, something that he also shared and engaged with, albeit only in spirit. The connection that the core worker-speaker tried to establish with the worker-audience indicates a sense of collectivity, which emerged out of the former's empathy and shared interests with the latter, even though they were now in differing circumstances and production networks.

Core workers claimed to have offered legal advice to fellow workers in the same company, which often happened during the break, lunch time, or after work. While most of them talked at ease about their knowledge sharing, two of the core workers told me that they have to walk a fine line to make sure that they would not be watched over by their bosses. In particular, they specified to me that they did not reveal to their co-workers that they are 'core workers,' or are participants of the LAC programme. One of them, Mr Hải, also tried to keep this fact hidden from the company union and management, and even went further in lying to a manager when asked how he was so knowledgeable about the law. Another core worker, Mr Lê, was willing to share general legal issues with his fellow workers during the work breaks, but preferred to talk through the case with a disadvantaged co-worker after work and outside the factory. Both these core workers believed that concealing their role would allow them to maintain close and good relationships with their co-workers while keeping themselves safe from the management's surveillance.

In most cases, after giving general verbal advice to workers in need, core workers referred them to the LAC for more specific advice on their situations and assistance with lodging of complaints and lawsuits. Only one core worker, Mr Anh, had directly engaged with other workers' lodging of disputes and lawsuits. As one who has experienced different forms of managerial mistreatment, on which I will give more details in Chap. 6, Anh shared with me how strongly he feels for others who were caught in similar situation and who were desperate for genuine support. When I was conducting fieldwork in December 2015, Anh had successfully helped a few workers in the Long Thành District to claim their benefits from the company managers, and he was in the process of assisting another worker with her claim. Disadvantaged workers learnt of Anh's legal assistance through word of mouth. They delegated Anh as their legal representative, to act on their behalf throughout the whole dispute resolution process from completing the paperwork to mediation and litigation. During litigation, Anh attended the court hearings, where he was able to 'defend' the litigant worker himself without the need for any lawyer. Therefore, it is understandable why Anh told me that 'I sued company X' when he recalled his involvement in other workers' lawsuits.

Anh has also been successful in helping other workers to obtain redress. In October 2015, he represented a male senior worker in his lawsuit against the company for illegal dismissal and won the case. Anh told me that the company in question 'sacked people in a reckless manner' (Interview 18 January 2016). The senior worker managed to claim full compensation from the company, and he was also reinstated to his previous position.

The senior worker's niece-in-law, Mrs Lan, who also worked in that company, had faced the same problem and was likewise referred to Anh for help. In January 2016, Anh succeeded in representing Lan in the labour mediation process. Anh told me that 'As we had won against the company in the previous case, it was much easier to solve this one. The company management agreed to mediate with us and we reached the resolution quickly' (Interview 18 January 2016). Anh's involvement in these cases illustrates the role of social networks in informing workers' resistance tactics, and indicates the possibility of employing legal measures to assist disadvantaged workers in contesting managerial behaviour.

I had the chance to accompany Anh to Mrs Lan's rental unit where they talked through the resolution outcome. The outcome was that the company had to pay Lan compensation equal to the income she would have earned for the number of days she was out of work, as well as to reassign her to her previous role in the company. In response to Lan's worry that the manager might exert pressure on her after she returned to work, Anh told her 'not to worry or be afraid' and that he was willing to offer further help in the event that the company caused her any trouble. Outside the purview and surveillance of the management, the workers' residential areas became a safe ground for the core workers to help their co-workers make sense of injustice and, where possible, take measures to improve their working conditions.

Looking at the interactions amongst workers across social spaces and background in these situations invites comparison to how legal aid can be of value in other authoritarian contexts. Taking the case of China, Chan and Siu (2012, pp. 88–89) note that legal aid mainly focuses on addressing individual disputes and thus contributes only to workers' pursuit of individual rights. They see it as detracting from acts of resistance that can push for workers' collective rights and improve the situation of the working class as a whole. This sceptical proposition is based on a dichotomous view of individual and collective forms of resistance and does not acknowledge the potential for individual actions to embrace or trigger collective pursuits of justice. Chan and Siu also argue that legal aid and legal mobilisation are reactive rather than proactive, as they only occur following clear signs of employers' unlawful practices. The introduction of labour laws in authoritarian regimes like China therefore circumscribes the type of actions and demands that workers can pursue to become, in Marxist terms, a 'class-for-itself,' which implies a high stage of class consciousness (Chan and Siu 2012, p. 81).

The literature debate on class consciousness is vast, and it is beyond the scope of this book to fully address them. However, I wish to emphasise here that the sole focus on workers' overt actions, mobilisation, and demands overlooks other social and cultural factors that inform workers' consciousness and can generate their resistance. In the words of E.P. Thompson (1963, p. 10 and 269), these factors include 'traditions, value-systems, ideas, and institutional forms,' which underpin working-class experiences and contribute to class consciousness.[10] Informed by this cultural approach, I consider state law as constituting the values that underpin workers' experiences and contribute to their class consciousness. The observations thus far of the interactions between core workers and ordinary workers suggest that law does not stall the development of class consciousness. Social spaces outside the purview and surveillance of management are the breeding grounds for core workers to help their fellow workers identify exploitative and unjust practices, and overcome their disadvantaged position vis-à-vis management. These spaces allow workers to raise consciousness, among each other, of their individual and collective rights. Core workers' class consciousness—the way in which they identify with other workers as a collective with shared interests—is nurtured through their involvement in legal aid activities. While the core and ordinary workers in the province may not (yet) have become a 'class-for-itself' in Marxist terms, there is no evidence to suggest that their awareness of law is a factor that constrains their class consciousness.

Legal Aid and Labour Resistance from the Core Workers' Views

In this section I will move on to discuss core workers' views about legal aid, law, and workers' resistance to find out whether and how their access to law makes them different from ordinary workers. The core workers I spoke with shared common views about the role of legal aid in promoting workers' interests and almost all of them agreed on what constitutes rightful acts against management. They regarded the Oxfam project as useful and effective in bringing the law closer to workers in the province, and wished for the continuation of the project. One core worker remarked: 'The LAC and the legal aid program have helped bring some improvements to workers' plight in general; without them, many of our fellow workers would continue to be exploited and mistreated' (Interview, 28 February 2015). The core workers also felt positive about their own role and the legal knowledge they obtained. Some said they are 'responsible' for helping disadvantaged workers, while others saw themselves as contributing small good deeds to society. Their other commendations of the project's positive impacts included that it raises workers' 'understanding' (*hiểu biết*) of their rights and interests, helps workers 'face less coercion' (*đỡ bị chèn ép*), and makes their lives 'less miserable' (*đỡ khổ hơn*) (Interview, 30 January 2015, 5 February 2015, 7 May 2015, 27 December 2015).

In short, core workers saw the law as a potential 'weapon of the weak' (Scott 1985) that puts workers in a good bargaining position vis-à-vis their supervisors and managers. A male worker proudly said: 'The company management in general should be wary because workers now know more about the law' (Interview, 28 February 2015). Core workers especially emphasised that legal knowledge allows workers to 'protect themselves,' or 'defend their rights and interests,' a type of language that echoes the VGCL's legal aid objective and the labour news' campaigns on promoting legal aid services. Their thinking was different from the ordinary workers I spoke with, who had little or no interest in employing legal knowledge to contest management's behaviour. Though both core workers and ordinary workers had experienced injustice through the practice of the law at their workplaces, the former group saw the necessity of legal knowledge as a buffer against management abuse, while the latter felt hopeless and disillusioned about raising their voices.

Core workers' beliefs in the law were also influenced by their interactions with LAC staff and their observations of the staff's commitment.

They did not see the LAC as a part of the state or as holding corporatist interests. Core workers regarded the centre as genuinely attending to workers' interests, evidenced through their approachable manner, (free) generous support, and especially the high success rate of labour litigation. When encountering tricky issues and queries from fellow workers, core workers always, and only, refer them to the LAC and not the official unions. In observing and experiencing the dedication of LAC staff, core workers placed their trust in the LAC without regard to the practical limitations that it might face in holding state authorities accountable for law enforcement. Among all interviewed core workers, Mr Hải was perhaps the most positive about the LAC. He talked of an LAC legal counsellor, who trained him from the early days of the project, as a source of inspiration with her outstanding dedication towards the workers' plight. He said that, similar to the lawyer, the counsellor has always 'tried to demand something beneficial for the workers' (Interview, 30 January 2015), even though an informed outsider might judge that those workers were not necessarily right.

Core workers' attachment to the law has led them to have a critical view of strikes, and especially spontaneous strike actions, since they contravene legal procedures. This does not mean that they were against workers' collective actions, but they supported actions with a proper procedure informed by labour law. For instance, one of them specified:

> In some circumstances, some workers get so hot-tempered that they instigated strikes without [going through] any procedures.[11] Instead, if someone wants to mobilise their fellow workers, they should stand up, state their aim of representing workers, and take the initiative to collect workers' demands. They can seek help from the LAC to write a complaint letter and send their complaints forward. (Interview, 18 March 2015)

This extract depicts what makes a good workers' representative, who acts in an overt rather than underground manner, and whose course of action is based on collective interests rather than individuals' immediate needs. It demonstrates core workers' awareness of the law and the reality of the under-representation of workers' voices in the workplace. With little faith in the current union system, they see the potential for workers' resistance to take root in an awareness of collective interests and a knowledge of the capacity of collective voices, being enabled by an institution that they trust. Again, they throw total support behind the legal assistance of LAC lawyers and believe that such assistance would lead to a positive outcome.

However, as discussed in Chaps. 3 and 4, aggrieved workers often refrain from speaking up against management for fear of losing their jobs, or choose not to disclose their names when writing complaint letters. In the broader context of strikes, a worker whom the manager considers a strike instigator or finds to be vocal during a strike can easily face retaliation. That worker can either be dismissed, or transferred to a different work position in the company until he/she is bored and voluntarily quits the job.

I followed up with the previous depiction of workers' representatives by raising the issue of retaliation with three core workers: 'I think that if workers expose themselves or go through the complaint process, they can be easily identified by the boss and face some punishment. So workers prefer not to stand up and act in that overt manner.'

Two core workers thought that retaliation would beget further resistance. For instance, one said:

> Workers who stand up and act against management should not be afraid. If they are sacked, they can sue the employer for the illegal unilateral termination of contract. If they are transferred to a different position in the company, this process must follow what is stipulated in the Labour Code. Briefly, the transfer must result from a negotiation between the employer and employee, and the employee must be notified within three days before the actual transferral. Also, the total duration of transfer must not exceed 60 days. So if any of those conditions is violated, a worker can also sue. (Interview, 30 January 2015)

Rather than directly addressing my concern, another core worker raised a complaint related to his previous unsuccessful attempt to mobilise his fellow workers against their company's failure to raise wages.

> I told my fellow workers about the company's failure to raise wages but they continued to keep their silence because they did not want to risk their jobs. Their thinking is not right. How can they lose their jobs when they are in a labour contract, a labour relationship with the employer, and their rights and interests still apply? (Interview, 11 April 2015)

In short, these core workers believed that resisting workers would be able to mobilise their fellows against the company's legal violation *and* protect themselves against illegal acts of retaliation by the management if they knew the law. They did not use the exact word 'strike leader' or 'strike organiser' (*người lãnh đạo/tổ chức đình công*), the type of language used by union and labour officials, but 'the one who stands up/rises up' (*người đứng lên*) to indicate the ideal person capable of contesting management abuses. They believed that the law will do justice to law-abiding acts and is the only right way to demand justice.

There is, nonetheless, one core worker who spoke critically of the legal procedure for strike. Minh used to work for a chemical production company, which ultimately went bankrupt and closed its business. He is now working for a local state agency and, though no longer a factory worker, is still actively engaged with legal aid activities. He is one of the most fluent speakers among the core workers I met, and demonstrates the most experiences in his evaluation and comments about labour law in relation to workers' interests and rights. In his view, the legal procedure for strike is 'unacceptable':

> If workers follow the right legal procedure, they have to wait until the 13th day [since the dispute emerges] to be able to go on strike. Clearly, workers' grievances by that time would have all cooled down. When workers ask me about their intention to go on strike, I told them to go ahead, otherwise, who would protect their rights and interests? Who would listen to their voices? (Interview, 7 May 2015)

Minh also spoke against giving advice to workers about lodging petitions and letters to the state and unions, which he thinks is either ineffective or would put the letter writers at risk. Apart from these critical views, in general Minh is not different from other core workers in acknowledging other aspects of the labour law that benefit workers' interests and the utility of legal education. Indeed, he also laments that the core worker project could have been more effective had the organisers paid more attention to the quality of their training and had there been more active reception from participant workers. His understanding and conformity with the law accompanies a critical judgement of its rule, which I will show to be key characteristics of core workers' legal consciousness and mobilisation.

Members of the core workers' project do not only include workers on the assembly line but also those in managerial and supervisory positions. Mrs Hà has been a production supervisor for four years in a wood manufacturing company. As migrants from a Northern Province moving to work in Đồng Nai, Hà and her husband have lived in workers' rental units, and for that reason, she had a chance to join a mobile legal aid session and later the core workers project. Her position as someone who stands in between workers on the shop floor and the company management makes her a distinctive figure among core workers. The Taiwanese wood company where she works has been affected by wage-related strikes almost every year from 2010 to 2014. In the most recent strike, in 2014, workers were dissatisfied that the company's wage rise was being applied only to workers who had been employed for less than five years, with longer-term people receiving no increase.[12]

Hà's initial explanation to me regarding the wage rise issue was similar to that of other interviewed workers in Chap. 3: she referred generally to the state's 'wage rise' at the start of the year when workers were kept waiting for the company's decision. The lack of a two-way dialogue between the management and the workers has led to either workers' dissatisfaction after a wage rise decision was issued or the management's deliberate delay in announcing its decision which eventually exhausted workers' patience. Later she explained that the underlying problem with ongoing labour disputes lies in the company's failure to establish a wage table, an issue that she herself has posed to the company union's chairman:

> I have asked the union chairman why the company does not have the wage table which includes the percentage of wage rise. He told me that he had collected workers' opinions and demand for the wage table for several years. However the company has not addressed this. In a strike last year, workers demanded for a wage table but it still was not addressed. (Interview, 22 January 2015)

While ordinary respondent workers justify their demands for a higher wage rise based on their sense of fairness and equality, Hà clearly identified such demands as rooted in the company's failure to adhere to the Labour Code. Without explicitly saying that the company's conduct is illegal, Hà has effectively justified workers' demands throughout their strike actions by repeating management's refusal to see to workers' problems.

Hà then followed up with the union's failure to satisfy workers' demands: 'The union chairman is sandwiched between two sides. He can only find some way to negotiate [workers' concerns] with the boss. If the boss had a good heart, he would be listening'[13] (Interview, 22 January 2015). Her last sentence interestingly suggests that the management's moral commitments are a key to the actual realisation of workers' lawful demands. It was at this point that Hà started to move freely between legal and moral reasoning to defend workers' actions.

Her sympathy with the workers on the shop floor became evident when she told me about workers' frustration with the meal quality and unreasonable discipline in her company. In addition to the wage issue, she opined that the other problems further fuel workers' grievances amidst the management's continuing refusal to address them. Although she initially showed some ambivalence in her judgement of workers' strikes, she seemed to be supportive of their demands and actions. The following transcript details her reactions and attitudes when strikes broke out in the past few years:

> In my situation it is not a matter of participating or not participating in strikes. I am situated between workers and the management. When strikes happen, I can't continue to work, but I also can't stand outside the company gate. I therefore choose to go home. In general I know that workers' going on strike is wrong, but I understand that they were so angry. I can't do anything about their action. Nor can I talk in favour of the company. (Interview, 22 January 2015)

Her account demonstrates an awareness of the legal procedures for strikes, which workers have contravened by taking actions spontaneously without going through a complaint process. Her inaction when strikes take place indicates the quandary of standing by workers' action, officially deemed to go against labour law, when the company management is not in the right. When I later followed up by asking about the company's treatment of workers after a 'successful' strike, Hà changed her stance and defended their actions:

> After a strike for which the management had to raise wages and workers were successful in getting their demands, the management in turn put pressure on the workers, they pushed workers a lot. They supervised and checked workers more closely. [...] However, workers had gone on strike to demand their rights and interests. In general they hadn't done anything wrong, and they don't need to be afraid of their action. As far as I know, workers asked the Department of Labour or the LAC about their demands before and during strikes. (Interview, 22 January 2015)

Hà's narratives, like those of other core workers, represent a tension between a legal and moral evaluation of strikes. She considered workers' actions to be unlawful but later suggested that their demands are 'legitimate,' as 'workers only demand the minimum level of wage according to law, no more than that.' She sees that, in stipulating certain rights and interests that lay the grounds for workers' demands, the Labour Code contributes to shaping rather than constraining labour resistance. Such contribution, as she made clear in the aforementioned transcript, is possible through the legal consultation offered by the Department of Labour and the LAC. By throwing her support behind workers' demands, Hà has come to treat their experiences as shared injustices and condoned what she initially saw as legally wrongful actions.

Hà spoke positively of her connections with workers on the shop floor, mentioning that many of them approached her about legal issues after learning of her engagement in the core workers project. She is also positive about how workers improved knowledge of labour law over time, allowing them to judge the management's conduct and take necessary action. Yet she understands that law itself is not an all-powerful or determinant force, and hints at management's ethical role as a key to ensuring workers' interests.

Concluding Remark

This chapter has discussed the ways in which legal aid influences workers' views towards law and justice, and the media discourse that reflects the increasing role of legal understanding in promoting labour rights in Đồng Nai. It highlights the catchphrase of 'defending their rights and interests' as a thread that runs through VGCL's legal aid objective and core workers' motivation to spread the law more widely to workers' community in the province. I have also stressed the importance of social spaces outside the purview of the state and management, such as workers' rental units, in enabling and facilitating the exchanges between core and ordinary workers. Through their activities in the Oxfam-funded project, core workers have come to appreciate the role of legal aid, perceive workplace grievances as legal problems, and consider the legal pathway as necessary for disadvantaged workers to break their silence against abusive management. In their view, labour law must be actively engaged with, through legal education, legal aid, and legal mobilisation, in order for fair practices to be established and sustained.

Notes

1. As the Chinese state is concerned with preserving stability and social order, scholars have argued that the state's encouragement of citizens' use of law is aimed at controlling grievances and conflicts (Friedman and Lee 2010; Gallagher 2017).
2. These organisations often face burdensome registration procedures, scant funding, and close monitoring from the state (Becker 2014; Chan 2012). They were set up by former migrant workers and professionals concerned with workers' rights. While organisations that vocally advocate for workers' rights and collective actions are co-opted and repressed by the state, others which provide social welfare services that serve the state's interests work in tandem with the state and union. These organisations provide disadvantaged workers with free legal assistance, such as advising them on claim-making strategies, and social welfare support (Friedman 2009; Chan 2012; Becker 2014). Yet the largest organisation providing legal aid for employees in China, as indicated in Gallagher's 2017 book, is the Legal Aid Centre affiliated with the Shanghai law school.
3. These core workers, whose roles will be discussed in the next chapter, have a good relationship with the LAC.
4. This means a wage level for newcomers, which is much lower than the wage level that senior workers have been paid during their employment.
5. Information obtained by the author from the 'Conference on experience sharing and developing models of support for migrant employees' (Organised by Centre of Research—Consultation for Social Work and Community Development and Southern Institute of Social Sciences, Hồ Chí Minh City, Vietnam, 17 December 2015).
6. As much as I wish to interview ordinary workers to see how they opine about the core workers and the legal sessions, I was unable to do so due to the timing of my fieldwork (which took place almost one year after the project's heyday had passed) and the difficulty of recruiting ordinary workers who had joined any of the legal session.
7. Information obtained at the 'Conference on experience sharing and developing models of support for migrant employees' (Hồ Chí Minh City, Vietnam, 17 December 2015).
8. This session was organised after Oxfam ended its funding to the project. However, the format and content of the legal sessions remained the same.
9. The Vietnamese pronoun is *chúng ta*. I will discuss this semantic use later in the chapter.
10. In Thompson's thesis, class is not a fixed category that is structurally determined by productive relations. It is always in the making and manifests

'when some men [...] feel and articulate the identity of their interests as between themselves, and as against other men' (1963: 269).

11. The people referred to here are different from informal strike leaders who mobilise workers around certain complaints and sometimes may be asked to get involved in the process of strike resolution (Pringle and Clarke 2011).
12. Đồng Nai Labour Federation (2014), Report on the work of taking care of material and mental lives for workers and the situation of strikes and work stoppages.
13. The Vietnamese word is *nghe*, which means listening or hearing, and in some context also means following someone's words or advice.

References

Albiston, C. (2006). Legal Consciousness and Workplace Rights. In B. Fleury-Steiner & L.B. Nielsen (eds.). *New Civil Rights Research: A Constitutive Approach*. Dartmouth, UK: Ashgate Press.

Becker, J. (2014). *Social Ties, Resources and Migrant Labor Contention in Contemporary China: From Peasants to Protesters*. Lanham: Lexington Books.

Chan, A. & Siu, K. (2012). Chinese Migrant Workers: Factors Constraining the Emergence of Class Consciousness. In Carrillo, B. & Goodman, D. S. (eds.). *China's Peasants and Workers: Changing Class Identities*. London: Edward Elgar.

Chan, C. K-C. (2012). Community-based Organizations for Migrant Workers' Rights: The Emergence of Labour NGOs in China. *Community Development Journal*, 48 (1), 6–22.

Đồng Nai Labour Federation (2014). *Report on the work of taking care of material and mental lives for workers and the situation of strikes and work stoppages*.

Ewick, P. & Silbey, S. (1992). Conformity, Contestation and Resistance: An Account of Legal Consciousness. *New England Law Review*, 26, 731–749.

Friedman, E. (2009). External Pressure and Local Mobilization: Transnational Activism and the Emergence of the Chinese Labor Movement. *Mobilization: An International Journal*, 14 (2), 199–218.

Friedman, E. & Lee, C. K. (2010). Remaking the World of Chinese Labour: A 30-Year Retrospective. *British Journal of Industrial Relations*, 48 (3), 507–533.

Gallagher, M. (2006). Mobilizing the Law in China: 'Informed Disenchantment' and the Development of Legal Consciousness. *Law & Society Review*, 40 (4), 783–816.

Gallagher, M. (2017). *Authoritarian Legality in China: Law, Workers and the State*. New York: Cambridge University Press.

Gillespie, J. (2011). Exploring the Limits of the Judicialization of Urban Land Disputes in Vietnam. *Law and Society Review*, 45 (2), 241–275.
Lao Động (10/11/2015). Cty TNHH Yupoong Việt Nam: Gần 2000 lao động bất ngờ bị chấm dứt hợp đồng. http://laodong.com.vn/cong-doan/cty-tnhh-yupoong-viet-nam-gan-2000-lao-dong-bat-ngo-bi-cham-dut-hop-dong-395289.bld. Accessed 24th June 2016.
Lao Động Đồng Nai (11/5/2014a). Công nhân lo lắng vì bị điều sang công ty khác. http://laodongdongnai.vn/Ban-doc/Bam-doc-voi-cong-doan/0B824D/cong-nhan-lo-lang-vi-bi-dieu-sang-cong-ty-khac.aspx. Accessed 15th August 2017.
Lao Động Đồng Nai (14/5/2014b). Chủ bỏ trốn, công nhân khốn đốn. http://laodongdongnai.vn/Ban-doc/Bam-doc-voi-cong-doan/0A0004/chu-bo-tron-cong-nhan-khon-don.aspx. Accessed 15th August 2017.
Lao Động Đồng Nai (8/7/2014c). Trả lương sai, phải bồi thường cho người lao động. Available at http://laodongdongnai.vn/Ban-doc/Bam-doc-voi-cong-doan/2E1645/tra-luong-sai-phai-boi-thuong-cho-nguoi-lao-dong.aspx. Accessed 15th August 2017.
Lao Động Đồng Nai (10/9/2015a). Bảo vệ quyền lợi hợp pháp cho người lao động (Bài cuối). http://laodongdongnai.vn/Ban-doc/Bam-doc-voi-cong-doan/2EB404/bao-ve-quyen-loi-hop-phap-cho-nguoi-lao-dong-bai-cuoi.aspx. Accessed 15th August 2017.
Lao Động Đồng Nai (12/4/2015b). Mòn mỏi hơn 4 năm đi kiện. http://laodongdongnai.vn/Ban-doc/Bam-doc-voi-cong-doan/23805F/mon-moi-hon-4-nam-di-kien.aspx. Accessed 15th August 2017.
Lao Động Đồng Nai (26/5/2015c). Gần 3 năm đi đòi trợ cấp tai nạn lao động. http://laodongdongnai.vn/Ban-doc/Bam-doc-voi-cong-doan/22945D/gan-3-nam-di-doi-tro-cap-tai-nan-lao-dong.aspx. Accessed 15th August 2017.
Lao Động Đồng Nai (27/1/2015d). Khốn khổ vị đột ngột bị cho nghỉ việc. http://laodongdongnai.vn/Ban-doc/Bam-doc-voi-cong-doan/0A961D/khon-kho-vi-dot-ngot-bi-cho-nghi-viec.aspx. Accessed 15th August 2017.
Lao Động Đồng Nai (3/9/2015e). Bảo vệ quyền lợi hợp pháp cho người lao động (Bài 1). http://laodongdongnai.vn/Ban-doc/Bam-doc-voi-cong-doan/2EB404/bao-ve-quyen-loi-hop-phap-cho-nguoi-lao-dong-bai-1.aspx. Accessed 15th August 2017.
Lao Động Đồng Nai (6/9/2015f). Bảo vệ quyền lợi hợp pháp cho người lao động (Bài 2). http://laodongdongnai.vn/Ban-doc/Bam-doc-voi-cong-doan/2EB404/bao-ve-quyen-loi-hop-phap-cho-nguoi-lao-dong-bai-2.aspx. Accessed 15th August 2017.
Lao Động Đồng Nai (8/9/2015g). Bảo vệ quyền lợi hợp pháp cho người lao động (Bài 3). Available at http://laodongdongnai.vn/Ban-doc/Bam-doc-voi-cong-doan/2EB404/bao-ve-quyen-loi-hop-phap-cho-nguoi-lao-dong-bai-3.aspx. Accessed 15th August 2017.

Lao Động Đồng Nai (18/5/2016a). Sa thải lao động trái luật, công ty bồi thướng 88 triệu. http://laodongdongnai.vn/Ban-doc/Bam-doc-voi-cong-doan/03205D/sa-thai-lao-dong-trai-luat-cong-ty-boi-thuong-88-trieu-dong.aspx. Accessed 15th August 2017.

Lao Động Đồng Nai (28/9/2016b). 1 vụ án, 4 lần xét xử vẫn chưa có hồi kết. http://laodongdongnai.vn/Ban-doc/Bam-doc-voi-cong-doan/4B904F/1-vu-an-4-lan-xet-xu-van-chua-co-hoi-ket.aspx. Accessed 15th August 2017.

Legal Aid Centre – Đồng Nai Labour Federation (2009). The project of mobile legal consultation for migrant workers in Long Bình ward, Biên Hòa city, Đồng Nai province (Number 20/DA-TVPL)

Legal Aid Centre (2013). *Report on Activities of the Legal Aid Centre*, Biên Hòa.

Pringle, T. & Clarke, S. (2011). *The Challenge of Transition: Trade Unions in Russia, China and Vietnam*. Basingstoke: Palgrave.

Scott, J. (1985). *Weapons of the Weak: Everyday Forms of Peasant Resistance*. New Haven & London: Yale University Press.

Thompson, E. P. (1963). *The Making of the English Working Class*. New York: Pantheon Books.

Trần, A. N. (2013). *Ties that Bind: Cultural Identity, Class, and Law in Vietnam's Labor Resistance*. Ithaca: Cornell Southeast Asia Program Publications.

Tuổi Trẻ (9/11/2015). Công ty chấm dứt hợp đồng, hàng ngàn công nhân điêu đứng. http://tuoitre.vn/tin/chinh-tri-xa-hoi/20151109/cong-ty-cham-dut-hop-dong-hang-ngan-cong-nhan-dieu-dung/999928.html. Accessed 24th June 2016.

Vietnam Television Online News (13/11/2015). Yupoong Việt Nam vẫn quyết định chấm dứt hợp đồng với 2000 lao động. http://vtv.vn/xa-hoi/yupoong-viet-nam-van-quyet-dinh-cham-dut-hop-dong-voi-2-000-lao-dong-20151113220005921.htm. Accessed 24th June 2016.

CHAPTER 6

Core Workers' Legal Mobilisation

This chapter explores three case studies of core workers' role in contesting practices at their own companies and the challenges of collective legal mobilisation. Existing literature on legal mobilisation and rights campaign in other contexts has demonstrated the link between institutional support for rights and the individuals' or activists' willingness to pursue their claims or collective causes (McCann 1994; Merry 2006). Such institutional support includes the recognition of certain rights claims through court cases, official announcements by state authorities, and the availability of legal aid resources that provide access to justice. In the previous chapter, we learn that the core workers' legal training and the media reporting of the Legal Aid Centre's success at the courts help promulgate the rhetoric of rights protection to the wider workers' communities. To the core workers, they give hope and confidence in the law. Would their hope and confidence be sustained when they themselves resort to law to confront mistreatment and injustice at work?

In the previous chapter, I mentioned briefly the difficulty of one core worker in garnering his fellow workers' support for bringing unlawful practices to the official unions and authorities. This worker ultimately quit his job and applied to work in another company that pays a higher income. The two core workers that appear in this chapter also face difficulty in mobilising their fellow workers; yet, instead of keeping silence or resigning, one of them opted to go her own way in petitioning, and the other took time to encourage his colleagues to stand by his pursuit. In order to

T. P. Nguyen, *Workplace Justice*, Critical Studies of the Asia-Pacific,
https://doi.org/10.1007/978-981-13-3116-9_6

fully understand core workers' ability to mobilise and use the law effectively, we need to take into account their individual circumstances and their own experiences at work. How do they challenge and move around managerial tactics and enthuse with fellow workers to collective action?

Support for Letter Writing

Mr Lê has worked for nine years in the storage section of the food processing company, which has been discussed at length in Chap. 3. He and his wife, who works in the same company, have two small sons. This company was fraught with spontaneous strikes and work stoppages between 2010 and 2014. Workers' grievances were mainly about the unclear piece rate payment and the company's failure to pay the premium overtime rates. As mentioned before, despite perpetual exploitation, many workers on the production line have given up their lunch break to produce as many pieces as possible and did not complain about excessive overtime hours and weekend work in their interviews with me. Lê nevertheless raised his concern about the excessive working hours that he and his fellow workers are enduring. In his conversation with me, he also raised the issue that the company's overtime hours go beyond the legal limit of 30 hours per month. Besides complaining about the lack of premium rates for Sunday work, Lê also pointed out that the premium rate for night shifts has not been properly calculated or shown up in workers' payslips, something that other respondent workers did not raise. The following transcript is an example of his detailed explanation about the company's problems in law enforcement:

> Besides the piece rate problem, the working hours per month, including overtime, often exceed the maximum legal limit of 300 hours. I can show you the attendance records of my group; it's common that many of us work more than 300 hours a month. No premium overtime rates are applied for night shifts and Sunday work, which are 30 percent and 200 percent, respectively. (Interview, 5 February 2015)

Despite his detailed legalistic explanation, Lê shared the same complaint with the other workers that wages in his company are 'not enough to live by' (Interview, 5 February 2015), which effectively connects his concern about law enforcement with others' concern about livelihoods. Ultimately, while having a clear sense of the company's legal violation, Lê has not mobilised his fellow workers nor stood up as a workers' representative during the strikes. He lives in a workers' rental unit close to his many fellow workers, who, like him, are migrants to Đồng Nai Province. His legal knowledge and living arrangements provide a fertile ground for him to become a strike organiser or leader, similar to those featured in Trần's stories of labour protests (2013). Yet, he has not followed such a path as his concern for job security keeps him from speaking out on behalf of workers' collective interests. Lê has learnt that he might lose his job if he were to take any overt action against the company management. This happened to a young male worker in 2014, who had worked there for one year before he engaged in a confrontational action against the management. In the strike in 2014, he raised a banner with workers' demands at the company's gate and blocked the manager's car to put pressure on him to meet his demands. Though Lê and other respondents did not personally know him, they knew about his job loss shortly afterwards.

Lê therefore chose to contribute to workers' resistance in a covert rather than in an explicit manner, by throwing his support behind complaint writing. He helped some of his fellow workers write a collective letter to the management before the strike in 2014. He gave advice about the appropriate language and some relevant legal terms to others, who took the initiative to write the letter and collect other workers' signatures. Lê no longer retained the letter but clearly remembered its five demands: (1) transparent calculation of the piece rates, (2) payment of the premium rate for Sunday work, (3) a year-end bonus, (4) an increase in meal portions, and (5) a transport allowance. Even though Lê earlier complained to me about the excessive overtime hours, this issue was not raised in the complaint letter. The reason is that a reduction in overtime work would result in a reduction in workers' monthly income and consequently affect their livelihoods. The absence of this issue concerning overtime in the letter demonstrates the tension between legal understanding and actual demands that are more closely linked to workers' everyday subsistence. According to Lê, after the letter was sent to the labour inspectorate at the Department of Labour, some resolution meeting happened at the company office, which he did not attend, but which saw no change to the company's policies. Soon after that, the workers who wrote the letter quit their jobs.

In short, Lê's legal knowledge leads him to understand the legal problems behind workers' exploitative situation and the management's failure to pay workers the correct income according to law. However, his legal consciousness has not substantially changed his workplace experiences or led to concrete actions against injustice. Concerned about managerial retaliation, Lê has preferred to assist his fellow workers with individual issues rather than raise collective awareness about legal violations. His indirect role in complaint writing with regard to collective issues can be seen as the only pragmatic way for him to raise workers' grievances in accordance with legal procedures without risking loss of his job.

A Sole Petitioner

Mrs Nguyên is also supportive of complaint writing, but, unlike Lê, she is overt in her role and initiates complaint letters. Nguyên has worked for six years in a joint-stock garment company[1] in Đồng Nai, which employs 700 workers. She is a single mother of a school-age daughter. As she told me, the company where she works has not been affected by factory strikes but is fraught with legal violations. Before taking the initiative to speak up on behalf of her fellow workers, Nguyên herself was involved in an individual dispute with company management which saw her turning to semi-official channels to solve her problem.

Her individual dispute started in 2011 when she claimed that she was transferred from the storage section to a sewing position against her wishes. This happened after she participated in a training programme coordinated by her employer and a skill training college. After failing to have the manager reassign her to the storage section, she was then transferred to a quality control position for which she received a lower wage. Nguyên decided to lodge a complaint letter to the upper-level union office. Subsequently, the company management's mistreatment of Nguyên was briefly reported in the local labour newspaper,[2] in which her name was abbreviated and the company's name was not revealed. After the publication of the news, a resolution meeting took place between the upper-level union officials, herself, and her employer. However, the outcome was not in her favour. Then, while remaining in the job, she was subjected to numerous arbitrary decisions and disciplinary actions from the managers.

Nguyên did not make it explicit to me whether the unfavourable outcome of her individual dispute pushed her to take further and bolder action against the company's conduct. However, it is clear that she then stopped pursuing her own case and started a new petition in relation to complaints and grievances of a collective nature. In 2014, with assistance and consultation with the Legal Aid Centre (LAC) lawyer, she decided to lodge a complaint letter on behalf of her fellow workers against the management's conduct. The letter she showed me was directed to the leaders of different state agencies in the province—the People's Council, the People's Committee, the National Assembly's representatives, and the People's Mobilisation Committee, as well as the local news channel. She previously sent a copy to the labour inspectorate of the Department of Labour, but due to their unresponsiveness, decided to forward the problem to other state agencies.

Mrs Nguyên started the letter with her name, phone number, and postal address. She then referred to the employment positions and workplace behaviours of her and her fellows. The collective nature of her complaints is mixed with her own individual action and self-ascription, evidenced through an interchangeable use of the pronouns 'I' and 'we' throughout the letter. For instance, the letter starts with:

> Now I am writing this letter to urgently request the authority to consider and solve our problems. We have worked at sewing plant 3 of company X for many years. During this time I have always tried to complete the assigned tasks and have never violated any company regulations.

Nguyên then provided more details about employees' working situation and the company's profits and business awards:

> Due to the enormous pressure of completing the quota and ensuring products' quality, we employees always have to brace ourselves for the tasks. Thanks to our contribution, the company has achieved such things as: accomplishing the planned targets every year, having its market further expanded, and exporting more products. In particular, the company is annually acknowledged as the leading company of the province and receives all sorts of commendations and rewards. Furthermore, the company is also granted the title 'Labour hero in the reform era.'[3] How can the company achieve all these titles? It is thanks to employees' contributions and labour. Yet the company has coerced and exploited us employees.

Here Nguyên demonstrates her grasp of the reality of production: the company meets its deadlines and expands its profits at the cost of workers' labour and exploitation. She is astute in pointing out the irony involved in giving the title of 'labour hero' to a company that does not even meet its legal responsibilities to its employees. Furthermore, the extract also suggests that there should be some reciprocal exchange in the labour-management relationship: if the workers meet management's demands despite their excessive nature, then management should be grateful for their service. The company's coercive and exploitative practices in the face of labour loyalty are seen as indications of the company management's ingratitude to the workers, who deserve good treatment and recognition for their hard work.

She then accuses the company management of problematic wage policies, unclear bonuses, and lack of insurance payment. She explicitly refers to legal regulations in her allegations, and gives evidence and reasons to demonstrate her arguments, as can be seen in the following example:

> As far as I know, the common minimum wage of 1,150,000 dong only applies to state employees and officers. Private enterprises must apply the regional minimum wage of 2,700,000 dong according to the legal regulations. However, I don't know why my company has kept calculating our wages based on the common minimum wage to pay employees. When we asked the management and [company] union about this issue, they responded that the state agency allowed them to do so. I asked, which agency and who allowed the company to do so, and they kept silent. Who and which agency dared to allow the company to act *against the law*? [italics added]

The extract illustrates workplace problems similar to those discussed in Chap. 4 with regard to workers' income and the lack of responsiveness by the company management towards workers' queries. Yet the writing manner in this case is clear-cut and confrontational, with the writer judging management conduct in terms of its illegality. I shall further note that the continual shifting between 'I' and 'we' in the previous extract highlights Nguyên's individual defiance in the face of a shared problem. She has managed to prove that her voice matters: the management's silence in response to her query can be understood as a compromise in a context that would otherwise see a reverse effect upon ordinary workers who have little legal support in their contestation of abusive practices.

The last rhetorical question interestingly demonstrates how the writer perceives and situates law within workers' relationship with the state and the management. While Nguyên freely cited relevant legal provisions in the preceding sentences, she later seems to view law as a supreme authority that shall circumscribe the power of the state and the management. As law has been daringly evaded and manipulated on the shop floor, Nguyên wants to assert to the perpetrators and their accomplices that they have committed outrageous acts against the law's authority. Her reference to the state agency when talking with the management and union not only evokes the state's responsibility of law monitoring but also calls on the state to honour the letter of the law. Her rhetorical question therefore is an outright challenge to the state and management in their complicity. The question also indicates a strong sense of injustice derived directly from workers' legal understandings and practices of labour law that is not observed in other letters analysed in the preceding chapter.

The letter moves on with further details:

> According to the legal regulations, the company has to raise wages for employees every year. We have worked here for many years but our wage has been raised only once from 1.67 to 2.01 [the wage level]. This will affect employees' rights and interests when we retire. We raised our question but the company said that, if we wanted to have a wage rise, we had to take a skill examination, to show that we can make a certain quantity of clothes in a certain time. As we are doing jobs like quality control, housekeeping, etc. [i.e. non-productive areas], how can we make the products? Such conduct is *against the law*, as the company evades its responsibility to employees. [italics added]

The accusation here was raised on behalf of all employees but seemed to centre specifically on those employed in non-production sections where Nguyên was assigned. Several issues can be drawn from this short extract. First, the writer refers to law to highlight the illegality of the company conduct, including its failure to raise wages and the rationale for its decision. This use of law is different from that of the letter writers analysed in Chap. 4, when law is mentioned to support moral claims of unfairness. Second, the reference to 'rights and interests' in this context constitutes both legal and moral claims. Legally, the pensions that workers receive each month will be calculated based on their basic wage at the time of their employment, and therefore, a low basic wage would later allow for little retirement benefit. Yet it also implicates a moral obligation of employers, derived from the legal commitment described earlier, in ensuring employees' welfare and livelihoods. The way Nguyên frames her argument demonstrates an awareness not just of workers' legal benefits, which have been infringed upon by the management, but also of the ethical consequences borne by the workers in the long term.

The letter moves on with further legal reasoning, and alerts the state authorities to the company's deliberate cover-up of its illegal conduct:

> According to the labour law, employees who work overtime shall be paid a rate of 150%, 200% or 300% for weekdays, weekend, and public holidays, respectively. We are paid by piece rate, and these should be calculated based on the premium rates mentioned above. However, the company only pays us the normal rates.
>
> According to the regulations, overtime work shall be done on a voluntary basis. However, in practice, the company forced employees to sign a paper and compelled them to work overtime.
>
> In addition, every time an examination team came to the company, the company forced employees not to reveal that our overtime hours exceed the limit as the law allowed. In order to 'cope' with the state, the company forced employees to sign their cards off at the end of the normal working time, then go back to work.

Here Nguyên accuses the company of not just illegal pay rates but also of forcing workers to do overtime and then forcing them to cover this up. The way she frames this cover-up is different from that of other complainants discussed in Chap. 4: she does not see this as a form of lying but as a twofold legal evasion. While the threat from the management is not made explicit in the quote, it is presumed that workers are in fear of losing their jobs if they do not comply with the management's demands.

In addition, the letter also raises further complaints about inconsistencies in reward and bonus payments. According to the Labour Code, rewards and bonuses are non-compulsory and are often issued on the basis of business profits. As it is difficult to apply the statutory legal terms in this case, the letter writer shifts towards a different type of reasoning. If the workers in Chap. 4 at times invoked the morality of workplace treatment in hope for the union's sympathy, the writer in this case wants to make a convincing case based on the following commonsense observations and judgements:

> Regarding our reward, we don't know if there is any reward scheme in our company. In many instances, the amount of reward that we signed[4] is high but the actual money received is very low. We don't know what the company has done with the difference.

She moves on to give an example of the New Year bonus in early 2014, when the company announced a good bonus for employees and asked them to sign the payment list, but then failed to pay it in the end. Here she tactically exposes the truth: it is not just the workers' labour that goes to make company profits but also their promised reward:

> We are confused: what happened to the money? Isn't it that our money is now used as part of the company cadres' savings to earn their interest?[5] We think that this matter is not only to do with labour relations but is a sign of cheating and grabbing other people's property.

The accusation raised in the extract, framed in the language of labour relations, moves into the common language of cheating and stealing. It refers to the company's violation as being not just an issue of labour law but also of being a civil impingement on other people's property. The writer has moved freely between making claims derived from the Labour Code and other claims outside of it to stretch her legal accusations beyond its statutory terms. This explains why at the end of the letter, the writer explicitly suggests that 'the company's conduct indicates criminal behaviour' that requires further intervention of the state beyond administrative measures.

Besides requesting the state to investigate and solve the company's illegal conduct, the letter also astutely requests a solution to rectify existing workplace problems, which makes it stand out among all other pleas and requests discussed thus far in the book:

> The current law has stipulated different forms of democracy in the companies. Therefore, besides resolving previous issues, could you give orders to enhance democratic practices in the company, especially with respect to bargaining and dialogue? Doing so would ensure that employees' voices are heard at the very grassroots level, and their rights and interests are made transparent and can be monitored by employees themselves.

The current Labour Code contains several references to workplace 'democracy'.[6] For instance, Article 5, on 'rights and obligations of workers,' stipulates that workers have the right to 'implement regulations on democracy and consultation at the workplace to protect their lawful rights and interests.' Article 6 also adds that an employer has the obligation to 'comply with regulations on democracy at the grassroots level.' While the term 'democracy' reappears in further provisions concerning workplace dialogue and communication between employers and employees, there is scant attention in the rest of the Labour Code to the functioning of workplace democracy and its significance within labour relations. Here, Nguyên is asking for workers' voices to be heard, for the workers to be able to know their rights and interests, and for workers themselves to have oversight of these issues through bargaining and communication channels. It is not only a call for proper implementation of labour law but also a plea for the workers' role in the production process to be properly acknowledged and enforced. None of the workers I interviewed nor the letters I analysed made reference to this term. Understandably, those workers obtain most of their information about law through their informal social networks, and have limited access to legal aid and dispute institutions.

Overall, having undergone some training about labour law and possessing a good knowledge of workers' legal rights, Nguyên has made good use of her knowledge and legal aid support to fight against managerial conduct. Her letter is similar to the kind of rightful claims brought against the abusive power of political and economic elites in authoritarian regimes (O'Brien and Li 2006, pp. 2–3). In making these claims, resisters exhibit a consciousness of their rights and in turn appropriate state law to mobilise support and demand justice. Apart from her confrontational language and her expansive use of labour law, the writer has been careful to wrap her accusations and requests with officially sanctioned rhetoric. These violations and mistreatments are also cast against the title 'labour hero' of the company awarded by the state, referred to at the start of the letter. There seems to be a moral outrage alongside the frustration with the company's illegal conduct.

As the resolution of her complaint letter failed to bring a favourable outcome for her and her fellow workers, Nguyên sent another denunciation letter to the provincial bodies and labour authority in June 2015. This letter is, by name and nature, more serious than her previous complaint letter. She restates her previous allegations and adds that 'the chief labour inspector checked the company but I don't understand how come the company committed more violations after that.' Similar to the last letter, workers' grievances are framed in a confrontational and legalistic manner:

> According to the legal regulations, overtime hours must not exceed 4 hours per day, 30 hours per month and 300 hours per year. As the company has

> recently had many orders, it gives workers voluntary overtime sheets, forcing them to sign and organising overtime consecutively from 4pm to 6pm. However, to 'legitimise' the overtime hours according to the regulation, the company has forced workers to sign off their cards at 5pm. I didn't sign the overtime sheet and didn't want to work overtime but the company forced me to do so and did not let me go home.

The extract also reveals Nguyên's attempted refusal to obey the management's order to work overtime. It is an outright resistance to an unlawful act of coercion and a further ploy to cover it up. Her attitude is different from that of other complainants, discussed in Chap. 4, who admitted that they reluctantly followed company rules rather than risk being disciplined or dismissed afterwards. By mentioning her outright disobedience of the management's order, she seems to want to distinguish herself from her fellow workers, few of whom are willing to speak up, while at the same time drawing attention to the shared injustices they all face. In this regard, Nguyên has tactically put forth her individual voice and resisting behaviour to support her arguments of broader problems of a collective nature.

Apart from the previous legal accusations, this denunciation letter also contains an issue that touches upon human dignity and bypasses an aspect of labour law. This last accusation is the shortest, but perhaps the most sharply worded, of all the complaints raised in the letter:

> The company these days also enforces a rule that violates human rights: after two months of internship, a [female] employee has to do a pregnancy test and will have a labour contract signed only if tested not pregnant. This practice is humiliating especially for unmarried people.

In legal terms, this practice violates Article 154 of the Labour Code, which stipulates that an employer is obliged to 'ensure the implementation of gender equality in recruitment, employment and training.' Nguyên's accusation is not directed at it being a discriminatory policy towards female employees, but a humiliating act. While there is a strong social stigma against premarital pregnancy in Vietnam (Gammeltoft 2014), demanding unmarried women take this test is seen as demoralising. The complaint in this case is not framed within the public/legal but the private/moral sphere and implicitly appeals to the state's moral obligations to female workers.

Attached to the typed pages is a page in her hand writing in which she invokes the Party's rhetoric, its moral authority, and campaigns on cadres' conduct. The language and sentiment expressed in her hand writing are different from the predominantly legalistic language in her previous complaint and denunciation letters. It seems that when legal reasoning was exhausted, she decided to opt for an emotional appeal to justice. This stands in contrast to the situation of a worker named Thắm, whose letter made the headlines and was discussed in Chap. 4, as Thắm and her fellow workers, after their spontaneous strike actions had failed, considered engaging with law as a last resort. Nguyên herself is not a Communist Party member, yet she derives her judgement from the Party's political campaigns that she sees have laid the ground for one's legal and moral behaviour. She wrote this letter shortly after the Party Congresses took place at the local levels in Vietnam, which saw the passage of key development agendas and the election of new local leadership.

I quote here the hand-writing section of the letter in full to do justice to its extraordinary nature:

> During this time, all citizens and party members across the country, including Đồng Nai province, are following the law, self-educating and self-training according to the moral lessons of Hồ Chí Minh, in order to make certain achievements before the Party Congress at the local level. Unfortunately, there is an enterprise that *violates the law*, despite being awarded the title 'hero in the reform era' and having a Party cell. Within the party cell, there are party cadres that have *verbally abused and humiliated* employees. Yet those cadres are always nominated for reward and are holding the positions of the union chairman or vice chairman in the company. So, who will demand equality (*công bằng*) and legitimate rights and interests for employees?
>
> Once more, with all respect, I urge the leaders of all state agencies of Đồng Nai province to promptly intervene to save our lives. We are genuine employees who have no rights, lack equality, and experience a lot of coercion by the business.
>
> Because of the wish to demand equal rights and interests for employees, I have sent my petition letters, which have been handled by the state authorities and especially the labour inspectorate. However, those cadres only worked in a cosmetic manner and protected the business; they also forced me to sign a meeting minute in which I have to confirm that I will stop sending my complaints and denunciations. Such command has given the ground for the company to *punish and repress me in a brutal manner*.

> I am wondering if there is no justice (*công lý*) or equality in our lives, in our society. I guess that I might be *agonised and pushed until death* before my letters are resolved. [italics added]

This letter is an extraordinary manifestation of the call for labour rights combining Nguyên's knowledge of labour law and official rhetoric and fundamental moral principles. Her pitiful claim that employees 'have no rights' while experiencing 'a lot of coercion' implies a breach of both ethical and legal standards on the part of the business and indirectly, of the state, for condoning the business' conduct.

The combination of different rhetoric and reasoning in Nguyên's letter shows that law is the dominant, but not omnipotent, factor in shaping her consciousness. Similar to Thắm's published letter, Nguyên's letter also raises the abuse of legal rights and human dignity and passionately calls on the state for those rights to be protected. The difference is that, while Thắm derives her demands mostly from her and other workers' experiences on the shop floor, Nguyên arrives at her plea by extensively drawing upon political rhetoric which has been ironically betrayed by the people in high positions supposed to act upon its principles. As such, despite the legally adept complaint language in Nguyên's type-written letters, her appeal to justice is not so different from that of other ordinary workers: she also holds the state authorities accountable for the workers' plight and stretches the boundary of law and legal rights to push for an honouring of workplace ethics. More importantly, in connecting workers' grievances to (the lack of) justice and equality 'in our society,' Nguyên eloquently weds her aspiration for workplace ethics to the fundamentals of the Vietnamese state's socialist vision of equality and progress.

Mrs Nguyên's language of resistance contributes a Vietnamese case study to the existing debate on the role of legal discourse in social justice in American socio-legal scholarship. Central to this debate is whether legal discourse is useful to popular resistance and activism, or instead circumvents the types of claims and actions that people and activists can take in seeking redress and bringing about social change (McCann 1994; Lovell 2012; Albiston and Leachman 2015). George Lovell has refuted the negative proposition while revisiting this debate in his book on American citizens' complaint letters in the 1930s and 1940s. Lovell asserts that, while these citizens readily deploy discourse and language adopted from state law, the law does not 'set an outer limit on writers' demands' (p. 202). In fleshing out the underlying values of the letters, I concur with Lovell in his call for a revival of interest in legal discourse and resistance. The complaint writers in his study are found to either see law enforcement as illegitimate and unjust, or project their own views of justice as resistance to law's authority. These observations resonate with Nguyên's expanded demands in her typed and hand-written letters, which raise accusations about management's violation of workers' dignity and a call for equality in workplace relationships. If the American citizens employ extra-legal claims in the hope that the government officials will rule in their favour, Nguyên also hopes that her emotional pleas deserve more attention from the authority. Her alternative expressions of justice, based on lay morality and the state's socialist vision, complement and reinforce, rather than contest, the call for justice supposedly granted by law.

Nguyên after all remains a sole petitioner. Similar to other core workers, Nguyên has claimed to build rapport with her fellow workers by advising them about their legal rights and helping them to claim individual benefits. However, this has not sufficed to transform her own struggle into collective actions. The only part her co-workers were willing to play was to let Nguyên see their payslips and use them as evidence for the writing of the letter. For instance, her second denunciation letter mentions the names and incomes of two female workers, as well as her own, as examples of the company's unlawful wage policy. Apart from that, Nguyên has taken the path of collective petitioning on her own, being the only worker that signed and lodged the letters. She repeated that other workers were afraid of losing their jobs and facing managerial discipline. Nguyên revealed to me that, following her petitioning, the company manager and supervisor warned workers on the shop floor against talking or even 'coming close' (*tới gần*) to her. In one instance, a female fellow worker raised her voice about an unfair practice to the manager and was questioned whether Nguyên was implicated in her speaking. Her co-workers therefore would rather keep their silence and so keep them safe from further trouble.

In short, Nguyên's access to labour law and legal aid has confirmed her conviction that her struggle is legitimate and that her demands should, by law, be met. Her letters contain language derived from labour law, the Party's rhetoric, and a moral judgement of managerial conduct. In other words, law, morality, and political discourse interweave with each other in shaping her claims and expressions of injustice. It is her faith in legal justice and, more dimly, the ethics of state officials that underpin her ongoing struggle with a labour institution that has been notoriously skewed against Vietnamese workers' interests (Sidel 2008).

Small-Scale Mobilisation

Mr Anh also acted with law to demand workers' rights and interests, and he had a more positive experience in mobilising his fellow workers. Anh has been employed in a steel company in Hồ Chí Minh City (HCMC) for two years. Before moving to the city, he worked in a garment company in Đồng Nai Province. Like Nguyên, he had deployed legal weapons to solve his individual dispute with his previous employer, but managed to win his case.

His dispute with the previous company started when he refused to obey the orders of a female officer who was not in charge of supervising him. This female officer later arbitrarily accused Anh of threatening her to the human resource manager. Subsequently, the human resource manager transferred him from his manual task to an administrative position, which Anh sees as unsuitable to his skills and educational background. After his refusal of the transfer for this reason, Anh was ordered to sit in the security office doing nothing for the whole day, and was subject to strict surveillance. He appealed verbally and in writing to the union of the industrial zones, the Labour Federation, and his case was made known to a labour journalist. The journalist reported his story in detail, expressing the sympathetic attitudes of the Labour Federation, who hinted at intervening if the company management persisted in its discipline.[7]

After the publication of his case, the company management reassigned him to his previous position, yet put him under strict control. At the start of a work day, he received a task 'report,' which showed the number of tasks that he had to finish within a day. He said: 'It made me bored and angry' (Interview, 27 February 2015). Not long afterwards, he was dismissed after the New Year holidays. The company claimed that he took extra leave days without any notice. He did not dispute the company decision and quit the company.

In recounting his story, Anh told me: 'By law, an employer can sack an employee if the employee takes five days off in a month or 20 days off in a year, in an undisciplined way. That is not my case' (Interview, 27 February 2015). It was unclear to me whether Anh had a thorough understanding of labour law at the time he quit, but he recalled clearly his decision to sue his employer about 10 months later. With the LAC's assistance, he won the case and received full compensation from his employer, including wages for the days he was out of work, insurance benefits, and a two-month wage penalty. His successful litigation, with the assistance and moral support of the LAC lawyer, contributed to Anh's confidence in the enforcement of labour law. Anh joined the core workers' project shortly afterwards. Subsequently, he employed this experience and his legal knowledge to take forward a collective labour dispute.

The steel company, his new employer, used to be a state company and became a joint-stock company in the 2000s. The company however continued to apply the common minimum wage, which is the legal wage for state employees, rather than applying the minimum wage set for foreign and private business sectors. With consultation from the LAC, Anh learnt that such a wage policy is illegal and decided to act against the company management.

The following transcript from our interview summarises the situation of Anh's co-workers: 'You know, many workers have been employed for more than 10 years but their wages are very low, standing somewhere around 3 or 4 million dong' (Interview, 22 March 2015). His statement points to the imbalance between workers' long service to the company and the low wages they receive. Anh then went on: 'Those workers don't know about labour law and have so far accepted the amount given by the company' (Interview, 22 March 2015). He attributes the disadvantageous position of his co-workers to their lack of legal knowledge and their passive compliance towards the company's wage policy. He seems to see the issue as their ignorance rather than the company's malpractice, and, as such, has decided to embark on his resistance by taking his time to inform other workers about their legal rights.

Apart from his legal knowledge, there is another reason concerning workers' livelihoods that explains Anh's decision to initiate workers' actions:

> I stand up [against the company] since I know the law and I am not afraid of being sacked. It is possible that the company management will sack me if I sue them. But I am not so needy or desperate for this job. If I quit this job, I can find a new job at some other place. Other workers are different: They are older than me and moving jobs is difficult, so they need to attach themselves to this company. (Interview, 27 February 2015)

Anh's explanation sees other workers' acceptance of the company's pay rate as relating to job security and seniority. He understands that losing one's job is a possible outcome when one resists, and realises that his flexibility will allow him to overcome such a scenario better than other workers. However, the extract does not indicate a trade-off between resistance and one's own livelihood. Instead, it shows that workers' needs and lawful rights should be fulfilled without them falling into exploitative relationships with the company management.

As I mentioned in a previous section, core workers are aware that taking strike action is illegal, and Anh is no exception. He even went further in articulating his attitudinal change towards strikes as a result of the legal training: 'Before I learned about the law, I thought that going on strike is right. Later I knew that it is wrong, because it goes against procedures.' His attitude subsequently influenced his plan to act:

> After I talked to my fellow workers about the company's wage policy, they really wanted to go on strike but I talked them out of doing so. I told them, 'I will rise up (*đứng ra*) and work out the paperwork and procedure [to sue the company].' I told them to wait until after the Lunar New Year. Then, if the company did not raise our wages, I would ask for some advice and write the complaint letter. (Interview, 27 February 2015)

The Lunar New Year holiday had passed when I had this conversation with Anh in 2015. What he meant in his conversation with his fellow workers was that they should wait until receiving their first payslips after the holiday. Anh's discouragement of striking can be seen as a result of both his legal understanding and his moral integrity. In his view, it is problematic to condone illegal reaction, or act in an illegal manner, in response to unfair conduct. He therefore believes that the rightfulness of workers' resistance will stand them in good stead in their pursuits, despite being aware that the complaint process will take a long time:

> I understand that the time taken for the authority to address our letters is long and is a *disadvantage* to employees. For instance, if I write the letter and lodge it at the end of March, it may not be addressed until May. However, we have to accept that. (Interview, 27 February 2015)

Anh's critical judgement of the lengthy legal process does not affect his legal compliance. Consequently, his further actions, including mobilising the support of his fellow workers, were taken within the administrative channel sanctioned by the Labour Code.

After our conversation, there was some delay in the writing of the complaint letter, due to the company management's verbal promise to raise workers' wages following the voicing of their concerns and queries. The complaint process did not start until October 2015, when Anh and 14 fellow workers working in the same group and shift together signed and lodged a complaint letter to the company management. Of course, Anh's mobilisation of others was not without challenges. Anh told me how he took his time to get other workers to his side and that it only worked with workers who 'are not afraid [of management's threat and retaliation]' (*không sợ*) (Interview, 14 January 2016). There were hundreds of workers in other groups and shifts that Anh was unable to mobilise or even approach.

The workers' letter reads:

> We are a collective of workers in company X, together writing this letter to request the company management consider raising the basic wages for workers according to the Government's regional minimum wage regulations. Our understanding is that the regional minimum wage for HCMC is 3.100.000 dong. If employees have manual skills and have worked for a long time, their wages should be at least 7 percent above the minimum wage. However the basic wages of many workers like us are currently below this level.
>
> The Government decree number 103/2014 on 11/11/2014 has been in effect since 1/1/2015, but up until now the company has not raised basic wages for workers. Therefore, the contribution towards our social insurance based on such wages is too low and does not guarantee the rights and interests of employees.
>
> With due respect, we request the company management to consider this issue, otherwise we have no choice but to send our letter to the state agencies.

Similar to Mrs Nguyên's letters, this letter refers to the government policy and employs legal reasoning to justify workers' demands. As this letter is directed at the company management, it reads more like a gentle request and reminder rather than containing a strong confrontational language. The subsequent inaction and silence from the management saw these 14 workers send their complaint to the labour inspector of the Department of Labour in HCMC. I did not get to see the second letter, but, according to Anh, the content of both the letters is the same. The legal language employed in their collective request letter demonstrates Anh and his fellow workers' belief in law as a potential bargaining tool vis-à-vis the management, and also in the state as a guarantor of their legal rights amid the management's arbitrary conduct.

So far, the resistance narratives of core workers have brought to life aspects of labour law that are not present or clearly articulated in the narratives of ordinary workers. In all of them, the legal knowledge they have obtained leads them to understand existing abuses and exploitation as legal problems and be aware of their right to contest this under the law. Their accounts suggest the potential of law and workers' access to law and legal aid to achieve social change, specifically, to alter managerial practices and improve workers' situations. However, different from Lê, Anh and Nguyên are not shy about exposing themselves and their intent in acting against the management. Lê and Nguyên both have family commitments, while Anh does not, but Nguyên's and Anh's desire for justice has overridden their worry about managerial retaliation and surveillance. The resistance of Anh and Nguyên further challenges the view that workers' pursuit of individual rights and the gaining of individual redress deter them from taking actions that benefit workers as a collective. These workers' individual actions do not stop them from acting on behalf of, or mobilising, others to demand better wage and benefits. Of these three workers, Anh has been the most successful in raising his fellow workers' awareness of the company's legal violations and mobilising them to act. Yet, while Lê has survived his covert resistance without negative reactions from the management, the other two have been subjected to managerial discipline and mistreatment following their overt actions.

Dispute Resolution and the Formation of Critical Consent

By submitting themselves to the law and deferring to its authority, core workers at the same time get caught in rules and practices that oftentimes work against their interests. Notable studies on labour resistance in China and Vietnam have presented evidence of weak law enforcement by labour institutions and the courts, leading workers to shift from arbitration and litigation to street actions or to simply give up on their cases (Lee 2007, p. 177; Trần 2013, pp. 279–280). In more details, Gallagher (2006) shows that legal aid plaintiffs in her study exhibit a legal consciousness of 'informed disenchantment,' a declining trust in legal institutions for their complex nature and failure to deliver redress. It is evident that law can contribute to workers' resistance in varying ways, and is not always conducive to attaining justice for the workers.

In this section I investigate the process of resolution and the outcomes of Nguyên's and Anh's petitioning. Do these workers' experiences in engaging with the system confirm their expectations in the legal system or lead them to change their tactics? In order to fully understand these workers' legal consciousness, it is necessary to look beyond their actions and the meaning of their writing towards the process of resolution and what they realise or obtain from their resistance. A part of this issue has appeared briefly in Nguyên's hand-written letter mentioned before; this section will show in detail the reason for her frustration and grief expressed in the letter.

Overwhelmed by the Powerful

After Nguyên's first complaint letter, the labour inspectors held a resolution meeting with her and the company management. Despite the collective nature of her complaints, she was the only worker invited to the meeting as the person who lodged and signed the letter. She complained to me about participation in the meeting: 'There is no impartiality for employees. The person representing the company union at the meeting is the union chairman who is also the vice manager. How can the vice manager act as an employee representative?' (Interview, 1 February 2015). A union official of the provincial Labour Federation was also present, but only to take notes. During the meeting, she recalled how the labour inspectors skirted her concerns, put psychological pressure upon her, and tended to talk in favour of the company management. The patron-client relation between the labour inspectors and the management was clear to her as they had lunch together after the resolution meeting. She also suspected that the chief inspector had notified the management of her complaints before the meeting, as the company asked her to withdraw her petition before the meeting took place.

The more this woman understands the function of labour law and its meaning concerning workers' benefits, the more frustrated she becomes concerning its implementation. Following the resolution meeting, the labour inspector sent a formal letter of response to her, indicating that the company was found to be wrong in two out of the five issues being raised. Yet no punitive measures nor follow-up investigation was outlined. As she clarified to me, the company still had not addressed these two problems and the lack of transparency still persists in its wage and bonus payment. She remained further subordinated to the management and labour authority precisely by conforming to the ideals of the law and its institutions.

As briefly mentioned earlier, Nguyên's language in judging the company's conduct is strong and straightforward with a clear awareness of workers' legal rights and injustices, expressed in phrases like 'against the law/legal regulations,' 'violate the law,' and 'rampantly "steal" employees' money.' Such language stands in contrast to the formalistic side-stepping tone of the labour inspector's response letter to her: 'The company's conduct is not yet right/appropriate according to the regulations'; 'the chief inspector requested the company manager to stop/do this'; and 'the inspection team requested the company to check the issue and coordinate with the company union to respond with clarity to employees.'

The inspector's language is as soft as the investigation carried out within the company during the time of the complaint resolution. For instance, two of the complaints raised in the letter concern the premium overtime rates that are not paid and how workers are coerced into working overtime. The inspector reported that the company applied premium rates at the same rates as were stipulated. Regarding the second issue, the inspector responded: 'After we checked and talked directly to several employees, we found no sign of the company's coercion.' In our conversation, I shared with Nguyên the speculation that the 'several employees' that the inspector talked to had either been silenced through intimidation or were pre-selected by the company management. Overall, in response to her five complaints, the inspector found one violation in relation to employees' social insurance and assured her that the general manager had been 'requested' to correct the company's wrongdoing. This refusal to properly address workers' concerns and the continual siding with management are illustrative of the weak regulation of labour laws, where the administration of the law does not provide fairness but rather the protection of a company's wrongful practices. Nguyên's expression of her distrust is thus a rejection of authoritative claims towards law (Lovell 2012, p. 143) that purport to generate her compromises and silence.

Throughout her resistance and experience with labour law, Nguyên has developed a form of legal consciousness which I call 'critical consent,' that is, an adherence to the ideals and principles of law coupled with an acute recognition of its practical limitations. The word 'consent' incorporates what Ewick and Silbey (1992, p. 747) describe as acts of deference to legal procedures and authority, but speaks more broadly to an individual's beliefs in what is right or wrong according to the law. My understanding of consent here is also different from the notion widely used in the literature on labour process, where consent is an outcome of managerial coercion and a threat to extract labour and elicit obedience (Burawoy 1979; Burawoy and Wright 1990). Nguyên's consent comes out of her access to legal training and is reinforced through her experiences and trust in legal aid. Her consent to the law becomes a major thread in her resistance against low pay, disrespect, and maltreatment.

Nguyên's situation bears some resemblance to the 'informed disenchantment' of litigant workers in China (Gallagher 2006), who approach the legal system with a high expectation of justice yet are later let down in their actual experiences. However, while 'informed disenchantment' refers to the workers' sense of personal efficacy as they navigate the legal system (Gallagher 2006, p. 785), the notion of 'critical consent' refers more broadly to workers' views of how law should work in shaping the behaviour of workers, management, unions, and the state. The term 'critical' highlights core workers' evaluation as to how and why the implementation of law is not impartial and just, rather than their feeling of disappointment after the legal procedure did not function as was expected. Such evaluation results in the statement of a need for a moral role to be taken up by the agencies and actors in charge of legal implementation.

As detailed earlier, her frustration with the resolution and its outcomes did not stop her from pursuing her case by lodging the second denunciation letter. Nonetheless, Nguyên was also thinking of other extra-legal strategies, not because she had given up her consent to law, but because of the potential for other strategies to amplify her call for justice. In our conversation, she kept mentioning the case of female worker Thắm, whose letter to the VGCL Chairman made the headlines, as I discussed in Chap. 3. She hinted at her intention to appeal to the Chairman if the company's violations persisted. She also tried to contact two labour journalists in the hope that media reports would put further pressure on management to change their behaviour. While one labour journalist became silent after a few initial correspondences, the other journalist advised her to seek assistance at the legal aid centre of the *Labour* newspaper in HCMC. Nguyên also hopes that her letter might reach a good-hearted official who would take her complaints seriously and deal with the company's conduct thoroughly. Nguyên herself was in touch with one such union official a few years ago. When I visited her at her unit in early 2016, she recalled one of the announcements that this official had made on television when he ran for a seat in the provincial People's Council, that he would 'give his whole-hearted dedication to caring for employees' lives.' Touched by his words, Nguyên made contact with him and shared with him what she faced and endured at work. She understands that the official could not intervene in her case, yet shows appreciation for his television promise which gave her mental support during the early days of her petitioning.

For the past two years, at each stage of her resistance journey, Nguyên has faced and will face a personal choice to either continue working at ease and staying silent or raising her voice and risk disciplinary action. To her, this petitioning journey is both a legal and moral battle against abuse and exploitation:

> Other workers told me that if I left the company, the management would be very happy but they would suffer. I know the law and I dare to speak up; I am the only one among 700 workers. I didn't give up because I know there are people more miserable than me. I am a core worker belonging to the labour federation so I'm not afraid, and the company can't sack me. (Interview, 1 February 2015)

The transcript is telling in two regards. First, Nguyên is proud of being a core worker, and of her legal understanding, which she thinks has been a 'shield' for her to remain in the job. Had the management treated her as an ordinary worker, who is unaware of labour law, they might have found some way to sack her and got away with their illegal dismissal. Nguyên told me: 'They [the management] should think twice about getting rid of me. If I bring them to the court, the case would badly affect their reputation and their title [the "labour hero" title granted by the state]' (Interview, 1 February 2015). Second, her access to law imbues in her the sense of responsibility and courage to speak up against unfair practices, which is also bolstered by her emotional binding with fellow workers. I believe that, in the previous transcript, Nguyên wanted to highlight that she is one of those suffering rather than setting herself apart from her fellow workers. It seems to me that, eventually, her deployment and exhaustion of the legal weapon all contributed to her moral cause of making workers' lives, including hers as a single mother, less miserable.

Justice Can Be Done

While the resolution of Nguyên's complaints was mishandled through the patron-client network between the management and labour authority, Anh's letter resulted in management's surveillance of him and ongoing evasive tactics. Anh faced strict discipline at work after the lodgement of the complaint letter. In October 2015, he took a day off from work without asking for managerial permission. The management later called him in to a meeting with the human resource manager and the union chairman. He recalled:

> They discussed with me three options. First, I could write a resignation letter of my own accord. Second, the company would unilaterally terminate my contract with a 30-day advance notice. Third, the company would sack me. Given my mistake [of taking a day off without permission], are they right in giving me those options? (Interview, 28 December 2015)

The rhetorical question he raised to me illustrates that legal provisions become a benchmark for him to judge the management's conscience and conduct. Following the meeting, Anh did not dispute any of the management's proposals and quit his job. Three weeks later, in mid-December 2015, someone from the company came to his place to re-employ him,[8] to which Anh finally agreed. The company also paid him compensation for the number of days he was out of work, and an extra two month's wages.

During the time Anh was out of work, the labour inspectors had a meeting with the management in regard to the complaint letter but without any worker participation. After that, the management held individual meetings with all workers who had signed the letter, excluding Anh. The management asked these workers to sign an agreement accepting wage increases[9] starting on 1 January 2016. Anh was unhappy that his fellow workers followed the management's order, but it was too late for him to intervene in the outcome. Again, in Anh's view, his fellow workers' passive consent to the management order is to be blamed for the failure of workers to successfully resolve wage issues with the management:

> I wasn't there to tell other workers not to agree to what the management told them, and therefore they all accepted it. If I were to be called upon to the meeting, I wouldn't agree with the management. I would present to them the government decree. You know, the company kept saying to employees that its business has difficulties, but *employees' lives are also*

difficult. There are people employed for more than 10 years but their wage level is really low [italics added]. (Interview, 14 January 2016)

Again, Anh firmly believes that he is able to employ the legal regulations as buffers against the company's excuse for its legal non-compliance. He seems to expect that his legal language is weighty enough for the management to attend to his voice and rectify their conduct. Eventually, Anh also criticises the lack of morality on the part of the management: the management's excuse for its evasion of the law also means an ignorance of their moral obligations to workers' lives. Here his general framing of workers' wages as low is quite similar to the justification given by ordinary respondent workers and letter writers. It represents a subjective and comparative judgement of an income level based on workers' seniority and their working lives at large. Broadly speaking, Anh's account suggests that the labour-management relationship should function on the basis of both legal and moral considerations.

Anh's experiences with the law in his individual and collective resistance have been more positive than Nguyên's experiences, though at the same time he confronted abuse and unfair discipline from both his bosses. First, Anh won the lawsuit against illegal dismissal. Second, while his mobilisation through complaint writing led him to be dismissed, Anh also thought that his letter and his legal knowledge were the reasons for the management's re-employment of him. He kept mentioning to me the necessity of knowing and keeping up to date with government decrees and legal amendments, as this allows him to effectively 'talk' (*nói chuyện*) with the management.

Anh's legal consciousness can also be characterised as one of critical consent, as he understands the benefits and limitations of law in workers' pursuits of justice. Up until this point, except for his previous complaint about the lengthy time of petitioning, to Anh, the practices of law when needed had reenforced his position vis-à-vis the management and been on the side of the workers. While the letter that he convinced other workers to lodge relies exclusively on a legalistic mode of reasoning, he is well aware of the moral implications behind this legality. The narratives that surround his bold actions have effectively brought to life the minimum wage principle that provides for a guarantee of employees' welfare written within the Labour Code.

Yet, after the Lunar New Year 2016, Anh and more than 50 other workers were dismissed. The reason given was that the company was undergoing restructuring and had to reduce its staff. In Anh's case, however, the company dismissed him on the ground that he had taken two weeks' leave without permission and thus violated the company regulations. In fact, Anh did ask his employer for permission to take leave in order to take care of his sick father, but his request had been rejected. Anh knew that the company's decision to sack him bypassed the legal procedure, which designates that an employer who wants to sack an employee on a disciplinary ground must call the employee to a meeting to consider his/her case before handing down the dismissal. Having known that, Anh decided not to dispute the company's decision and quit. Yet this does not mean that he gave up on making claims for his rights. About six months later, he took the company to the court with the LAC's assistance and won a compensation of more than 50 million dong. Anh afterwards did not seek further factory work and instead turned to some unstable casual jobs to get by.

Conclusion

This chapter has analysed the way legal aid contributes to labour resistance through the cases of core workers. It draws attention to the role of legal aid in promoting workers' rights and interests, which has rarely received adequate discussion in studies of labour relations in Vietnam. While the success of the LAC in demanding redress for the workers, as evidenced in this chapter, has been mixed, it is undeniable that it has raised workers' awareness of legal violations and enabled or facilitated their acts of resistance. At the same time, the evidence also cautions against a unilinear approach towards legal aid and workers' collective attempts to stand up for their rights, considering the surveillance, threat, and potential retaliation faced by core workers and their co-workers.

Core workers' roles as both legal aid providers and beneficiaries have contributed to shaping their views concerning labour law, justice, and how to demand justice for themselves and fellow workers. The case studies of three core workers touch on the different experiences and positions of these workers within their workplaces, where they have encountered legal violations and labour disputes. In putting their legal knowledge and awareness into practice, these core workers have either assisted with collective letter writing or been directly involved in writing complaints. Unlike other workers discussed in Chaps. 3 and 4 who only refer to labour law in sweeping terms, the core workers actively engage with legal procedures, terms, and regulations in articulating their views of the workplace relationship and in responding to their grievances. These legal regulations underpin core workers' judgements of what is right and wrong, what is fair and unfair in employers' and workers' behaviour, and allow them to hold managers and state authorities accountable for illegal conduct. Core workers' involvement in legal aid activities endows in them a belief in a rightful struggle and the courage to stand up against injustice.

Many accounts expressed by the core workers concur with existing studies that cast doubts on the role of law in advocating for labour rights in authoritarian contexts, due to the legal constraints placed upon the collective actions of workers and labour activists. These scholars argue that law-based actions fail to generate pursuit of broader labour rights beyond what have been granted in the law. In addition, state legislation also places restrictions on the types of claims that workers and activists can make and thus outlaws demands or actions that contravene its content or procedure. Yet, this chapter also acknowledges that state law has become a benchmark for core workers to judge and identify exploitative conduct, and has offered a potential pathway for them to break their silence. Aside from the outcomes or effectiveness of their actions, what is important is that the law does not constrain labour resistance per se but influences the way in which workers choose to act against injustice. I stress that, as can be seen from the core workers' narratives, law does not necessarily alter, challenge, or negate existing social values and norms, such as those that concern mutual respect, reciprocal obligations, and the socialist ideals of equality. Their language of resistance does not stop at a call for a proper implementation of law, but also brings out the moral values imbued in management's legal obligations and extends the legal rights claim to assert a broader call for social justice.

The investigation of Anh's and Nguyên's experiences with dispute resolution following their resistance sheds light on the complexity of core workers' legal consciousness. Their critical consent denotes an adherence to law's rules, regulations, and principles, as well as recognition of its weaknesses in protecting workers' rights and interests. Their individual actions, and the way they interact with other workers, further suggest that legal consciousness nurtures rather than constrains their sense of class consciousness. The two case studies covered here also demonstrate the potential of legal aid in enabling workers' collective mobilisation, rather than just their individual pursuits of justice.

Notes

1. This was formerly a state-owned company which underwent equitisation, or partial privatisation, as the Vietnamese state restructures its economy.
2. Nguyên did not proactively approach the journalist but was introduced to him when he planned to report on workers' mistreatment cases.
3. The criteria for this title are outlined in the Prime Minister's decision 38/1999/QD-TTg, and include a business' contribution to the local, sectoral, and national economic development; technological development and innovation; human resource and capital development; conformity with the Party agenda and state legislation; and property protection.
4. The company issued a list detailing the amount of reward that each worker would receive, and asked him/her to sign on that list. This was done *before* the actual payment.
5. Here she speculates that the cadres have taken workers' bonuses to the bank to earn interest.
6. Despite being a one-party authoritarian regime, the term democracy (*dân chủ*) is not alien to the Communist Party's rhetoric and document, especially those concerning the promotion of people's participation in local civil affairs.
7. I have withheld the reference to the news to protect Anh's identity.
8. The company's efforts to re-employ Anh took me by surprise. Anh did not know exactly why: 'I don't know how or why the company knew that it was in the wrong. Maybe because the company was afraid that I would later take it to the court. It could be because of our petition letters. Maybe the labour bureau called the company and asked about me. The district labour bureau has known me well through my legal aid to other workers' (Interview, 14 January 2016).
9. Anh did not tell me whether such increases would lift their wages up to the levels prescribed in the government guidelines.

References

Albiston, C. R. & Leachman, G. M. (2015). Law as an Instrument of Social Change. In J.D. Wright. *International Encyclopedia of The Social & Behavioral Sciences* (2nd ed.). Oxford: Elsevier.

Burawoy, M. & Wright, E. O. (1990). Coercion and Consent in Contested Exchanges. *Politics & Society*, 18 (2), 251–266.

Burawoy, M. (1979). *Manufacturing Consent: Changes in the Labour Process under Monopoly Capitalism*. Chicago & London: The University of Chicago Press.

Ewick, P. & Silbey, S. (1992). Conformity, Contestation and Resistance: An Account of Legal Consciousness. *New England Law Review*, 26, 731–749.

Gallagher, M. (2006). Mobilizing the Law in China: 'Informed Disenchantment' and the Development of Legal Consciousness. *Law & Society Review*, 40 (4), 783–816.
Gammeltoft, T. M. (2014). *Haunting Images: A Cultural Account of Selective Reproduction in Vietnam*. Berkeley: University of California Press.
Lee, C. K. (2007). *Against the Law: Labor Protests in China's Rustbelt and Sunbelt*. Berkeley, Los Angeles & London: University of California Press.
Lovell, G. (2012) *This is Not Civil Rights: Discovering Rights Talk in 1939 America*. Chicago: The University of Chicago Press.
McCann, M. (1994). *Rights at Work: Pay Equity Reform and the Politics of Legal Mobilization*. Chicago & London: The University of Chicago Press.
Merry, S. E. (2006). *Human Rights and Gender Violence: Translating International Law into Local Justice*. Chicago & London: The University of Chicago Press.
O'Brien, K. & Li, L. (2006). *Rightful Resistance in Rural China*. Cambridge: Cambridge University Press.
Prime Minister of Vietnam (1999). Decision 38/1999/QD-TTg on the targets and criteria of the title Labour hero and Hero of the people's armed forces in the reform era.
Sidel, M. (2008). *Law and Society in Vietnam: The Transition from Socialism in Comparative Perspective*. Cambridge & New York: Cambridge University Press.
Trần, A. N. (2013). *Ties that Bind: Cultural Identity, Class, and Law in Vietnam's Labor Resistance*. Ithaca: Cornell Southeast Asia Program Publications.

CHAPTER 7

Conclusion

This book has captured the extent to which values, language, and practices derived from labour law contribute to shaping Vietnamese workers' views of workplace relations and providing justifications for their resistance. The main objective has been to examine, through workers' stories, how values embedded in the labour law regime interact with other values and practices that come from outside labour law, and drawing attention to the varying ways in which labour law contributes to their quest for workplace justice. In this conclusion, I will first revisit existing scholarship on law and popular resistance in Vietnam and, comparatively, China, before explicating the socio-legal approach taken in this book and summarising its key findings.

In studies of social disputes and resistance in post-socialist China and Vietnam, three patterns can be identified with regard to citizens' use of law in their pursuits of justice. I have concentrated on the way citizens articulate their problems and frame their demands in relation to state law, rather than on the procedural aspects of their actions, and whether they fall within or outside legal mechanisms. In this categorisation, the first pattern is acting 'within law,' with people eagerly deploying legal language and drawing on laws and regulations to justify their claims against officials' abusive and corrupt conduct. This pattern can be seen to incorporate behaviour termed 'rightful resistance,' thanks to the state's political propaganda and propaganda promoting the rule of law following economic reform (O'Brien and Li 2006; Pei 2010; Diamant et al. 2005; Labbé

T. P. Nguyen, *Workplace Justice*, Critical Studies of the Asia-Pacific,
https://doi.org/10.1007/978-981-13-3116-9_7

2011; Kerkvliet 2014). Aggrieved citizens' mobilisation of laws, alongside official state rhetoric, suggests a development of 'rights consciousness' (O'Brien and Li 2006, p. 7), which has been considered a hallmark of social and political change in closed and repressive political settings.

The second pattern involves resisting 'with law' and using law in an instrumental way, whereby people turn to legal language not to condemn particular illegal actions or call for stringent law enforcement, but to convey an alternative set of values and judgements. As demonstrated in Thireau and Hua's study of Chinese workers' complaint letters (2003), through references to 'law' or 'Labour Law,' complainants wish to amplify an appeal to justice premised on ethical norms and behaviour (pp. 97–99). Law is invoked to 'argue that a given threshold between the acceptable and the unacceptable, the tolerable and the intolerable, has been crossed' (p. 98). Similar to rightful resisters, the aggrieved workers in this study also pushed for state agencies' intervention, but they did so on the basis of shared views of fairness rather than on an endorsement of legal rights. From an analytical point of view, this study of workers' complaint letters also cautions against equating legal language with a demand for legal rights and, relatedly, legal rights consciousness.

The third pattern identified in the scholarship is acting 'against' law, which involves people challenging or defying legal regulations in their claim-making. This type of resistance implies a contradiction between regulations and practices associated with state laws and people's views and ideas of justice. Collective action against the expropriation of land, which is among the most common type of disputes in post-socialist Vietnam and China, dominates this form of resistance. Contesting villagers have framed their claims to retain the land based on their spiritual and emotional attachment to it (Gillespie 2011; Kerkvliet 2014), or in terms of a collective entitlement and persistence of their livelihoods (Hsing 2010; Sargeson 2012). These claims are a rejection of the way in which laws are used and abused by the state in favour of private investors, and of official rhetoric that associate law with justice and legitimacy. Other studies of disruptive actions by wage claimants and construction workers in China (He et al. 2013; Pun 2016) likewise suggest that the claimants' view of fair pay in exchange for their labour plays out strongly in their protests and conversations with government officials. Of course, the line between these patterns of acting with, within, and against the law can be blurred: disputes that incorporate rightful claims at the start can shift towards claims that critique and reject law's authority. Studies of popular resistance in both

China and Vietnam demonstrate that the power and relevance of law in society is subject to people's experiences in political encounters or commonplace contexts (Merry 1990; Ewick and Silbey 1998; Engel 1998). Their use or avoidance of law and its institutions is not just determined by how they view and perceive law, but also by the way in which they experience other social institutions, norms, relationships, and practices.

The first two patterns of acting, with and within law, are found among the workers covered in this study. It is more difficult to conclude about workers' resistance against the law, given the overlap between law and non-legal sets of values underpinning workers' pleas and demands. Indeed, my objective of evaluating the role and meaning of law in resistance cannot be adequately fulfilled by treating law merely as a set of written rules acting upon society. Instead, law provides one of the cultural resources and schemas that shape social behaviour, interactions, and individuals' consciousness. Throughout the explication of workers' written and verbal accounts, I have analysed labour law as a combination of (1) the labour law regime, that is, legal institutions and processes set out in the Labour Code; state policies and regulations associated with the Code; and measures, such as the establishment of strike action teams and legal aid activities, introduced by the state to enhance implementation of the Code and associated policies and regulations; (2) the language used in the Code and other aspects of the labour law regime, and the values and understandings embedded in it; and (3) the practices through which the Code and associated state policies and regulations are implemented (or not implemented) by officials, factory managers, and others. This conceptualisation of law allows me to grasp how meanings, values, and practices of law unfold in workers' experiences on the factory floor in the lead-up to their action and in their aspirations for justice. It also overcomes the limitations within labour resistance studies which, inspired by political economy and moral economy approaches, downplay the enabling effects of law on workers' struggles for their rights or pay little attention to the role of law in shaping individuals' views of justice.

Informed by the socio-legal inquiries that look at people's disputing behaviours, and their legal consciousness, this book takes a close look at workers' workplace and social experiences, lay language and interpretations, and cases of both deployment and avoidance of law. These include events, incidents, and particularly grievances prior to workers' acts of resistance, as well as workers' views and perceptions of law throughout their recounting and interpretations of their experiences. From an analysis of selected case studies in Đồng Nai, the chapters demonstrate that labour law is only one factor shaping workers' articulation of what is fair and unfair, as it is also one aspect of what generates their resistance to injustice. The way workers turn (or do not turn) to labour law depends on their perceptions of the relationship between the law and the morality of workplace behaviour. These perceptions, in turn, are constructed through their experiences on both the shop floor and with legal institutions and processes, and are shaped also by socialist ideology and long-standing cultural norms. While I do not attempt to make generalised statements on the experiences of workers in other industrial regions in Vietnam, the struggle of workers to be paid reasonably and treated fairly, as discussed so far in this study, reflects many other struggles elsewhere in the country.

An empirically oriented and interpretative approach is particularly fruitful in capturing the complex, varying, and multi-faceted nature of workers' consciousness. Workers' retelling of shop floor interactions, their justifications for strike actions, their complaint letters and petitions, and their accounts of dispute resolution paint intricate pictures of desperation and hope, rights violation and rights claims, courage and disappointment, obedience and resistance. Lacking a representative trade union and abandoned by the state that claims to serve their interests, Vietnamese workers have struggled to assert their voices and improve their conditions through ways that can put their employment and income at risk. Most of the workers I engaged with went through a process of 'naming' and 'blaming' of what is unfair and problematic, and about a third also took action to claim their rights or what they felt they deserved. In their stories, labour law matters in different ways: at times it entrenches workers' suffering and deters them from resisting; at other times it enables them to overcome their silence and offers a rhetorical tool for them to have their pleas heard. While many workers do not use the labour law regime to seek justice, others make full use of it and are able to evaluate its utility.

The broader literature on law and society in post-socialist regimes tends to treat law and other institutions and sets of moral norms and precepts as oppositional, conflicting, or separate from each other (see, e.g., Phạm 2005; Gillespie and Nicholson 2005; Koh 2007; Yang and van der Wal 2014; He and Feng 2016). In these works, morality is associated with traditional norms and cultural beliefs that have shaped the functioning of politics and society throughout their history of development. State laws, which emerge during the course of economic transition, bring with them new rules, ideas, and thinking that are not compatible or clash with pre-existing social norms and behaviour. As with the case of other Southeast Asian countries, the tendency of individuals to follow and invoke traditional norms and thinking at times reflects a form of resistance against formal legality (Chua and Engel 2015, p. 213)

Contemporary Vietnamese society, in particular, has seen a limited penetration of state laws. Despite a rather comprehensive legal reform and system developed since the 1990s, interactions between and within state and society are still heavily shaped by customary norms, precepts, and informal practices: from patron-client networks between business and the state, to local government's policy implementation and the courts' handling of disputes. Labour relations are no exception: despite the state and VGCL's rhetoric of promoting legal compliance and legal understanding, in their actual practice of settling labour disputes, such as strikes, local governments and unions have often deployed a verbal appeal to sentiment to seek compromise between disputing parties. In addition, a conflictual relationship between law and morality is evidenced through numerous protests and petitioning in Vietnam where, as in China, disadvantaged people contest, reject, or bypass the letter of the law and invoke moral justifications for their claims and demands. In a similar vein, the ways in which disadvantaged people appeal to the state also illustrate the eminence of the state's moral obligations embedded in socialist propaganda. Little is known, though, about how the Constitution or constitutional values penetrate social relations and state-society interactions in Vietnam.

While acknowledging the eminence of moral norms, this book does not treat law and morality as always separate or oppositional, but instead posits that their relationship is fluid and complex. Such relationships manifest in the varied ways in which factory workers justify their grievances and articulate their desire for fairness. In the following paragraphs I will unpack this relationship while summarising three focal issues explored throughout the chapters.

The first issue concerns the way in which workers make sense of their relationship with management, their workplace problems, and the role of the state and unions. Most of the workers interviewed, as well as those who wrote complaints, perceive this relationship in moral terms: they expect management to respond to workers' living needs and, when it comes to remuneration, to treat them in a fair and reciprocal manner. Their ethics and expectations are similar to the moral economy of peasants in pre-capitalist societies and the state workers employed in the socialist era. Only a minority of letter writers and the core workers evaluate employment relationships based on their understanding of labour law and expect management to fulfil their legal obligations to workers.

These different constructions of labour relations are accompanied by different framings of workplace problems. My analysis of interviews and letters reveal common problems and grievances concerning unfair and low wages, excessive working hours, discipline, coercion, and abuse of female workers' rights and workers' dignity, and problematic bonus distribution. Workers most commonly describe these practices as unjust, but without referring to law. Instead, for example, they complain about immoral behaviour on the part of management, the uneven implementation of wage rises, management's ignorance and their pursuit of personal interests, unequal treatment between workers in different sectors, and dismissal when business is slack. They perceive their situations as 'unfair,' or 'unbearable,' or their wage rise as 'unreasonable,' and complain at length about past experiences of coercion, harsh discipline, and punishment. From an outsider's point of view, workers' accounts reveal management's evasion and/or violations of the Labour Code, but the workers themselves do not articulate their sufferings as a violation of the Code and, therefore, as stemming from illegal practices. In calling attention to their problems, workers refer to a combination of their material needs, their skills and productivity, their emotional bonds with and contribution to the business, and the treatment they deserve (but do not receive) as dignified human beings.

Only a minority of letter writers and the core workers interpret their grievances through the lens of labour law. They are able to point out what is problematic in management conduct from their varying understandings of the law. In both an explicit and indirect manner, they bring in legal terms and regulations and, where possible, provide evidence to show that the management have contravened them. They perceive their situations as 'illegal,' or 'against the law,' and desire the legal protection of workers' 'rights and interests.' In an exceptional case, the complaint letter of Mrs Nguyên further calls for an implementation of workplace democracy, an entitlement under the Labour Code, which allows workers to raise their voices and monitor management's conduct. At the same time, core workers understand that workers' grievances are also outcomes of management's lack of care and their failure to meet their moral obligations to workers.

The way in which workers relate to the state and official unions is best seen in their appeal to these institutions, either in going on strike or in lodging their complaints and petitions. In this market regime, workers do not hold the state directly accountable for their problems. They nonetheless still believe that state and union officials, as those endowed with power and authority, are able to circumscribe managerial power and save workers from their suffering. Their appeal to compassion and sentiment is influenced by the state's socialist ideology, specifically its promise to care for the welfare of the Vietnamese working class and its projection of an image of the socialist society as 'rich, equal, democratic and civilised.' However, as seen in the cases of the food processing workers discussed in Chap. 3 and Nguyên's resistance in Chap. 6, the state's and union's failure to deliver justice is sometimes deemed a problem of moral integrity and can erode workers' trust in those institutions.

My second set of findings address the question of how workers use the language of labour law to voice their grievances and make claims. Most of the workers interviewed and those who lodged their complaints show a general understanding of the terms and regulations set out in the Labour Code and government policy concerning workers' wages, overtime, working conditions, and bonuses. They commonly couch their understanding of these terms and regulations in lay language such as 'raising wages twice,' or a rough estimation of working hours. The specific term, 'rights and interests,' found in the Labour Code, is often used to justify workers' strike actions and appeals to the state and management. Both lay language and legal terms are, however, used primarily to amplify moral judgements embodying the norms of reciprocity, subsistence, and fair treatment, as mentioned earlier. In comparison, their use of law is very similar to that of Chinese workers who lodged their complaints at the Letters and Visits offices in the study by Thireau and Hua (2003) and the Chinese migrant workers in the construction industry, who were the subject of research by Pun (2016). A few workers who lodged their complaints at the union offices in Chap. 4 derive their judgements of management's immoral conduct from their understanding of labour law, before driving home their emotional call for the union's intervention.

Only the core workers employ legal language to explicitly condemn illegal, rather than immoral, practices, and call for a proper implementation of law. Their understanding of fairness and motivation for action is mostly shaped by their legal training and access to legal aid. However, in their rightful resistance, core workers also tactically combine their legal claims with moral ones. These moral claims are shaped both by the values underpinning certain articles of the Labour Code on wages and social insurance benefits and by the norm of subsistence and socialist values of equality. In short, law and morality complement and are intertwined with each other in workers' resistance and appeals for justice.

The third and last set of issues addressed here relate to workers' notions of rights. I find that workers invoke different notions of rights. The first, which is most clearly expressed, is legal rights endorsed in the Labour Code. These rights are articulated in conjunction with legal allegations of business' rights infringement and references to articles of the Labour Code and other formal regulations. The second notion of rights is not explicit but can be inferred from workers' appeals and their experiences of (un)fairness. In these accounts, they deploy the legal term 'rights and interests,' but their use of this term implies an understanding different from the way in which the term is used in the Labour Code, where rights, as separate from interests, refer to seven basic rights set out in Article 5 and to other terms agreed upon in the labour contracts and collective bargaining agreements. This second notion of rights captures workers' moral worldviews of the labour-management relationship, valorising the guarantee of livelihoods, secure employment, and ethical treatment as workers' entitlements. The last notion of rights concerns rights to equality, respect, and rights as human beings. These understandings of rights are in the minority: they are only expressed in Thắm's published letter and alluded to in Nguyên's hand-written petition. They emerge from these workers' acute feelings of demoralisation and maltreatment, and are likely to have been learnt from their understanding of the socialist propaganda, which continues to be widespread in post-socialist Vietnam as well as from the Vietnamese Constitution.

There is no clear-cut boundary between the aforementioned notions of rights, even though workers often express them in different and separate ways. While the second and third notions of rights may be broader, basic, and more fundamental than the legal rights explicitly endorsed in the Labour Code, the moral values that underpin understandings of all these rights, as I have mentioned earlier, overlap and complement each other. The analysis thus suggests that it is essential to examine rights consciousness as part of workers' broader views and social engagements, and their experiences of workplace relationships, rather than only from their legal understanding or access to law. A focus on legal rights, as seen in some studies inspired by the rightful resistance literature, risks neglecting other values and notions of rights that workers absorb from outside law. Despite their different acts of resistance and ways of problem framing, workers in my study all exhibit some form of rights consciousness[1] and a will to stand up for their rights when they are abused or neglected by management and/or the unions and the state.

Both core workers' access to legal aid and their trajectory of resistance allow for further elaboration on their views and evaluations of law, and reflect on the concept of 'legal consciousness.' This notion, as employed by Ewick and Silbey (1992), for example, is broader than (legal) rights consciousness in the sense that it captures the dynamic process through which people's views of law emerge, develop, and change as a result of their experiences with legal institutions. I study core workers' legal consciousness through their interactions with other ordinary workers and how they try to raise their consciousness, their views of legal aid, their mobilisation of other workers against injustice, and the outcomes of their resistance. Core workers, first of all, see law as a potential resource for workers to understand what is right and wrong in workplace behaviour, and act against managerial abuse if possible. They believe that workers' access to law will put them in good stead in bargaining with management and contesting their practices.

Core workers' engagement with labour law further leads them to be critical of its practices. They see that the implementation of the Labour Code, as in dispute resolution, is not impartial and just, and can put workers at a disadvantage. In their accounts, legal aid offered by the union has helped fill the institutional void in taking care of workers' rights and interests, but such support is fragmented rather than sustained. The two core workers, who initiated the lodgement of complaint letters to the labour authorities, started their journeys with a belief in the labour law regime and a hope that it would achieve justice. When dispute resolution processes were manipulated and tampered with by management and local state authorities, these core workers did not give up hope in the labour law regime, but saw a greater role for the goodwill and moral considerations of the state and management in response to workers' demands. Their consciousness, which I describe as 'critical consent,' embodies a multi-layered perception of law and the delivery of legal justice, and a paradox of pursuing justice through the labour law regime despite being aware and critical of its limitations.

For the past five years in Vietnam, the relative decline in open protests and strikes does not mean that the struggles of factory workers, both in and outside the shop floor, are subsiding, or that conditions for labour rights protection have improved. Indeed, the struggles for better workplaces and recognition of workers' dignity are ongoing and smouldering, sometimes both enabled and stifled by the very legal and political system that are supposed to protect their rights and benefits. This book has sought to capture the nuanced and tacit way in which law contributes to workers' views and understandings of the unfair situations they are in, and enables them to contest those situations. In focusing on and elucidating the different values underpinning workers' demands and acts of resistance, this study seeks to enhance understanding of why workers resist, by shedding light on workers' perspectives, expectations, grievances, and aspirations as they unfold through their resistance stories. Understanding the values implicated in these perspectives in turn allows for a critical reflection on the role of different institutions and practices in shaping and generating workers' resistance. By introducing and incorporating labour law as one such set of institutions and practices, I have shown how it interacts with other institutions and practices in the state-society relationship in Vietnam in informing and contributing to workers' perspectives, sentiments, and expressions of workplace (in)justice.

The findings of this book call for a rethinking of the role of law in post-socialist context, showing that labour law serves as a moral resource for workers to judge management's conduct. These findings pave the way for future empirical research on law, legal consciousness, and resistance in relation to other contentious social issues in Vietnam, and for an analytical reframing of law in post-socialist societies. Despite many limitations in its enforcement, state law brings about social change through informing and shaping people's expectations. This subtle effect of law does not always lead to overt actions or articulations to contest problematic practices, but is an important indication of increasing consciousness of fairness, justice, and rights. And sometimes social change resulting from law manifests in overt actions, inspired by legal aid and legal access, aimed at altering existing practices and improving workers' situations. The core workers' narratives, in particular, are clear testimonies to the relationship between labour law and social change, as they demonstrate the moral underpinnings of law in workers' evaluations and the potential of legal actions to alter workplace practices. Of course, in Vietnam, where law is often bent and non-legal practices are often deployed by the powerful to serve their personal interests, such an end is difficult to achieve.

Note

1. Since workers in my study do not demand for new rights to be recognised in the law or for rights that challenge existing state laws and policies, their consciousness might be considered as similar to what Elizabeth Perry described as 'rules consciousness' to refer to the nature of citizens' claims and protests in China (2007; see also Li 2010). However, in another article, Perry made clear that she is critical of the depiction of rights that adopts a Western idea of citizen rights and, as such, overstates their political impact (2007, pp. 45–46). Perry instead offers an intricate discourse analysis of rights, drawing from Chinese philosophical thoughts, socialist propaganda, and fundamental social norms.

References

Chua, L. & Engel, D. (2015). State and Personhood in Southeast Asia: The Promise and Potential for Law and Society Research. *Asian Journal of Law and Society*, 2 (2), 211–228.

Diamant, N., Lubman, S. & O'Brien, K. (eds.) (2005). *Engaging the Law in China: State, Society, and Possibilities for Justice*. California: Stanford University Press.

Engel, D. (1998). How does Law Matter in the Constitution of Legal Consciousness?. In B. G. Garth & A. Sarat (eds.). *How Does Law Matter?*, Illinois: Northwestern University Press.

Ewick, P. & Silbey, S. (1992). Conformity, Contestation and Resistance: An Account of Legal Consciousness. *New England Law Review*, 26, 731–749.

Ewick, P. & Silbey, S. (1998). *The Common Place of Law: Stories from Everyday Life. Chicago: University of Chicago Press.*

Gillespie, J. & Nicholson, P. (eds.) (2005). *Asian Socialism and Legal Change: The Dynamics of Vietnamese and Chinese Reform*. Canberra: ANU E Press & Asia Pacific Press.

Gillespie, J. (2011). Exploring the Limits of the Judicialization of Urban Land Disputes in Vietnam. *Law and Society Review*, 45 (2), 241–275.

He, X. & Feng, Y. (2016). Mismatched Discourses in the Petition Offices of Chinese Courts. *Law & Social Inquiry*, 41 (1), 212–241.

He, X., Wang, L. & Su, Y. (2013). Above the Roof, Beneath the Law: Perceived Justice behind Disruptive Tactics of Migrant Wage Claimants in China. *Law & Society Review*, 47 (4), 703–738.

Hsing, Y-T. (2010). *The Great Urban Transformation: Politics of Land and Property in China*. New York: Oxford University Press

Kerkvliet, B. J. (2014). Protests over Land in Vietnam: Rightful Resistance and More. *Journal of Vietnamese Studies*, 9 (3), 19–54.

Koh, D. (2007). Modern Law, Traditional Ethics, and Contemporary Political Legitimacy in Vietnam. In S. Balmé & M. Sidel (eds.), *Vietnam's New Order: International Perspectives on the State and Reform in Vietnam*. New York: Palgrave Macmillan.

Labbé, D. (2011). Urban Destruction and Land Disputes in Periurban Hanoi During the Late-Socialist Period. *Pacific Affairs*, 84 (3), 435–454.

Li, L. (2010). Rights Consciousness and Rules Consciousness in Contemporary China. *The China Journal*, 64, 47–68.

Merry, S. E. (1990). *Getting Justice and Getting Even: Legal Consciousness among Working-Class Americans*. Chicago & London: The University of Chicago Press.

O'Brien, K. & Li, L. (2006). *Rightful Resistance in Rural China*. Cambridge: Cambridge University Press.

Pei, M. (2010). Rights and resistance: The changing contexts of the dissident movement. In E. J. Perry & M. Selden (3rd ed.), *Chinese Society: Change, Conflict and Resistance*. London & New York: Routledge.

Perry, E. (2007). Studying Chinese Politics: Farewell to Revolution?. *The China Journal*, 57, 1–22.

Pham, D. N. (2005). Confucianism and the Conception of the Law in Vietnam. In J. Gillespie & P. Nicholson (eds.). *Asian Socialism and Legal Change: The Dynamics of Vietnamese and Chinese Reform*. Canberra: ANU E Press & Asia Pacific Press.

Pun, N. (2016). *Migrant Labor in China: Post-Socialist Transformations*. Cambridge: Polity Press.

Sargeson, S. (2012). Villains, Victims and Aspiring Proprietors: Framing 'land-losing villagers' in China's Strategies of Accumulation. *Journal of Contemporary China*, 21 (77), 757–777.

Thireau, I. & Hua, L. (2003). The Moral Universe of Aggrieved Chinese Workers: Workers' Appeals to Arbitration Committees and Letters and Visits Offices. *The China Journal*, 50, 83–103.

Yang, L. & van der Wal, Z. (2014). Rule of Morality vs. Rule of Law?. *Public Integrity*, 16 (2), 187–206.

Appendix: Fieldwork Notes

When doing fieldwork in Đồng Nai, I was not affiliated with an academic institution or organisation, nor did I have any previous contacts with factory workers there. I am aware that the information that my respondents shared with me was shaped by their perceptions of me as an outsider, as an outsider who does not share their experiences and is not able to offer practical help with any of their work-related problems, as well as the relationships between them and other key informants. My encounters with factory workers in a food processing company exemplify the observations regarding researcher and participant relationship. I managed to recruit these workers, thanks to the introduction of a core worker, Mr Lê, who was also willing to provide me with the most information about his workplace. We first met each other at a year-end party of the core workers in the province, and by chance shared the same table. Lê knew that I was a student researching labour disputes, while I also knew that he worked in one of the strike-prone companies that I planned to investigate. Lê had previously helped to recruit workers for other labour research projects, so was willing to introduce me to his wife and four other co-workers, who lived in the same workers' rental area with him. With Lê's introduction, his wife and the four other workers agreed to be interviewed. The bond between my key informant and prospective respondents in this case is much closer, compared to most other workers who were only acquaintances to my infor-

T. P. Nguyen, *Workplace Justice*, Critical Studies of the Asia-Pacific,
https://doi.org/10.1007/978-981-13-3116-9

mants, or were known to my informants through indirect contacts. The interviews took place in a daily conversational setting between workers and me as an outsider. At times my key informants were also present and helped facilitating the interviews. While about a third of my respondents showed some hesitation or little interest in describing in detail their grievances or issues relating to labour disputes, the rest were willing to share their stories. Half of these respondents, mostly women workers, spoke with vigour and strong emotion, with some being thankful to me for listening to their stories.

Only five of ordinary worker interviewees were male. This is despite the fact that I did not intend to focus on female workers in designing my project. The first reason for the predominance of women is that four out of the six selected companies, which are in the footwear and garment industry, employed a majority of female workers. The second reason, which I only realised towards the end of my first field trip, is my gender. Some of my key informants assumed that, as a female, I would be more comfortable talking with females than with males. When I first requested them to introduce potential interviewees in a certain company to me (without any gender specification), they came back to me with several female workers. It was not until later, when I made a further request and one informant asked me: 'Are you okay interviewing male workers?,' that I realised my gender mattered in this process.

At the same time, I found that female workers were more willing and at times more passionate about sharing their stories than men. In addition to providing answers to my questions, many digressed at length, enabling me to understand more about their working lives and how different issues and events contribute to shaping their attitudes and behaviour. When I compared male and female workers' accounts, I found minor differences in the way they talked about their grievances. Female workers had more complaints than male (such as problems with company-provided meals and managerial attitudes), and the former mentioned their family and living expenses while the latter did not. I have factored in gender difference in workers' articulation of their problems in my analysis.

Index[1]

[1] Note: Page numbers followed by 'n' refer to notes.

T. P. Nguyen, *Workplace Justice*, Critical Studies of the Asia-Pacific,
https://doi.org/10.1007/978-981-13-3116-9

Kolibri 360 GmbH
Ferdinand-Jühlke-Straße 7
99095 Erfurt, Deutschland
produktsicherheit@kolibri360.de